HEALTH CARE FACILITY ELECTRICAL SYSTEMS

Based on the 2021 *NFPA 99: Health Care Facilities Code* and 2020 *National Electrical Code®*

Stephen Lipster

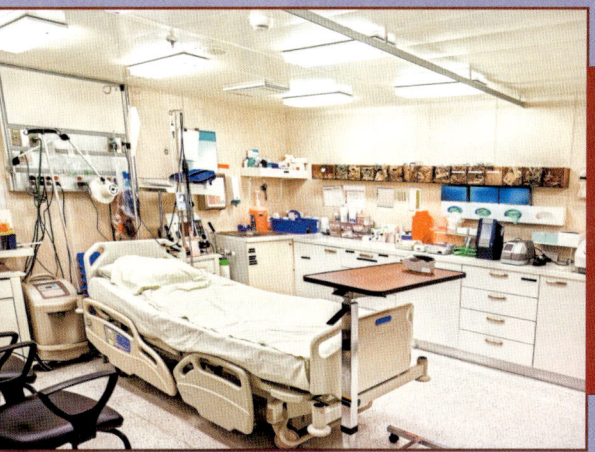

electrical training
IBEW - NECA
ALLIANCE

Health Care Facility Electrical Systems, Based on the 2021 *NFPA 99* and 2020 *NEC®* is intended to be an educational resource for the user and contains procedures commonly practiced in industry and the trade. Specific procedures vary with each task and must be performed by a qualified person. For maximum safety, always refer to specific manufacturer recommendations, insurance regulations, specific job site and plant procedures, applicable federal, state, and local regulations, and any authority having jurisdiction. The *electrical training ALLIANCE* assumes no responsibility or liability in connection with this material or its use by any individual or organization.

Contents

Contents

Acknowledgments

NFPA 70®, *National Electrical Code®*, and *NEC®* are registered trademarks of the National Fire Protection Association, Quincy, MA.

The *electrical training ALLIANCE* wishes to thank the following companies and individuals for submitting photos for inclusion in this edition.

American Society for Healthcare
    Engineering (ASHE), Chicago, IL
Bill Koplitz/FEMA
Eaton

Hatzel & Buehler, Inc., Circleville, OH
Jace Anderson/FEMA
Lawson Electric, Chattanooga, TN

QR Codes

American Society for Healthcare Engineering
Centers for Disease Control
International Association of Electrical
    Inspectors

Milwaukee Tool
The Joint Commission

Health Care Facilities Electrical Systems Advisory Team

David Anderson, Mid-City Electric
Gary Beckstrand, Utah Electrical JATC
Chad Beebe, American Society for
    Healthcare Engineering
Joe Burton, Mid-City Electric
Mark Christian, *electrical training
    ALLIANCE*

David Dagenais, Wentworth/Douglass
    Hospital
Jim Dollard, IBEW Local Union 98
Palmer Hickman, *electrical training ALLIANCE*
Robert Kennedy, Lawson Electric Co.
Gary Krupa, Veterans Health Administration
Hugh Nash, Nash Consult
Mike Shutts, The Superior Group

Health Care Project Team

Gary Beckstrand, Technical Editor, *NEC* CMP-15 Principal
Gerald Dix, Training Director, Hampton Roads JATC

Features

Headers and **Sub-headers** organize information within the text.

Code **Excerpts** are "ripped" from the 2020 *National Electrical Code*, 2021 *NFPA 99*, or other codes and standards.

Figures, including photographs and artwork, clearly illustrate concepts from the text.

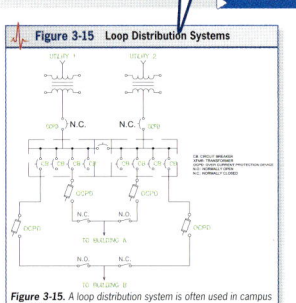

Vignette boxes offer additional information related to Health Care Facility Electrical Systems.

For additional information related to QR Codes, visit qr.njatcdb.org Item #1079

Quick Response Codes (QR Codes) create a link between the textbook and the Internet. They can be scanned using Smartphone applications to obtain additional information online. (To access the information without using a Smartphone, visit qr.njatcdb.org and enter the referenced Item #.)

Features

Clear, easy-to-read **Contents** pages in the front of the textbook and inside each Chapter enable the reader to quickly find important grounding and bonding content.

Chapter 2

Table of Contents

An **Appendix** conveys information specific to working in health care facilities during the COVID-19 pandemic.

Work in Existing Health Care Facilities

A growing trend in health care facility construction is the almost constant changes to existing facilities as health care organizations adopt new technology and medical processes to assure patients receive the best care science can provide. Recent studies have shown that the demolition and construction processes negatively impact patients and others with compromised immune systems. These facts have driven wide-ranging changes in the construction work environment, changes that affect every Electrical Worker engaged in their trade at an existing health care facility. Furthermore, patient information privacy laws and regulations, as well as appearance expectations, all affect existing health care facility workplaces.

Objectives

- Explain why an Electrical Worker's appearance and conduct is especially important when working in a health care facility.
- Describe who should be involved in the development of a risk assessment and what items should be addressed.
- Understand why an Infection Control Risk Mitigation Plan (ICRMP) is important and how it is enforced.
- Distinguish and describe the differences between barriers used in health care facilities during construction projects.

The **Introduction** and **Objectives** at the beginning of each chapter introduce readers to the concepts to be learned in each chapter.

Appendix

INTRODUCTION

At the time of this writing, many valuable lessons of the COVID-19 pandemic are still being learned. It is not an exaggeration to say that the pandemic has reinforced the wisdom of Infection Control Risk Assessment/Mitigation Plans (ICRAMP). At the same time, it is challenging to perform an effective ICRAMP when the threat is not entirely understood. Health care organizations have taken a four-pronged approach when reviewing construction activities during the crisis:

- Issue a stop-work order on projects that are not considered vital to the health care organization's newly focused mission. Some projects have been delayed and will resume when the pandemic has passed. Others, particularly those in the planning stages, have been canceled and funds reallocated to other more critical activities.
- Build temporary facilities in buildings not designed for health care activities, such as convention centers and athletic facilities, or build stand-alone temporary facilities on undeveloped property. Because these facilities are temporary, the local authority having jurisdiction (AHJ), working in concert with an accreditation organization, may allow the temporary facility some respite from code and standard requirements. From an Electrical Worker's perspective, these are "new builds" and may not require an ICRAMP. Under any conditions, the procedures and protocols an employer has in place to protect one another from the transmission of COVID-19 must be carefully followed.
- Continue existing projects deemed essential, with enhanced ICRAMP protocols and procedures to combat the spread of the novel coronavirus.

- Begin emergency fast-track remodel and retrofit activities to address specific physical plant alterations needed to treat patients with COVID-19 more effectively.

WORKING DURING THE PANDEMIC

Addressing the final two bullet points above will be the focus, as those scenarios impact the Electrical Worker employed in a functioning health care facility. While each project in a working health care facility is unique, with a unique set of ICRAMP protocols and procedures, specific COVID-19 additions to these procedures generally apply to several fronts.

Increased use of PPE, especially face masks and gloves, is mandated to help contain the spread of the virus. At the time of this writing, COVID-19 is thought to be primarily transferred from person-to-person via airborne contact; secondarily, the virus is believed to be transferred via surface contact from surface-to-person. The face mask requirement is designed to protect both the wearer and those that may come inside the six-foot social distancing boundary. The use of face masks has been shown to minimize transmission by trapping respiration droplets containing the virus. The use of rubber or vinyl gloves is employed as a means to stop the spread of the virus from surfaces to human respiratory systems. It is critical when wearing gloves not to touch the face or eyes, and it is crucial to change gloves as often as instructed. This will allow maximum benefit from the PPE to be achieved.

Increased cleaning protocols are also in place to combat the surface transmission of the virus. The daily cleaning and mop-down of workspaces is a requirement as well as the regular cleaning of shared hand tools and power tools. Hand tools should be cleaned with an approved disinfectant. Power tools

SUMMARY

Maintenance of electrical distribution equipment in health care facilities is a significant part of the electrical industry. Many electrical contractors are discovering that maintenance work is a vital and profitable part of doing business. Following equipment manufacturer recommendations, *NFPA 99*, and *NFPA 70B* guidance for well-timed, frequent maintenance procedures reduces downtime and accidents. Providing a reliable and safe supply of electrical power for critical life support and life safety is a vital element of any health care facility providing a high quality of care to a community. Several codes and standards, most recently *NFPA 99*, regulating electrical systems have adopted requirements for maintenance. Equipment maintenance programs must be in writing, detail rationale for the program, and document all crucial data. The most valuable NFPA document covering electrical systems maintenance is *NFPA 70B: Recommended Practice for Electrical Equipment Maintenance*. Because this document is not a standard or a code, but rather a recommended practice, until the next edition is release as a standard, it is not enforceable by the AHJ. However, it does play a vital role in guiding the work of the Electrical Worker. Due to the sensitive and critical role that these facilities play in communities, special care must be taken when performing such maintenance activities. Understanding the codes, standards, and documents that regulate these protocols and procedures is what sets a skilled Electrical Worker apart.

REVIEW QUESTIONS

1. For health care facilities to be eligible to receive Medicare and Medicaid payments from the United States Department of Health and Human Services, facilities must conform to the _?_.
   a. Center for Disease Control
   b. Centers for Medicare and Medicaid Services (CMS) Conditions of Participation
   c. Hospital Association of America
   d. *NFPA 99: Health Care Facilities Code*

2. CMS requires that maintenance shall be performed on hospital electrical equipment in accordance with the _?_.
   a. American Hospital Association Guidelines
   b. equipment manufacturer's recommendation
   c. hospital governing body maintenance guidelines
   d. industry standards

3. Essential electrical system generation specifically requires that equipment to be maintained to come online in _?_ upon a power outage. It also requires that generator sets be tested _?_ times a year in intervals of not less than 20, but no more than 40 days, as well as specific main and feeder circuit breaker inspection and exercise requirements.
   a. 10 seconds / 12
   b. 30 seconds / 6
   c. 60 seconds / 12
   d. 120 seconds / 6

4. *NFPA 70B: Recommended Practice for Electrical Equipment Maintenance* is not a standard or code, and therefore, not enforceable by an AHJ; however, when considering maintenance and testing, *NFPA 70B* is just as important to an Electrical Worker as *NFPA 70* is when installing electrical systems.
   a. True   b. False

5. When health care facilities engage outside electrical contractors to perform maintenance on the facility's electrical system, it is generally to perform specific preventive maintenance procedures on specific electrical equipment, or at the far end of the maintenance spectrum, on the entire branch of an essential electrical system.
   a. True   b. False

At the end of each chapter, a concise chapter **Summary** and **Review Questions** reinforce the important concepts included in the text.

Introduction

Health care is a large sector of the United States economy. As a sector of the construction economy, health care is equally as important. The health care build environment presents a unique set of requirements for designers, engineers, and builders. Health care facilities play an exceptional role in the community. They must be able to provide lifesaving care under any circumstance, and the reliability of electrical power is paramount to that mission.

Over the years, redundancy, a philosophy that dictates the loss of one electrical component will not adversely affect patient care, has been the keystone for reliable electrical power. It has been said that other than nuclear generation stations, no other occupancy is more regulated than health care facilities. This extreme level of regulation is designed to do one thing: ensure safe patient care in any circumstance. This book explores the various *codes* and standards that govern health care facility construction and operation.

The textbook and course of study are designed for two levels of delivery. Chapters 1 through 4 make up the first level and follow the electrical system elements of a health care facility as if an Electrical Worker were viewing a one-line diagram. The overall elements of a health care facility and why those elements are unique to health care are discussed in Chapter 1. Chapter 2 covers the different schemes that design engineers can use to get primary utility power to the health care facility, as well as the facility's essential electrical system generation. This is a key element of any health care essential electrical system. Chapter 3 discusses the internal electrical distribution systems inside the facility. Normal power, the three branches of the essential electrical system, and loading are all covered. Chapter 4 deals with the end use: patient care spaces and the requirements needed for a safe installation to the most vulnerable of persons, the patients.

The second level of delivery assumes the student has a good understanding of the first four chapters, as the final three chapters discuss specialty work within an existing facility. Chapter 5 covers health care facility electrical system maintenance and the best practices used in that sphere of work. Chapter 6 discusses remodel or retrofit work in existing facilities and the precautions a worker must take to keep patients safe. Chapter 7 also looks into some of the trends impacting health care organizations, and the effect these trends will have on health care construction in the upcoming years. A new appendix brings to light lessons learned from the COVID-19 Pandemic and provides valuable resources for Electrical Workers.

This book assumes the student has an understanding of *codes* and standards, as well as an understanding of electrical theory and installation practices. This work is not intended to be an installation manual, but it is hoped the text will provide the Electrical Worker with insight into the unique design and installation requirements of today's health care facilities.

About This Book

This textbook is the latest version of *electrical training ALLIANCE* works focused on the health care environment. Beginning with the 2008 *NFPA 70: National Electrical Code (NEC)* cycle, the *electrical training ALLIANCE* published the first health care textbook, *Health Care Systems: Properly Applying Codes and Standards*. This publication was revised for the 2011 and 2014 *NEC* cycles.

In 2016, the National Fire Protection Association Standards Council made several decisions affecting health care electrical systems, which moved *NFPA 99: Health Care Facilities Code* into prominence. The decision was made to publish a work that coincides with the new *Health Care Facilities Code*, which is currently one year behind the *NEC*. The move to a later publication date created an opportunity to review the entire body of work and dig deeper into electrical systems in health care facilities—to go beyond the application of *codes* to a thorough discussion of electrical systems from the utility to generation to end use.

While still resting on a codes and standards foundation, the latest textbook is more in-depth when exploring health care as electrical installation. System maintenance and its impact on construction and health care technologies, as well as the scope of work for an Electrical Worker, are discussed. It is all designed to keep the workforce knowledgeable, safe, and efficient in a rapidly changing environment, especially during the COVID-19 Pandemic.

About the Author

Stephen Lipster completed his apprenticeship in 1988 at The Electrical Trades Center of the IBEW/NECA program in Columbus, OH. After graduation, Lipster served the training trust as a trustee, an instructor, an instruction coordinator, and a training director. He also served the industry as a local union officer, a foreman, and a general foreman. Since 2019, he has served the IBEW/NECA apprenticeship program in Charleston, S.C., the Charleston Electrical Training Alliance, as director.

In 1996, Lipster was awarded the IBEW Founders Scholarship, a life-changing event. In 1999, with the help of the electrical industry and his family, Lipster graduated from The Ohio State University summa cum laude with a bachelor of science degree in technology education. He was asked to become the training director at The Electrical Trades Center and went on to author the NJATC's *Conduit Bending and Fabrication* textbook and the NJATC's *Concepts in Motor Control*.

In 2004, Lipster was appointed by IBEW President Hill and the NFPA to serve on the *National Electrical Code, Code*-Making Panel (CMP) 15. In 2006, he was appointed to the *Health Care Facilities Code* Electrical Systems Technical Committee, as well as the Fundamentals Technical Committee. Since 2019, he has served on these *Code*-making panels and technical committees as a special expert. A lifelong proponent of registered apprenticeship and code, Lipster currently resides in Charleston, S.C.

Introduction

Health care facilities are arguably the most critical structures in a community. These structures are complex and expensive to build. Health care facilities are important pieces of a community's health care system, and when a community's emergency management plan is considered, it becomes an extremely critical element of that plan. It is a place of healing, shelter, and refuge. Health care facilities are some of the most regulated environments on earth, governed by design, performance, and installation codes and standards that are all in place to assure patient safety, to ensure defend-in-place strategies are viable, and to guarantee that the facility functions in any type of emergency.

Objectives

» Explain the important role that health care facilities play in the communities that they serve.

» Identify critical health care facility systems and the difficulties electrical professionals will face when installing and maintaining them.

» Describe how the codes and standards were developed and how they apply to health care facilities today.

» Explain how codes and standards are enforced.

Chapter 1

Table of Contents

INTRODUCTION

The United States Department of Homeland Security defines critical infrastructure as "Systems and assets, whether physical or virtual, so vital to the United States that the incapacity and destruction of such systems and assets would have a debilitating impact on security, national economic security, national public health or safety, or any combination of those matters." Health care facilities, particularly large local and regional medical centers, are rightfully defined as critical infrastructure. **See Figure 1-1.**

The *International Building Code* (*IBC*) is used, among other things, to provide risk category classification for structures. These risk categories are in turn used to provide minimum design and construction criteria based on the facility's role in the community. Large- and medium-sized health care facilities are classified by the *IBC* as Risk Category IV buildings. This type of building includes physical assets essential to the health and well-being of human life, having the most value to the community and, therefore, the most stringent building design and construction standards. In addition to the rules detailed in the *IBC*, many communities opt to adopt the regulations found in the Article 708, Critical Operations Power Systems (COPS), in the *NFPA 70: National Electrical Code® (NEC 2020)*, for front line health care facilities, underscoring the impact and value these buildings provide to the community.

From a design and installation perspective, health care facilities are extensive and complex. For firms skilled enough to compete in the medical and health care construction market, these projects can boost firm portfolios. Health care facilities are unique in design, construction, and post-construction use. Many factors found in the discussion of the health care equation are exclusive to these structures.

> **Fact**
>
> The 2021 edition of *NFPA 99: The Health Care Facilities Code* defines *health care facilities* as: "Buildings, portions of buildings, or mobile enclosures in which human medical, dental, psychiatric, nursing, obstetrical, or surgical care is provided." The same document defines *hospitals* as: "A building or portion thereof used on a 24-hour basis for the medical, psychiatric, obstetrical, or surgical care of four or more inpatients."
>
> Reproduced with permission of NFPA from NFPA 99, *Health Care Facilities Code*, 2021 edition. Copyright© 2020, National Fire Protection Association. For a full copy of the *NFPA 99*, please go to www.nfpa.org.

Figure 1-1 Regional Health Care Facility

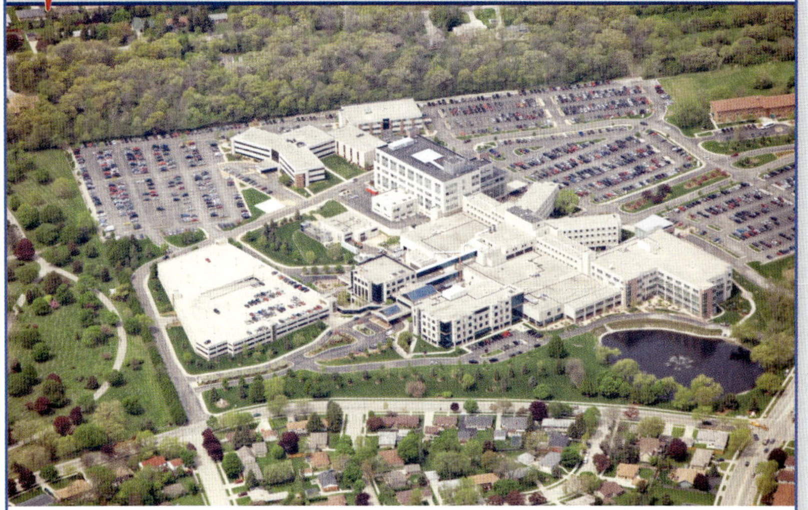

Figure 1-1. *Large health care facilities are often built in multiple phases.*

WHY HEALTH CARE FACILITIES ARE EXCEPTIONAL

Health care facilities are typically in use 24 hours a day, 365 days a year providing in-patient care. The systems that support these structures, including electrical, mechanical, communications, and diagnostic systems, and the care offered to patients within these structures must be robust enough to handle constant use. Redundancy is often designed in these systems to assure a sub-system can be taken offline for repair or maintenance without affecting the system's overall function.

Critical Operations Power Systems

The code making community reacted to the lessons learned from 9/11 in many different ways. For electrical installers, perhaps, the most substantial change driven by this tragedy is found in *NEC*, Article 708 *Critical Operations Power Systems (COPS)*. Article 708 provides guidance and regulations for power systems serving critical operations areas; these are spaces in critical infrastructure where the loss of power would "disrupt national security, the economy, or public health."

COPS designation is provided by the governmental authority who determines that the loss of electrical power would meet the requirements detailed above. Article 708 provides an increased level of reliability for wiring systems, distribution equipment, and generation and transfer equipment all designed to ensure the power stays on in a man-made or natural disaster.

Health care facilities must remain open during times of emergency and disaster when utility services may not be available for a considerable period of time. For this reason, reliable backup electrical power and fuel sources must be available for such emergencies. Health care facilities must provide not only lifesaving care but offer other assistance, such as food services, that are very critical to both patients and staff.

Narratives told in the aftermath of Hurricane Katrina and Superstorm Sandy clearly relate accounts of hospitals becoming places of refuge for communities, families, neighbors, and even pets during events of natural disaster and extreme distress. In some cases, hospital buildings were the only structures in the area left safe, standing, and providing shelter from the storm in good general working order. It is only natural that people would gather with their families and friends in the only "functionally working" structures available. **See Figure 1-2.**

Health care facilities must be designed and built to withstand natural and man-made disasters. Hospital emergency departments must be able to provide services to the community no matter what the disaster. Patients seen in the emergency department are diagnosed and cared for and, if necessary, admitted to general or specialized care units of the hospital to begin treatment or any procedure required to keep them alive and healthy. These facts add considerably to the design, construction, specifications, maintenance, and operating costs of health care facilities.

Recent case studies show when and where facility design and construction proved unequal to the forces Mother

Figure 1-2   Storm Damage in Louisville, MS

Figure 1-2. *When a tornado struck Louisville, MS on April 28, 2014, it caused extensive damage to the Winston Medical Center. Courtesy of Bill Koplitz/FEMA*

Nature threw at the health care facility, with both horrifying and eye-opening results. In some cases, even the best construction methods and efforts can come apart in a moment when faced with nature's awesome power. The Joplin, MO tornado of 2012 structurally devastated the local hospital, essentially taking it offline for some years while a new facility was constructed. **See Figure 1-3.**

In some ways, the events associated with Hurricane Katrina and Superstorm Sandy paint a different picture entirely. In these situations, health care facilities structurally held up to the challenge. However, critical systems, especially essential electrical systems, failed when they were needed the most. These failures are directly related to designers who placed emergency generators and transfer switches in floodplains, fuel in underground storage tanks, and day tanks in pits. When flooding occurred, the generators or fuel systems serving the generators became compromised, and the essential electrical system went offline for the duration of the event.

Man-made disasters, while much less prevalent, can be more devastating. While certain international protocols place hospitals outside acceptable acts of war, these protocols are being sorely tested by radical groups who choose not to honor centuries-old understandings and agreements. An event where domestic terrorists enter a medical center with an improvised explosive device and find their way to the heart of the facility to detonate the device has fortunately never been realized in the United States; the very thought of such an action is horrifying. Engineers can design against outside threats, but a well-placed device located in a carefully selected location would be devastating indeed.

The lifesaving and preserving activities that occur in health care facilities employ a range of systems that are unique to these institutions. Medical gas and vacuum systems, medical imaging equipment, essential electrical systems, transportation systems, ICU, NICU, operating rooms, procedure areas, and even things as innocuous as food service must remain online and in working order even if a disaster or another hazardous event has occurred. Lives are literally on the line in these facilities.

Systems used in a health care facility may have elements in common with

Figure 1-3   Tornado Damage in Joplin, MO

Figure 1-3. *A close view of St. John's Regional Medical Center in Joplin, MO shows the force of a 200-mph storm and the damage it can cause. An EF-5 tornado struck the city on May 22, 2011, causing serious damage to the generator enclosure. Courtesy of Jace Anderson/FEMA*

Figure 1-4   Parallel Diesel Generators

Figure 1-4. Essential electrical systems often require large diesel line-ups to assure patient and staff safety. Courtesy of Lawson Electric, Chattanooga, TN

systems found in other occupancies. For example, a hospital's essential electrical systems may look, from a design and installation perspective, very much like an electrical system found in a data center, financial institution, or educational facility. However, no occupancy in today's building environment has as many critical systems in one structure as a modern health care facility. **See Figure 1-4.**

One of the hard lessons learned from the COVID-19 pandemic is that interactions of many critical systems become more complex as the use of the health care space is pushed beyond design limitations. In other words, many patient care spaces that were designed for other treatment were converted to treat patients with respiratory problems. These conversions primarily affect HVAC systems and their controls that must be reconfigured to provide negative pressure to COVID-19 treatment spaces. At the end of the day, system flexibility will prove to be a major

take-away for the health care construction community post-COVID-19.

Infection control has been a concern for health care facilities for some time. Patients with compromised immune systems are particularly susceptible to potentially life-threatening infections. Efforts to control the spread of infectious agents are generally focused on heating/cooling/ventilation systems and domestic water systems. Construction processes have also been identified as a potential avenue for noise, dust, and infectious agents to travel to patient care areas. Many health care facilities are adopting strict work practices, especially on remodeling and renovation projects, that require contractors and their workers to follow protocols designed to minimize the spread of infection. In response to the COVID-19 pandemic, work and environmental controls, procedures, and protocols evolved; these rules and regulations may seem overtly restrictive, but are in place for the benefit and well-being of the patients. **See Figure 1-5.**

An often-overlooked aspect of a health care facility's responsibility to staff and patients is the food service. The food service must provide high-quality, healthy, sustaining meals for both patients and employees throughout any emergency situation. With this in mind, essential electrical systems often serve food storage and preparation areas. Pharmacies also have special environmental requirements, such as refrigeration and fume hoods that require reliable, essential electrical system power. Data collection, medical records storage and retrieval, and telecommunications systems, in general, also require service from the essential electrical system to remain online and operating.

Further stretching the design-build envelope is the fact that during an emergency, the occupants of health care facilities are very often incapable of self-preservation. The patients are not able to evacuate themselves from situations that endanger their lives. In any other structure, in an emergency situation, designers assume building occupants will be able to evacuate a structure under their own power with little help from outside resources. This is simply not the case with patients, particularly those in operating rooms, recovery rooms, intensive care units, and those otherwise unaware of their surroundings. Fire or weather-related events, such as tornados or even earthquakes, require special emergency procedures for a health care facility. Some patients may be confined to a bed or connected to life-saving equipment. Many years ago, defend-in-place strategies were developed to aid hospital workers in keeping incapacitated patients safe. This strategy involves relocating occupants to a safe location on the same floor or other areas of the facility during an emergency. These concepts have found their way into health care facility building codes. For example, *NFPA 101: Life Safety Code* provides certain smoke compartment configuration regulations unique to health care facilities that allow defend-in-place concepts in these occupancies. *NFPA 99: Health Care Facilities Code* also makes many provisions for defend-in-place strategies that are unique to health care facilities.

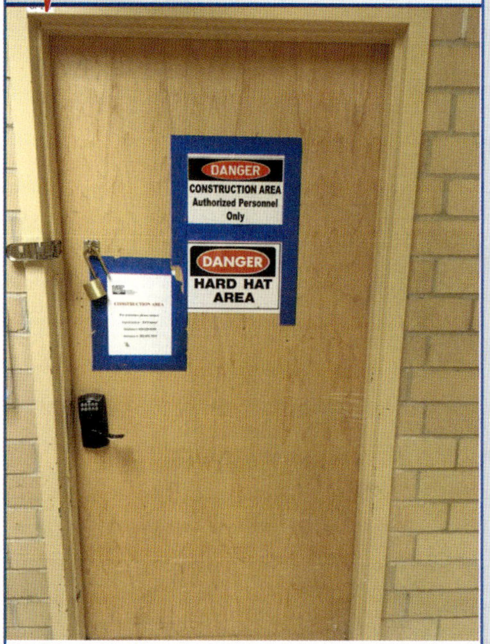

Figure 1-5. During remodeling operations, health care facilities have cleanliness and access control requirements designed to control the spread of infectious disease in the facility. Courtesy of Hatzel & Buehler, Inc, Circleville, OH

PATIENT SAFETY OVERARCHING PRINCIPLE

The reason health care facilities exist is to care for those who are ill, infirm, or incapacitated in one form or another. These patients are extraordinarily vulnerable, and their inability to act for themselves during an emergency situation is the primary reason so many building codes and standards provide more rigorous regulations and requirements for health care facilities. The secondary, seldom considered reason for increased regulation is employee safety. Health care environments expose workers to more radiation, biohazards, and potential infection hazards than any other single workplace. Keeping health care workers safe is a continuing challenge, not just from an operational perspective, but also from a design and build outlook.

Toward the goal of patient and worker safety, many codes and standards have been developed; these can be broadly categorized as *building codes and standards* and *operational codes and standards*. While the distinction between building and operation is convenient, it is quite blurred in real life. For example, The Joint Commission, an operations accreditation and certification nonprofit organization, refers to *NFPA 99-2012: Health Care Facilities Code* for regulations regarding the design of health care facility systems. From a building perspective, the standards and codes used in health care facility construction can be further divided into two distinct groups: *design standards* and *installation* standards and codes. **See Figure 1-6.**

DESIGN STANDARDS

Design standards fall into two groups: codes and standards that only apply to health care facilities and those that apply to other occupancies as well as health care facilities.

Design Standards Exclusive to Health Care Facilities

The *Guidelines for Design and Construction of Hospitals*, developed by the Facility Guidelines Institute and published by the American Society for Healthcare Engineering, is the primary document for health care facility design. In order for a health care organization to become eligible to receive reimbursement from the Centers for Medicare and Medicaid Services (CMS), the health care organization must meet certain operational and facility criteria imposed by CMS. CMS requires health care facilities to be designed to the specifications detailed in the *Guidelines*. This extensive document

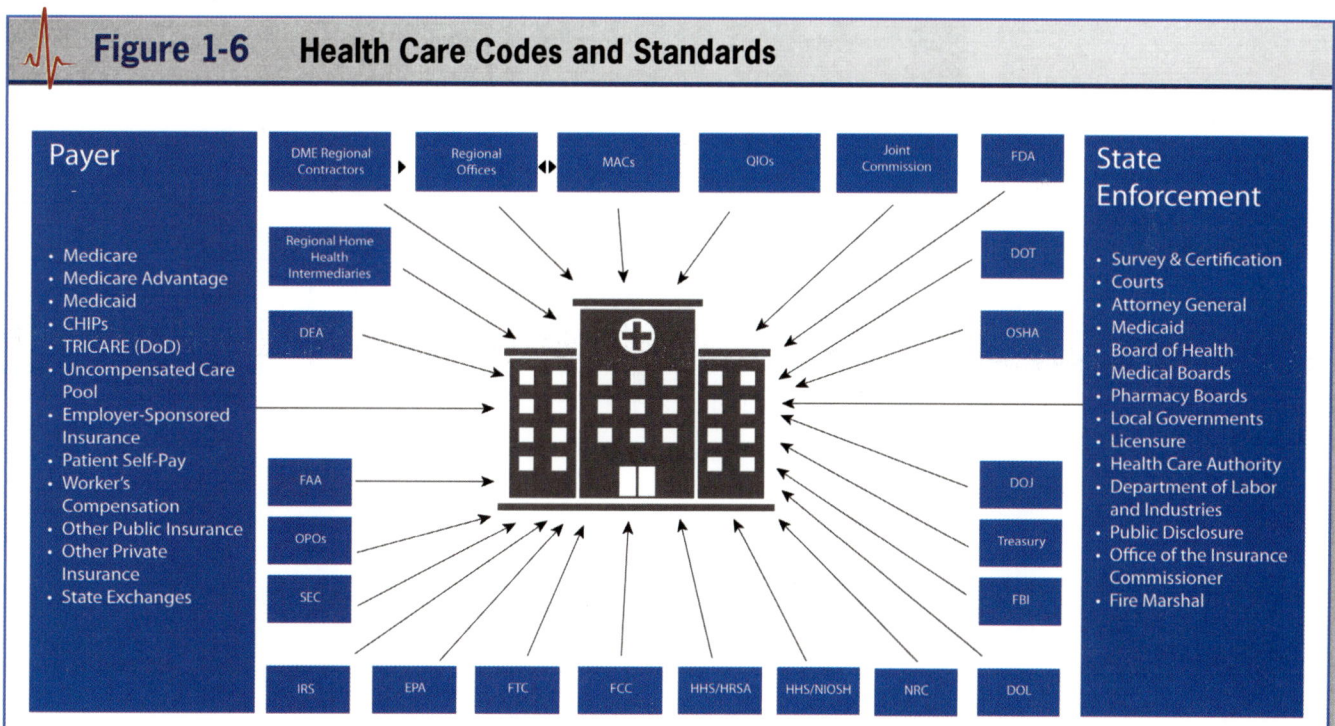

Figure 1-6   Health Care Codes and Standards

Figure 1-6. *A graphic representation of all codes and standards significant to health care facility construction and operation. Courtesy of the American Society for Healthcare Engineering (ASHE), Chicago, IL*

covers health care facility design requirements by both use and occupancy. The 2018 *Guidelines* reference 112 codes, standards, and documents from 56 different organizations as diverse as the National Fire Protection Association, the Society of Cardiovascular Patient Care, the National Sanitation Foundation, the American Water Works Association, and the American College of Surgeons just to name a few. For an Electrical Worker, among the most important referenced documents are *NFPA 70: National Electrical Code, NFPA 72: National Fire Alarm Signaling Code, NFPA 99: Health Care Facilities Code, NFPA 101: Life Safety Code, NFPA 110: Standard for Emergency and Standby Power Systems*, and *TIA 607: Generic Telecommunications Bonding and Grounding (Earthing) for Customer Premises*. It is said that the *Guidelines* are truly the gold standard of health care facility design.

A second document that is exclusive to health care facilities and is also specified in CMS regulations is *NFPA 99: Health Care Facilities Code*. First published in the mid-1980s, *NFPA 99* started life as an amalgam of 12 different NFPA documents that covered separate, specific areas in hospitals. These documents were combined, with a great deal of revision and modification, into the *NFPA 99* document that exists today. The most current edition of *NFPA 99* has 16 chapters and four annexes. The chapters include material covering electrical systems, features of fire protection, information technology and communication systems, plumbing, electrical

Outpatient Facility Guidelines

The Guidelines for Design and Construction of Hospitals (2018) are quite comprehensive, as an upper-level review of the contents will show. *The Guidelines* consist of three parts. Each part is then subdivided into as many as 14 sublevels. Here is a quick look at the document design:

1. General
    1.1   Introduction
    1.2   Planning, Design, Construction, and Commissioning
    1.3   Site
    1.4   Equipment
2. Hospitals
    2.1   Common Elements for Hospitals
    2.2   Specific Elements for General Hospitals
    2.3   Specific Requirements for Freestanding Emergency Departments
    2.4   Specific Requirement for Critical Access Hospitals
    2.5   Specific Requirements for Psychiatric Hospitals
    2.6   Specific Requirement for Rehabilitation Hospitals and Other Facilities
    2.7   Specific Requirements for Children's Hospitals
    2.8   Mobile Transportable Medical Units
3. Ventilation of Health Care Facilities – ANSI/ASHRAE/ASHE Standard 170-2013: Ventilation of Health Care Facilities

equipment, gas equipment, hyperbaric facilities, and heating ventilation and air conditioning. The great majority of *NFPA 99* is focused strictly on performance, maintenance, and testing. Performance has been interpreted to mean: Does the design requirements of a particular system meet the minimum requirements detailed in *NFPA 99: Health Care Facilities Code*?

This document is unique when compared to other codes and standards publications as it is not based on use and occupancy, but rather on *risk assessment*, or an analysis of the danger present to patients and workers in a particular physical space. Due to this nuance, *NFPA 99*'s "performance" jurisdictional boundaries have been broadly interpreted as design only. From an electrical construction perspective, this means the engineering drawings and documents must meet the requirements of *NFPA 99*, while the installation of the electrical system must meet the requirements of *NFPA 70: National Electrical Code.*

While this dichotomy may work in the world of codes and standards, in real world situations the line blurs. For example, the listing requirements of automatic transfer switches (ATS) differ between *NFPA 99* and *NFPA 70*. Should a designer specify an ATS that meets the *NFPA 99* design standard, but not the *NFPA 70* installation standard? Both the electrical contractor and the electrical inspector are left with a problem that can become very costly rather quickly when purchased equipment is not acceptable for the installation.

Risk Assessment

Risk assessment is a process everyone learns at an early age. Does the risk of punishment outweigh the reward of the forbidden candy bar? Is it safer to cross the street at the crosswalk, or will a shortcut be just as safe while being faster?

Health care facility risk analysis is a multi-person process that is focused on one goal: creating contingency plans for emergency action should a system go offline. CMS and other agencies require health care facilities to have extensive contingency plans in place to protect the patient in the event of failure.

The second use of risk analysis is an important requirement of *NFPA 99*, which involves using a documented risk analysis to assign risk categories to spaces during the design phase of proposed construction. Unlike the other design codes and standards, which define regulation requirements by the intended use of the space, *NFPA 99* requires a risk analysis of the risk of the space to determine the level of regulation in that space. *NFPA 99* has four risk categories that are to be used as the end result of the risk analysis:

4.1 Risk Categories. All activities, as well as systems or equipment that are new or altered, shall be designed to meet Category 1 through Category 4 requirements, as detailed in this code.

4.1.1 Category 1. Activities, systems, or equipment whose failure is likely to cause major injury or death of patients, staff, or visitors shall be designed to meet Category 1 requirements, as detailed in this code.

4.1.2 Category 2. Activities, systems, or equipment whose failure is likely to cause minor injury of patients, staff, or visitors shall be designed to meet Category 2 requirements, as detailed in this code.

4.1.3 Category 3. Activities, systems, or equipment whose failure is not likely to cause injury to patients, staff, or visitors, but can cause discomfort, shall be designed to meet Category 3 requirements, as detailed in this code.

4.1.4 Category 4. Activities, systems, or equipment whose failure would have no impact on patient care shall be designed to meet Category 4 requirements, as detailed in this code.

Risk Assessment (cont.)

NFPA 99 also states that, by default, spaces are Category 1 spaces. Risk analysis shall be done to provide spaces with Category 2, 3, and 4 levels of protection. The document also provides annex guidance to aid those on the risk analysis team:

A.4.1 Four levels of systems categories are defined in this code, based on the risks to patients and caregivers in the facilities. The categories are as follows:

(1) Category 1: Systems are expected to work or be available at all times to support patient needs.

(2) Category 2: Systems are expected to provide a high level of reliability; however, limited short durations of equipment downtime can be tolerated without significant impact on patient care. Category 2 systems support patient needs but are not critical for life support.

(3) Category 3: Normal building system reliabilities are expected. Such systems support patient needs, but failure of such equipment would not immediately affect patient care. Such equipment is not critical for life support.

(4) Category 4: Such systems have no impact on patient care and would not be noticeable to patients in the event of failure.

The category definitions apply to equipment operations and are not intended to consider intervention by caregivers or others. Potential examples of areas/systems and their categories of risk follow. A risk assessment should be conducted to evaluate the risk to the patients, staff, and visitors.

(1) Ambulatory surgical center, two patients with full OR services, Category 1

(2) Reconstructive surgeon's office with general anesthesia, Category 1

(3) Procedural sedation site for outpatient services, Category 2

(4) Cooling Towers in Houston, TX, Category 2

(5) Cooling Towers in Seattle, WA, Category 3

(6) Dental office, no general anesthesia, Category 3

(7) Typical doctor's office/exam room, Category 4

(8) Lawn sprinkler system, Category 4

A.4.1.1 Major injury can include the following:

(1) Any amputation

(2) Loss of the sight of an eye (whether temporary or permanent)

(3) Chemical or hot metal burn to the eye or any penetrating injury to the eye

(4) Any injury that results in electric shock and electric burns leading to unconsciousness and that requires resuscitation or admittance to a hospital for 24 hours or more

(5) Any other injury leading to hypothermia, heat induced illness, or unconsciousness requiring resuscitation or admittance to a hospital for 24 hours or more

(6) Loss of consciousness caused by asphyxia or lack of oxygen or exposure to a biological agent or harmful substance

(7) Absorption of any substance by inhalation, skin, or ingestion causing loss of consciousness or acute illness requiring medical treatment

(8) Acute illness requiring medical treatment where there is reason to believe the exposure was to biological agents, its toxins, or infected materials

It is important to note that the jurisdiction of *NFPA 99* varies from chapter to chapter. The chapters in *NFPA 99* that are used most by the electrical trade are Chapter 6, "Electrical Systems," and Chapter 7, "Information Technologies and Communication Systems," which only call out performance, maintenance, and testing requirements. Others, such as "Emergency Management," detail entire programs designed to protect patients and staff in emergency situations.

The last electrical document exclusive to health care facilities to be discussed is the *IEEE White Book, Recommended Practice for the Electrical Systems in Health Care Facilities*. The most recent *White Book* revision, completed by the Institute of Electrical and Electronic Engineers (IEEE), was released in 2007. This edition of the *White Book* was the final published revision in book form, as several years ago the IEEE elected to discontinue the color book series in favor of an online subscription service. Future guidance regarding health care facility electrical systems will be accessed online. **See Figure 1-7.**

The *White Book* details guidance to design engineers and health care maintenance staff regarding the design and operation of health care facilities' electrical systems. The *White Book* provides an unparalleled look at the desired interplay between normal electrical systems, essential electrical systems, on-site generation, and all the associated equipment required to provide safe reliable electrical power to patients and staff.

Codes and Standards Not Exclusive to Health Care Facilities

Surprisingly, prior to 2000, there was no single general building code for United States communities to adopt into law. Before the turn of the century, there were three regional building codes in use through the United States. The Building Officials Code Administrators (BOCA) published the *National Building Code*, which was used on the East Coast and some eastern midwestern states. The Southern Building Code Congress International (SBCCI) published the *Standard Building Code*, also known colloquially as the *Southern Building Code*, which, as the nickname suggests, was adopted by many southern states. Finally, the International Conference of Building Officials (ICBO) published the *Uniform Building Code*, adopted by western states and midwestern states.

For some time, these disparate codes served their constituents well. However, over time, significant differences between the codes and the various code-making processes began to create legal and usability issues for the code-making bodies. In 1994, the three organizations had a historic meeting. During the meeting, they resolved to create a single building code for adoption across the country. Most extraordinarily, when the single code project was complete, each organization promised to disband once the new code was suitably published. The promise to disband was the key to the merger. Once the national code was available for adoption, in theory, there would be no competing document to impinge on the success of the new national code. During that historic

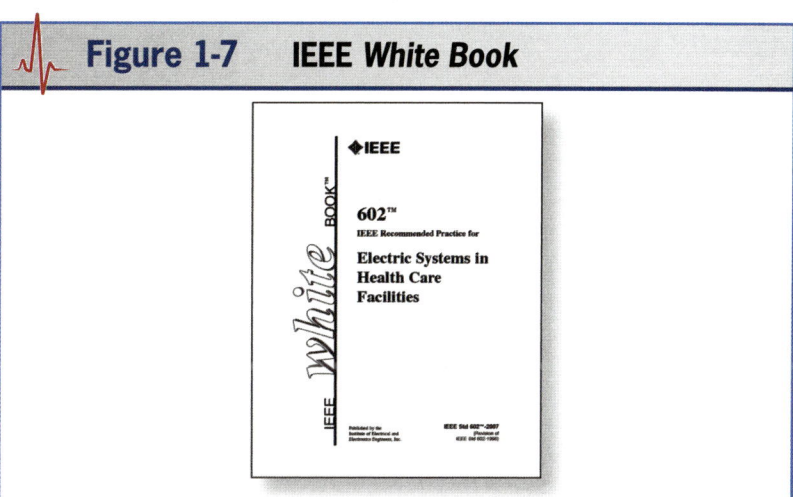

Figure 1-7. The 2007 edition of the IEEE White Book *was the last edition published in book form.*

meeting, the parties created the International Code Council (ICC), the organization that is responsible for the *International Building Code* to this day.

Beginning in 1994, the new ICC began the painstaking process of building a new code from scratch. The first edition was published in 1997 as a trial run. The second edition was published in 2000, and as promised, the SBCCI, the BOCA, and the ICBO all closed their doors, leaving the ICC as the sole publisher of general building codes for a short period of time. **See Figure 1-8.**

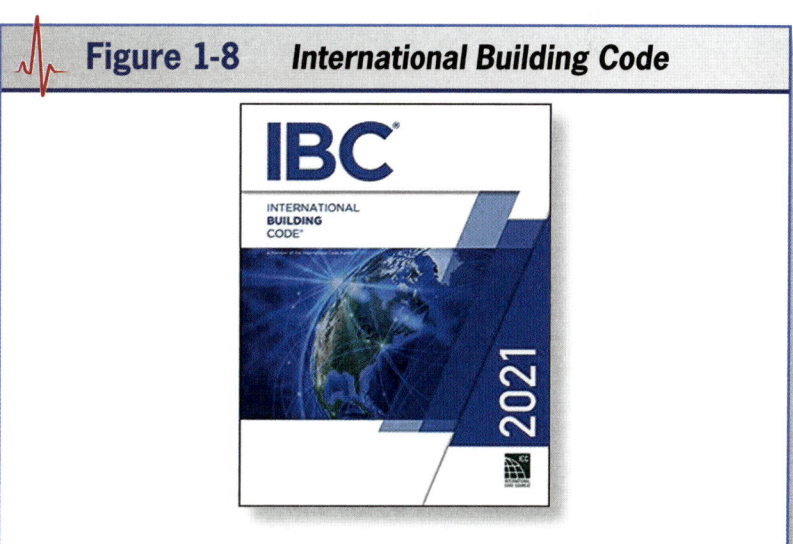

Figure 1-8. The International Building Code *is a base code standard used to provide safeguards from hazards associated with the construction of buildings.*

Early on, the NFPA and the ICC worked reasonably well together; both organizations agreed to support one another in the development of an *International Fire Code (IFC)*. Unfortunately, this period of goodwill did not last long. Soon the NFPA dropped out of the *IFC* project and began work on the *NFPA 5000* document, a general building code designed to test the ICC dominance of the market. In retaliation, the ICC threatened to begin work on the *International Electrical Code*, a document that would be in direct competition with the NFPA's flagship *National Electrical Code* (*NFPA 70*). Fortunately, the building and construction industry along with code users everywhere formed the "Get it Together" coalition and essentially insisted that both organizations call a truce and learn to work together. This intervention created an uneasy peace between the two organizations. Interestingly, *NFPA 5000* is still published and revised by the NFPA even though it has not been widely adopted by any jurisdiction. The ICC's *International Electrical Code* never got off the ground, although periodically there are rumors of its reincarnation. ICC does publish the *International Residential Code* which is an extract of NFPA's one- and two-family dwelling installation requirements from the *National Electrical Code* every three years.

Unlike *NFPA 99*, which specifically addresses health care facilities, the *IBC* is a use and occupancy standard. In other words, the intended use of the structure determines the requirements of the building construction. Toward that end, the *IBC* contains 35 chapters that collectively provide guidance on building classification, special requirements for special occupancies, and general requirements for all construction. In the 2018 edition, the *IBC* chapters are designated as follows:

- **Chapter 1: Scope and Administration.** Construction, alteration, repair, relocation and other types of construction activities. This chapter guides political jurisdictions regarding adoption, permitting, inspections, and enforcement.
- **Chapter 2: Definitions.** Provides specific usage information on key words used throughout the *IBC*. Unlike NFPA documents, all definitions are found in Chapter 2.
- **Chapter 3: Use and Occupancy Classifications.** As a use and occupancy code, this chapter is very important as it provides guidance on the classification of various structures which in turn determines the applicable construction regulations. Both hospitals and nursing homes are classified as Institutional Group I-2.
- **Chapter 4: Special Detailed Requirements Based on Use and Occupancy.** As the name suggests, this chapter provides detailed building requirements for structures defined in Chapter 3.
- **Chapters 5 through 34** provide general building requirements for everything from foundation details to roof requirements, and every structural and finish element in between.
- **Chapter 27: Electrical.** This is the chapter of most interest to Electrical Workers. Prior to 2015, it simply referred to *NFPA 70: National Electrical Code* and provided references to UL listing documents, guidance as to when an emergency electrical system was required, and maintenance references to the *International Fire Code*. The 2015 edition of the *IBC* saw dramatic revisions to the Chapter 27 emergency and standby power requirements, presumably in response to fact-finding reports issued after Hurricane Katrina and Super Storm Sandy. The listings found in Chapter 27 are important, as they clearly define legally required standby and emergency electrical systems in certain occupancies, as well as when certain systems (for example, emergency alarm systems) are in use within any structure.

- **Chapter 35: Referenced Standards.** A complete listing of every code and standard referenced in the *IBC*.

While not generally included in an Electrical Worker's curriculum, the *IBC* is an interesting and important document as it provides an accepted set of building regulations and often provides a mechanism for the *National Electrical Code* to be adopted into law.

Health Care and the *NEC*

Not surprisingly, the 1953 *National Electrical Code* was structured differently than the modern *NEC*. Consistent with today's structure, however, Chapter 5 of the 1953 *NEC* detailed the regulations for Special Occupancies. Article 510, "Specific Occupancies," had a section detailing the requirements for "Combustible Anesthetics," numbered 5135. This section is the first to mention requirements specifically devoted to health care. Article 510, Section 5135 was primarily concerned with the use of extremely flammable gas that was often used for patient anesthesia during that time. Cases of devastating fires were reported when these flammable gasses were ignited by an electrical spark.

In 1959, the *NEC* adopted a structure similar to the present-day editions. That *Code* also included the first entire article, Article 517, devoted to the more grammatically correct "Flammable Anesthetics." The 1971 edition of the *NEC* saw Article 517 restructured and renamed "Health Care Facilities"—the title it has retained to this day. Along with the name change came a large increase in the scope of the article beyond flammable anesthetics to include everything associated with the special installation techniques used in health care facilities.

Since 1959, health care has always had a dedicated article in the special occupancy chapter of the *NEC*. The installation and design requirements listed in Article 517 have grown in scope and depth over the years in response to the exponential growth of cutting edge technology, high-tech equipment, and the overall economic impact health care has on our national economy.

Although **Article 90** specifically calls out the *National Electrical Code* as an installation document, seasoned *Code* users know both design and performance elements are integral fundamentals found throughout the *Code*. The inclusion of design elements in the *NEC* makes sense as the installation of electrical systems requires quite a bit of design work on behalf of the installer. In 2011, and again in 2012, the Standards Council of the National Fire Protection Association essentially gave jurisdiction of all design and performance details found in Article 517 to the Electrical Systems Technical Committee of *NFPA 99: Health Care Facilities Code*. The rationale for this groundbreaking action was that this technical committee had jurisdiction over the design and performance aspects of health care facility electrical systems no matter what document was involved.

These decisions resulted in dramatic changes to the 2014 and 2017 revisions of the *National Electrical Code*. These changes have generally relaxed some of the important requirements for health care facility electrical systems, and have initiated a sometimes heated debate on which requirements are design and which requirements concern installation.

The specific electrical installation requirements for health care facilities are found in Chapter 5, "Special Occupancies," in Article 517, Health Care Facilities. This article contains seven parts.

Part I, General. This brief part details the scope of this article: "The provision of this article shall apply to electrical construction and installation criteria in health care facilities that provide care to human beings." The human aspect of this article is important as this language specifically exempts animal and veterinary care from the provisions of this article; although it is not uncommon to see the requirements of Article 517 detailed for these installations in individual job specifications.

This part also contains the extensive definition section of all the defined terms found only in Article 517, approximate total of 40 in the current edition.

Part II, Wiring and Protection. This important part deals with the specific requirements for patient care spaces. Section 517.10 provides information with regard to which wiring systems are covered and which are not covered in a patient care space. Section 517.13 requires redundant equipment grounding conductors for all receptacles and other equipment in patient care spaces. This concept is considered critical for patient safety and requires two intact and low-impedance ground paths to safely conduct stray current and allow the overcurrent protection device to open promptly, reducing the danger to patients. The section details the use of a metallic raceway or metallic cable jacket that qualify as an equipment grounding conductor in accordance with 250.118 as acceptable ground pathways, as well as requiring a green insulated equipment grounding conductor in the conduit or cable assembly to provide the wire type redundant equipment grounding conductor. **See Figure 1-9.**

Section 517.14 requires all panelboards serving a patient care space, whether supplied by the normal or essential power distribution systems, to be bonded together with an insulated green conductor not smaller than 10 AWG. This bonding assures a true equipotential ground plane in the patient care space.

Section 517.16 points out a unique installation requirement for isolated grounding receptacles, in that they shall not be installed within a patient care vicinity—pointing out to *Code* users the importance of applying special definitions contained in 517.2.

The number of receptacles and general installation requirements for Category 2 (General Care) patient care space is found in Section 517.18. General installation requirements for Category 1 (Critical Care) patient care spaces are found in 517.19. These sections also stipulate that all receptacles found in these areas shall be listed "hospital grade." **See Figure 1-10.**

Wet Procedure Locations are an area requiring special shock protection methods for patients and staff. These locations, as defined in 517.2, must be protected by GFCI equipment or isolated power systems.

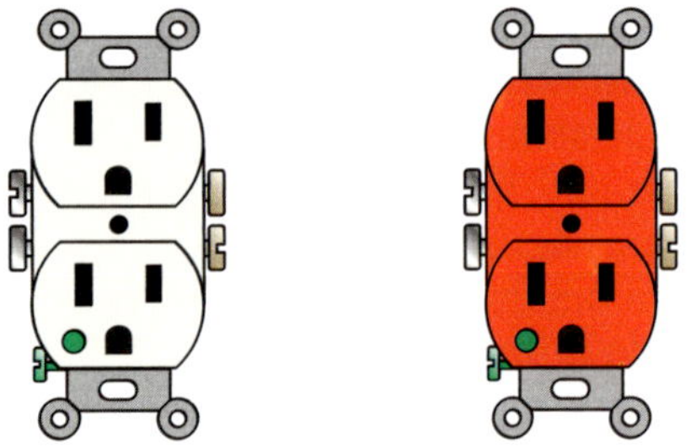

Section 517.21 provides an exception to general Ground-Fault Circuit-Interrupter Protection (GFCI) for personnel requirements, the exception states they are not required in bathrooms or toilet rooms of Category 1 (Critical Care)

Figure 1-9   Generic Patient Care Space

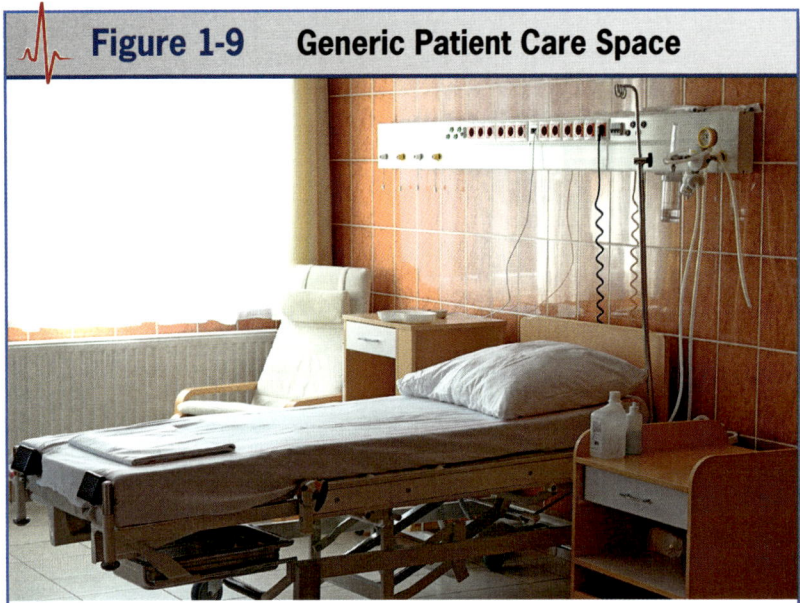

Figure 1-9. *A typical patient bed location requires the redundant grounding protection required in Section 517.13.*

Figure 1-10   Hospital Grade Receptacles

Hospital grade receptacles have greater contact tension.

Hospital grade receptacles are identified by the words "hospital grade" and a green dot on the receptacle's face.

Figure 1-10. *Hospital grade receptacles are required for general care patient bed locations.*

Space and Category 2 (General Care) space. If the governing board of the facility decides receptacles are necessary in these spaces, GFCI protection for the receptacle is required.

Part III, Essential Electrical Systems. Due to the extensive nature of these standby power systems in a health care environment, standby power systems are designated as essential electrical systems and are divided into three branches: life safety, equipment, and critical. It is important to note that 517.26 states the requirements of Article 700, Emergency Systems, only apply (with certain limitations) to the life safety branch. Moreover, it is also important to note that Article 517, as well as *NFPA 99*, is silent regarding the applicability of Article 701, Legally Required Standby Systems. This is significant as the *International Building Code* requires standby power systems in I-2 (Health Care) occupancies.

Part III also contains a requirement for the separation of essential and normal circuits, with some exceptions, such as within enclosures housing both normal and essential terminals. Provisions for the mechanical protection of essential circuits in patient care spaces, as well as receptacle identification requirements, are found in Part III.

This part also details the provisions for nursing home essential electrical systems which, dependent upon the level of care provided, may have two branches—critical and life safety—with the conditions found in other sections of Part III generally prevailing.

Part IV, Inhalation Anesthetizing Locations. This part is divided into two divisions: *Hazardous Anesthetizing Locations*, and *Other-Than-Hazardous Locations*. The reference to hazardous anesthetizing locations is a throwback to the flammable gases once used as anesthesia. These gases are no longer used in the developed world, but because the *NEC* is considered an "international electrical code," these provisions remain in the *Code* for the benefit of developing countries that may still use flammable gases.

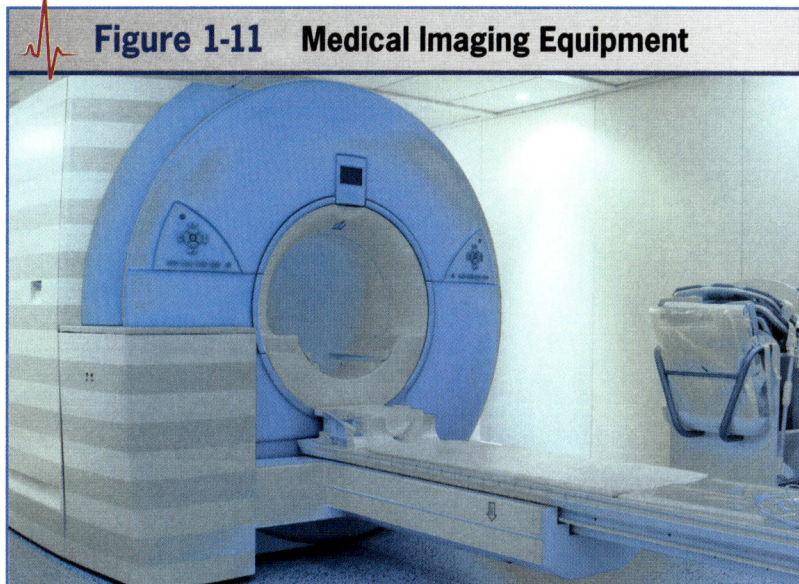

Figure 1-11   Medical Imaging Equipment

Figure 1-11. *Imaging equipment like a high-end tomography scanner should be carefully installed to the letter of the manufacturer's specifications.*

Other-than-hazardous locations require redundant grounding and mechanical protection of circuit conductors. Battery powered lighting units are also required to provide a source of illumination for the brief interval of time between the loss of normal power and the essential system coming online.

Part V, X-Ray Installations. This part details the requirements for the supply, rating, disconnect, and controls of x-ray equipment. This part is silent on other imaging equipment such as CAT scan and MRI devices. It is also a good example of technology outpacing the *Code*. When installing any imaging equipment, it is very critical to follow the manufacturer and listing instructions to assure a safe and usable installation. **See Figure 1-11.**

Part VI, Communications, Signaling Systems, Data Systems, Fire Alarm Systems, and Systems less than 120 Volts Nominal. Another example of technology outpacing the *Code*, the requirements contained in this Part primarily refer to Class 2 and 3 signaling circuits. Modern health care signaling and data acquisition equipment are now almost entirely wireless systems, rendering this Part essentially obsolete.

Figure 1-12   Current *Life Safety Code*

Figure 1-12. *The latest edition of NFPA 101: Life Safety Code was published in 2021.*

Part VII, Isolated Power Systems. The provisions of this Part details the requirements for these unique power supplies generally used as shock protection equipment in wet procedure area. Section 517.160 outlines conductor identification unique to this section of the *Code*, as well as the prohibition of wire pulling lubrication compounds, as two of the most important provisions found in Part VII.

There are other *NEC* articles that are important to health care facility installations. As mentioned, the requirements of Article 700 apply to the life safety branch of essential electrical systems, and one could argue that the provisions of Article 701, Legally Required Standby Systems, apply to the entire essential electrical system. Article 695, Fire Pumps, also has a special interest in health care installations as these important fire protection systems tend to be quite complex.

NFPA 101: Life Safety Code

In 1913, the National Fire Protection Association instituted the first committee on Safety to Life. The charge of this committee was to study notable fires involving tragic death toward a goal of decreasing loss of life in the event of a fire, as well as decreasing the frequency and severity of structural fires. The committee's first work stressed the importance of fire drills, adequate exits, and other egress means. Early publications authored by this committee were titled: *Exit Drills in Factories, Schools, Department Stores, and Theaters, Outside Stairs for Fire Exits*, and *Safeguarding Factory Workers from Fire*. In the 1920s, the committee published the *Building Exit Code*, which is the direct precursor to the modern *Life Safety Code*. **See Figure 1-12.**

The tragic Coconut Grove Nightclub fire of 1942 in Boston, which killed 492 people and injured hundreds more, drove home the need for an enforceable document that jurisdictions could adopt into law, providing better safety protocols and protection for their citizens. The *Building Exit Code* began a transformation to become that document shortly after the end of World War II. In 1963, the committee was restructured to become ANSI compliant, and the name of the document changed to *Code for Safety to Life from Fire in Buildings and Structures*. Through the years, the *Life Safety Code* has grown with each edition and has become one of the most referenced codes in North America.

The most recent edition of the *Life Safety Code* contains 43 chapters and four annexes. The first chapter is administrative and defines the scope and application of the document. Chapter 2, "Referenced Publications," provides the *Code* user a list of all NFPA and non-NFPA documents referenced by name in the *Life Safety Code*. Chapter 3, "Definitions," is an alphabetical listing of the definition of technical terms used in more than one chapter of the document. This chapter also points to the 11th edition of the *Merriam-Webster Collegiate Dictionary* for definitions not specifically located in Chapter 3. Chapter 4, "General," provides guidance on the general requirements for all structures, regardless of occupancy. Things like egress requirements, fire drill requirements, and maintenance, inspection, and testing are all found in this essential chapter. Chapter 5 provides performance-based options for general construction. Chapter 6, "Classification of Occupancy and Hazard of Contents," provides guidance on occupancy classification. Chapters 7 through 10 provide specifications on building elements such as egress, fire protection, and building equipment that are common to all occupancies. Chapters 11 through 42 provide regulations specific to certain classified occupancies. For example, the chapters specific to health care facilities are Chapters 18, 19, 20, and 21. Chapter 43, "Building Rehabilitation," addresses the requirements for life safety when an existing building is undergoing repair, renovation, modification, addition, reconstruction, or change in use or occupancy.

The health care facilities chapters of the *Life Safety Code* address occupancy-specific requirements. Chapter 18 details requirements for *new health care occupancies*, generally defined as new construction that provides sleeping accommodations to patients who are incapable of self-preservation. Perhaps the most far-reaching condition found in this chapter is the adoption of unique defend-in-place procedures in case of a fire emergency. The requirements, found in 18.7, are unique to these special occupancies and affect the manner in which fire alarm systems, fire sprinkler systems, and ventilation equipment are activated and used in a fire emergency. It is also important to note that the provisions of 18.7 are expressly permitted in other health care occupancies where self-preservation may not be a concern, specifically detailed in Chapters 19, 20, and 21.

Chapter 19, "Existing Health Care Facilities," provides direction on life safety requirements for structures currently occupied and classified as health care occupancies on an in-patient basis, such as hospitals or nursing homes that have been determined by the authority having jurisdiction as not being capable of self-preservation during an emergency.

Chapter 20, "New Ambulatory Occupancies," details the requirements for new construction regarding this fastest-growing sector of the health care market. These facilities are defined as providing service to patients on an outpatient basis and have been determined as not being capable of self-preservation during an emergency.

Chapter 21, "Existing Ambulatory Occupancies," provides regulatory requirements for existing structures providing service to patients who are not capable of self-preservation.

Many political jurisdictions adopt *NFPA 101: Life Safety Code* through their building regulation department. It is important to note that CMS also adopts the *Life Safety Code* as a condition for a health care organization to become CMS accredited.

Other NFPA Documents Important to Health Care Installations

- *NFPA 20: Standard for the Installation of Stationary Pumps for Fire Protection*
- *NFPA 72: National Fire Alarm and Signaling Code*
- *NFPA 90B: Standard for the Installation of Warm Air Heating and Air Conditioning Systems*
- *NFPA 110: Standard for Emergency and Standby Power Systems*
- *NFPA 111: Standard on Stored Electrical Energy Emergency and Standby Power Systems*
- *NFPA 241: Standard for Safeguarding Construction, Alteration, and Demolition Operations*

ENFORCEMENT

All the codes and standards (and all the millions and millions of working hours spent on *Code* development) are worthless unless the documents are adopted into law and vigorously and equitably enforced by a knowledgeable and professional building regulation department. Professional building officials are a crucial element to a safe, quality building environment. Health care facilities, by their very nature, are complex, not only from a codes and standards perspective but also from an enforcement point of view. Health care facility code enforcement can be divided into two camps: those involved in construction, usually defined as city or county authority having jurisdiction (AHJ), and those involved with the operations of the facility, called the governing body.

By and large, the enforcement of operational codes and standards by the governing body are peripheral to the study of health care facility electrical systems. The Electrical Worker does not need to be concerned with the health care organizations policy on the disposal of biohazard waste, for example. There are some operational codes established by the governing body of the facility that have a big impact on the construction environment. An understanding of these codes, and how their enforcement impacts health care facility construction, is in order.

Joint Operational and Construction Enforcement

For a health care organization to be eligible for Medicare and Medicaid reimbursement, the organization must meet certain standards required by CMS. These requirements include facilities built to regulations found in CMS requirements that include documents such as the *Guidelines for the Design and Construction of Hospitals*, *NFPA 101: Life Safety Code*, and *NFPA 99:*

Health Care Facilities Code. The great majority of health care organizations choose an accreditation process to show compliance with CMS regulations. They also use the Joint Commission as an accreditation body. The Joint Commission is often a part of the design team to make certain the building will be built to CMS standards and to assure that the health care organization building the structure will be eligible for the payments that will help pay for the structure. Operational standards greatly impact building construction.

Construction Enforcement

While health care facility construction code enforcement is often a local matter left up to the local AHJ, some states require an exhaustive "Certificate of Need" (CON) process before a building permit can be issued.

In 1974, new federal laws provided a funding mechanism for health care organizations who desired to build new facilities or substantially upgrade existing facilities. This law required states to develop a CON procedure to ensure that health care organizations were building structures that were needed by the community and not duplicating existing facilities, driving up health care costs.

All 50 states developed some form of CON procedure to allow local health care providers to access these federal funds. In 1987, the federal funding for this program ceased. Once the funding stopped, some states disbanded the

Joint Commission

The Joint Commission is a nonprofit organization that accredits health care organizations. This accreditation is a requirement for the health care organization to receive federal funds. This accreditation also assures the health care user that the facility meets certain minimum requirements. According to its website, the Joint Commission's mission statement is:

To continuously improve health care for the public, in collaboration with other stakeholders, by evaluating health care organizations and inspiring them to excel in providing safe and effective care of the highest quality and value.

For additional information, visit qr.njatcdb.org
Item #3998

Certificate of Need States

The following states/territories have "Certificate of Need" laws as of 2020:

- Alabama
- Alaska
- Arkansas
- Connecticut
- Delaware
- District of Columbia
- Florida
- Georgia
- Hawaii
- Illinois
- Iowa
- Kentucky
- Louisiana
- Maine
- Maryland
- Massachusetts
- Michigan
- Mississippi
- Missouri
- Montana
- Nebraska
- Nevada
- New Jersey
- New York
- North Carolina
- Ohio
- Oklahoma
- Oregon
- Puerto Rico
- Rhode Island
- South Carolina
- Tennessee
- US Virgin Islands
- Vermont
- Virginia
- Washington
- West Virginia

CON process, assuming market conditions would control unnecessary building costs. Other states maintained the CON process and statutes, feeling that some degree of control over health care construction spending was in the overall public interest. These CON states require the health care organization to complete what can be an arduous process before a building permit can be issued by a locality. For example, the CON process outline may include:

1. Allocation of beds and services
2. Review schedule for the allocation
3. Submissions of letters of intent to apply by health care organizations
4. Submission of applications by eligible applicants
5. Public comment period
6. Public meeting period
7. Application review
8. Award of certificate
9. Appeal period
10. Continual monitoring of the project(s) during the construction and commissioning phase

Getting a health care facility project off the ground can be delayed for years in a CON state.

Local Authority Having Jurisdiction

The authority having jurisdiction (AHJ) is usually the local city, township, county, or state building regulation department that has "boots on the ground" responsibility for inspection and verification of the design and construction of the building. The design and construction must qualify, to the letter, of whatever building and construction code that specific jurisdiction has adopted into law. While the process varies greatly from jurisdiction to jurisdiction, most AHJs have some form of plan review. Although the architect and engineer have a legal responsibility for the structure and systems, a thorough plan review by the AHJ should uncover any issues the design documents may have with the local codes adopted into law in that locality before construction begins.

Once a building permit has been issued, qualified inspectors make determinations of whether the installations meet the appropriate codes. Sometimes an installation is acceptable and will pass with no issues. More often, a few issues will be uncovered that can be fixed on the spot, and an "approved" card is issued for that portion of the work. Sometimes substandard work is uncovered that is so damaging that a "stop work" order is issued by the inspector until the unacceptable work can be repaired or replaced to meet specifications. Building inspectors are an important part of the construction team and are part of the enforcement process from the placement

International Association of Electrical Inspectors

One very effective organization representing AHJs is the International Association of Electrical Inspectors (IAEI). This group is very active in codes and standards development, working hard to ensure public safety. To quote from the website:

International Association of Electrical Inspectors (IAEI) has, since 1928, been a core leader in the electrical industry and has actively promoted safe products and safe installations. Active members and partners in the association include many diverse groups, including electrical inspectors, testing agencies, standards organizations, manufacturers, distributors, installers, and contractors. The association has a long and recognized history in comprehensive training in and promotion of safe products, electrical installations, and inspections in order to ensure compliance with electrical codes and standards.

For additional information, visit qr.njatcdb.org
Item #3885

of the first footer to the issuance of an occupancy permit.

Commissioning

A growing trend in health care facilities construction is the adoption of a commissioning process, certifying the building systems are installed and operating to specification before payments are made to contractors. This process can also include verification that medical equipment has been installed as per the manufacturer's directions, assuring the health care organization receives full benefit from equipment warranties.

Third Party Commissioning

The 2014 edition of the *Guidelines for Design and Construction of Hospitals* requires new and remodeled facilities to commission the following systems:

- HVAC
- Automatic Temperature Control
- Fire Alarm Systems
- Fire Protection Systems
- Essential Electrical Power

The *Guidelines* define *commissioning* as "... a quality process used to achieve, validate, and document that facilities and component infrastructure systems are planned, constructed, installed, tested, and capable of being operated and maintained in conformity with the design intent to meet the owner's project requirements." While this document only requires commissioning the systems detailed above, annex material strongly suggests the health care organization adopt a "total building commissioning (TBC)" strategy.

For the first time, the 2014 edition of the *Guidelines* requires that all commissioning activities be performed by a third party agency.

SUMMARY

Health care facilities are a critical part of modern society. They play an essential role in the communities that they serve. Understanding this position will help electrical professionals appreciate the importance of safe and quality installations of the electrical systems installed within them. Many codes and standards cover the design and installation of electrical systems that serve health care facilities. Understanding documents such as *NFPA 99*, the *International Building Code*, the *NEC*, and *NFPA 101* will give learners the foundation needed to become qualified professionals in the trade. Upon understanding how these codes and standards were developed and how they are enforced, it becomes clear how critically important they are for the safety of the patients, the health care professionals, and the community as a whole.

REVIEW QUESTIONS

1. The *IBC* categorizes medium and large hospitals as risk category __?__ buildings.
   a. 1
   b. 2
   c. 3
   d. 4

2. During times of emergency, health care facilities must remain open when utility services are not available for a considerable period of time. For this reason, reliable back up electrical power and fuel sources must be available for such emergencies.
   a. True   b. False

3. Health care facilities must be designed and built to withstand __?__ disasters. Hospital emergency departments must be able to provide services to the community no matter what the calamity.
   a. constant redesign and remodel
   b. extreme use
   c. natural and man-made
   d. terrorist attacks

4. A hospital's essential electrical system may look, from a design and installation perspective, very much like an electrical system found in a(n) __?__.
   a. data center
   b. educational facility
   c. financial institution
   d. all the above

5. Many health care facilities are adopting strict work practices, especially on remodeling and renovation projects, which require contractors and their workers to follow protocols designed to minimize the spread of __?__.
   a. airborne chemicals
   b. dust
   c. infection
   d. all of the above

6. The "defend in place" strategy involves relocating occupants to a safe location outside of a hospital facility or to another health care facility during an emergency.
   a. True   b. False

7. Which of the following is the primary document for health care facility design?
   a. *Guidelines for Design and Construction of Hospitals*, published the American Society for Healthcare Engineering
   b. *NFPA 70: National Electrical Code*
   c. *NFPA 99: Health Care Facility Code*
   d. *The International Building Code (IBC)*

8. Before 2000, there was no single general building code that communities in the United States could use to adopt into law for the construction of a health care facility.
   a. True   b. False

REVIEW QUESTIONS

9. The __?__ contains __?__ chapters that collectively provide guidance on building classification, special requirements for special occupancies, and general requirements for all construction.
   a. American Hospital Association Hospital Guidelines / 32
   b. *International Building Code (IBC)* / 35
   c. International Health Care Installation Standard / 47
   d. *National Life Safety Code* / 22

10. Historically, combustible anesthetics were used to reduce patient discomfort. Early editions of the *NEC* specifically devoted rules and regulations for health care facilities to prevent ignition and explosion of extremely flammable gas that was often used for patient anesthesia.
    a. True   b. False

11. __?__ specifically calls out the *National Electrical Code* as an installation document, but seasoned *Code* users know both design, performance, and prescriptive elements are integral fundamentals found throughout the *Code*.
    a. Article 90
    b. Article 110
    c. Article 300
    d. Article 517

12. The specific electrical installation requirements for health care facilities are found in Chapter 5, "Special Occupancies," in Article 517, Health Care Facilities. This article contains __?__ parts.
    a. 5
    b. 7
    c. 12
    d. 15

13. Section 517.13 of the *NEC* requires redundant grounding for all receptacles and other equipment in patient care spaces. This provision requires two intact, low-impedance ground paths to safely conduct stray current, reducing the danger to a patient. The section also details the use of a metallic raceway or grounded metallic cable jacket as an acceptable ground pathway, as well as requiring a green insulated equipment grounding conductor in the conduit or cable assembly, thus providing the redundant ground.
    a. True   b. False

14. Special bonding requirements of all normal or essential branch circuit panelboards in a hospital serving an individual patient care space require the installation of a 10 AWG or larger conductor with green insulated covering installed between the equipment grounding conductor terminal bus of each adjacent panelboard to create a true equipotential ground. This requirement is found in *NEC* __?__.
    a. 517, Part 1
    b. 517.13
    c. 517.14
    d. 517.19

15. Nursing home essential electrical systems, which are dependent upon the level of care provided, are generally required to have __?__ with the conditions found in other sections of Part III of Article 517.
    a. two branches: critical and life safety
    b. four branches: normal, critical, life safety, and equipment
    c. three to six automatic transfer switches
    d. all of the above

16. Communications, signaling systems, data systems, fire alarm systems, and other such systems less than 120 volts, nominal, are classified as __?__.
    a. Class A power-limited
    b. Class 2 and 3 signaling circuits
    c. communication and alarm systems
    d. power circuits

REVIEW QUESTIONS

17. The most recent edition of the *Life Safety Code* contains __?__ chapters and four annexes.

    a. 43
    b. 57
    c. 83
    d. 99

18. Health care facility code enforcement can be divided into two camps: those involved in construction, usually defined as city or county __?__, and those involved with the operations of the health care facility, called the __?__.

    a. authority having jurisdiction (AHJ) / governing body
    b. authority having jurisdiction (AHJ) / lead physician
    c. building code department / state health department
    d. inspector / advisory body

19. All 50 states have developed some current form of "Certificate of Need" procedure to allow local health care providers to access facility needs.

    a. True   b. False

20. The __?__ is usually the local city, township, county, or state building regulation department that has "boots on the ground" responsibility for inspection and verification of the design and construction of the building.

    a. authority having jurisdiction (AHJ)
    b. designer/architect
    c. general contractor
    d. governing body

Utility Power

A key element of health care electrical systems is redundancy. The failure of one element in an electrical system should not significantly affect patient care and safety. Redundancy applies to electrical utility services as well as on-site generator capability. Through the years, design engineers have developed several schemes in an effort to assure safe, reliable electrical power is always available for a health care facility's essential loads.

Objectives

» Explain how redundant utility power is applied to health care facilities and the multiple ways it is managed in the event of a service failure.

» Apply codes and standards to on-site generation of power and explain the installation difficulties electrical professionals must consider.

» Understand the concept of peak shaving and the pros and cons of its application.

» Describe the benefits of on-site power generation for nonessential loads.

Chapter 2

Table of Contents

POWER RELIABILITY

Electrical power plays an intricate role in allowing health care providers to diagnose and treat ill patients. Electrical power fuels diagnostic and treatment equipment, provides support for patient records, and allows additional critical activities needed to maintain life. It is no exaggeration to state that reliable electrical power is the lifeblood of a health care facility.

Power redundancy equals reliability. Every health care code and standard specifies that health care facilities must have standby or redundant electrical power supply systems. This is accomplished by using the local electrical utility to provide standard "normal" electrical service to the facility. The redundancy aspect of the equation is provided by on-site electrical power generation, usually diesel-engine driven generators. Occasionally the roles may be reversed: the on-site generation may be considered the prime or "normal" source of power and the redundancy is provided by the local electrical utility. Sometimes natural gas-fired engines are used to drive generators, rather than diesel engines. Either way, utility power and on-site generated power are both essential components of the equation, as are the common design schemes engineers use to assure health care facilities have the most reliable power systems possible. As we move into the future other redundant power supply systems will become available, namely uninterruptable power supplies (UPS) and microgrid type power systems.

UTILITY POWER

Normally, utility power is brought into a large institutional facility via properly-sized utility conductors, which are terminated to a large transformer bank that reduces the distribution voltage to the

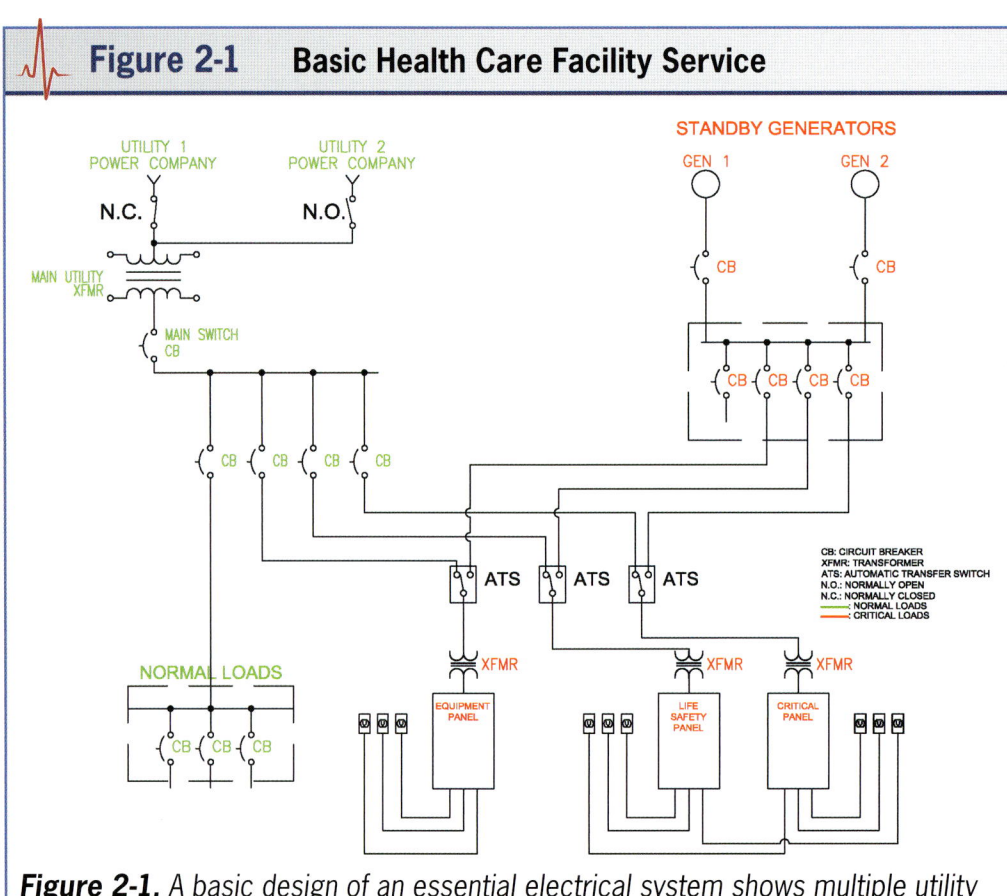

Figure 2-1   Basic Health Care Facility Service

Figure 2-1. A basic design of an essential electrical system shows multiple utility services and generators.

utilization voltage. From the load side of the transformer, power is brought to a service entrance main disconnecting means and then distributed throughout the facility using switchgear, feeders, panelboards, and branch circuits to provide power to the end user.

While the scenario is acceptable under code requirements, and is certainly cost-effective, it is almost never used in designing health care facility utility services; instead, engineers often use utility service designs that provide an additional layer of redundancy into the power equation. **See Figure 2-1.**

Two Separate Utility Grid Power Systems

Before electrical power deregulation in the 1990s, design engineers would often specify health care facilities have two utility services—one fed from the *local*, or *primary*, power grid in the general location where the health care facility is located, and the other fed from a separate, nearby *non-local, secondary* power grid. That way, if the local "primary" service had an outage, normal power would be maintained by the "secondary" service from a non-local power grid. Prior to deregulation, power

utilities would often provide infrastructure for these complex systems at little or no cost, as a community benefit.

Since deregulation, utilities require the user to pay for the development of these grids and they have become very expensive. Engineers often opt to use additional on-site generation capabilities rather than invest in the utility infrastructure. In any case, these dual grid design systems are very common and effective for providing redundant power, particularly in existing facilities, and are still used in new build situations in urban areas.

Although expensive, these systems have proven to be very reliable. As the saying goes, "Utility power is about 100% more reliable than generated power." The two-grid utility systems are used in health care facilities in a couple of different ways.

Manual Transfer of Power Supply Utility Systems

The most cost-effective solution for dual grid systems when changing connections from one power grid to the other is using manual transfer switches at the location where the primary utility supply grid meets the secondary utility grid. There are a few ways that

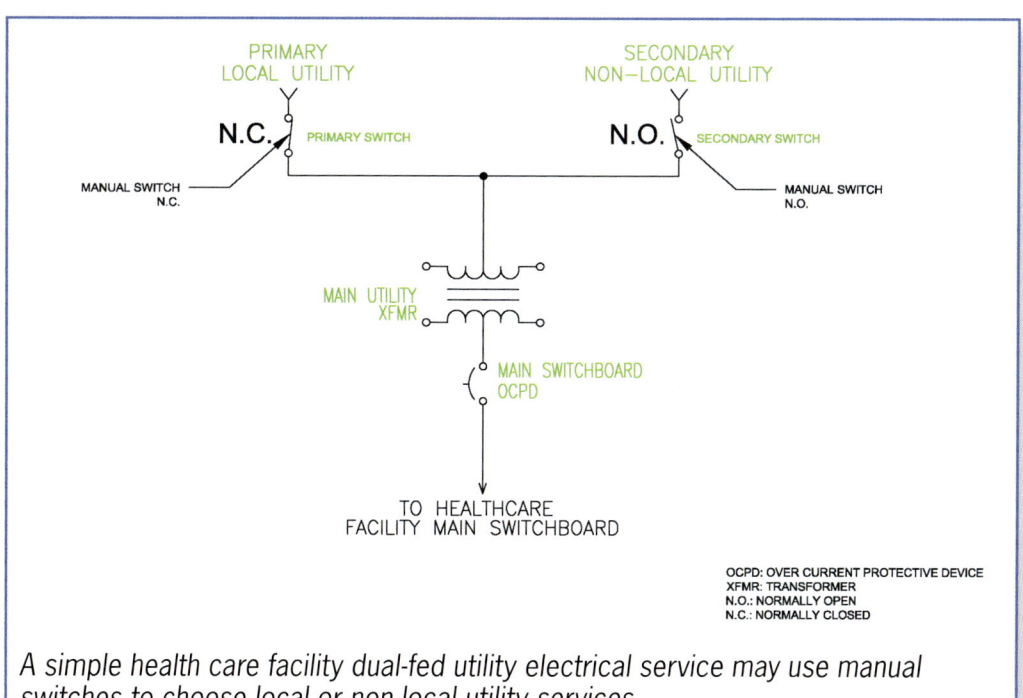

A simple health care facility dual-fed utility electrical service may use manual switches to choose local or non-local utility services.

this can be accomplished. Pole- or pad-mounted switches located at the spot where the primary and secondary utility distribution conductors are brought together are the simplest option. In this scenario, the primary local grid utility conductor switch is closed, providing normal power to the health care facility. In the event of a failure, a qualified person opens the primary utility switch and closes the secondary utility switch, providing normal utility power to the health care facility through the non-local grid. When power is restored to the primary utility conductors, the qualified person simply reverses the operation to put the health care facility back on the normal, local grid's primary power.

A second, slightly more sophisticated scheme, is to employ a manual transfer switch rather than rely on pole- or pad-mounted switches. In this case, the primary (local grid) and secondary (non-local grid) utility distribution conductors are brought into the line side of a distribution voltage-rated transfer switch. The transfer switch is closed on the primary

distribution utility conductors and open on the secondary distribution utility conductors. Should an outage occur on the primary utility conductors, a qualified person, usually a utility worker, manually changes the position of the transfer switch, opening the lost primary utility conductors and closing the energized secondary utility conductors, providing normal power to the health care facility.

These systems, although cost-effective, have some drawbacks. While providing redundancy for utility service, this system relies on a single set of utility conductors from the switchyard to the utility transformer. Most importantly, the entire normal system is reliant on a single transformer to provide normal utility service to the health care facility. These are glaring issues when considering reliable, redundant normal electrical power. **See Figure 2-2.**

Transfer of Power for Two Utility Services

Increased redundancy can be achieved under a two-grid system by providing two separate services from both the

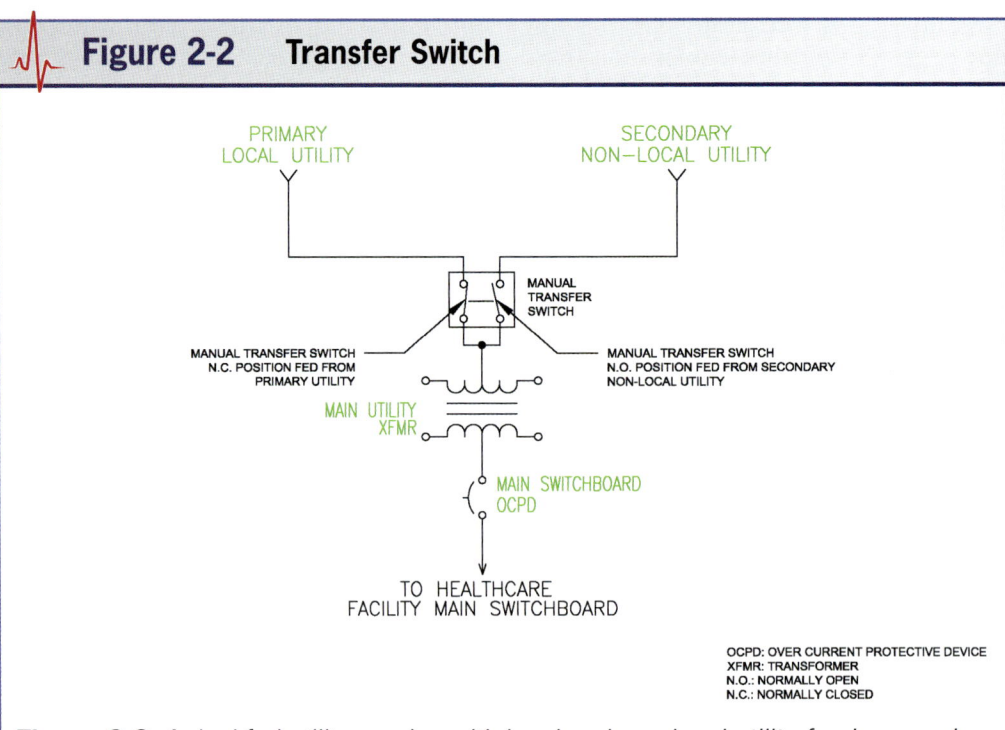

Figure 2-2   Transfer Switch

Figure 2-2. A dual-fed utility service with local and non-local utility feeders can be controlled by a manual transfer switch.

primary and secondary utility conductors, rather than just two utility distribution conductors. The two separate service conductor systems are much more expensive than the two-utility conductor scheme, but it provides additional redundancy by providing redundant distribution service conductors to redundant utilization voltage transformers to a main switchboard using a tie breaker to assure complete normal system redundancy. Most engineers will agree that the peace of mind provided by these two service systems is well worth the additional cost.

These two service systems employ two distribution utility services and two utility transformers; each service is sized to handle the entire load of the health care facility. Each transformer secondary is provided with a main disconnection means. Through the two main disconnects, each utility service feeds one-half of the main distribution switchgear. The switchgear is electrically divided by a tie-breaker into two distinct sections. This is commonly known as double-ended switchgear, which provides a distinct level of reliability. However, it can prove confusing and somewhat difficult to work on for an untrained worker.

During normal operations, the mains from both utility transformers are closed. The tie-breaker between the two ends of the switchboard is open, meaning that both the primary and secondary services are energized and under load with each carrying approximately one-half the entire load of the health care facility. If a power outage occurs on the primary service, a qualified person opens the main switch on the primary transformer and closes the tie-breaker in the double-ended switchboard. The secondary service would then energize the entire switchboard and assume the entire health care facility load.

When power is restored to the primary utility service, the tie-breaker is opened, and the primary service main is closed, bringing half of the health care facility load back to the primary service. Should the secondary service experience an outage, the process is reversed: the secondary main is opened, the tie-breaker is closed, and the primary service assumes 100% of the health care facility's load.

There are a number of advantages to this system. For example, from a maintenance perspective, it is invaluable to be able to shut down either utility transformer for testing, maintenance, repair, and replacement. Using both utility services helps justify the enormous cost of bringing two distribution feeders to the facility. Of course, the facility workers must remember that care should be taken to open the main switch of the utility transformer experiencing the outage *before* closing the tie-breaker to avoid back-feeding the grid with the entire energy of the second energized service.

This is a proven, extremely reliable system, with one glaring drawback—the

These two overhead utility services are feeding a health care facility. Each service is sized to carry the entire load of the facility. Courtesy of Lawson Electric Co., Chattanooga, TN

Figure 2-3   Two Services–Double-Ended Gear

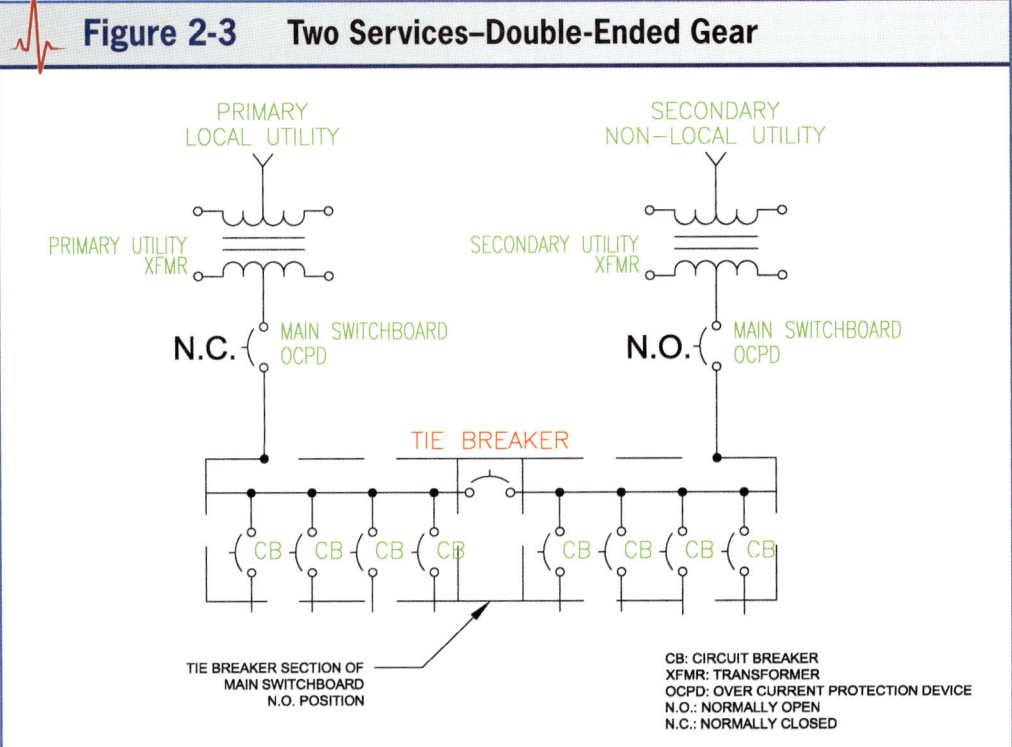

Figure 2-3. *A very reliable utility service configuration utilizes two services to feed double-ended switchgear. Note the position of the tie-breaker determines the load distribution.*

potential for human error. Under outage conditions, the pressure is on Electrical Workers to get the power back on as soon as possible. Naturally, this puts an enormous amount of stress on staff and mistakes can be made. Remember, the primary distribution feeder and the secondary distribution feeder come from two different grids, and even though they are, in all likelihood, fed from the same power plant, the two utility conductor systems are not synchronous. In other words, they are not in-phase with each other.

When restoring power to a normal situation after an outage, if the tie-breaker is not opened and the restored main is closed, a catastrophic event will tear the main double-ended switchboard apart as large asynchronous currents meet in a spectacular blow-up. The equipment will be destroyed and workers may be severely injured or killed. The entire normal electrical service will be out of commission for a long period of time as repairs and replacements are made, all in the name of desired redundancy. **See Figure 2-3.**

To avoid this catastrophic event, equipment manufacturers utilize a lock and key system to prevent human error. This system uses two keys that are "captured" by the system, or cannot be removed from the lock, when a switch is closed. This system requires a key to open and a key to close both the utility main switch and the tie-breaker. Only two keys exist in these systems—the two keys will fit the locks on both main breakers and the tie-breaker. A key cannot be removed while the breaker is in the "on" position and can only be removed when the breaker is in the "off" or deenergized position. This system prevents all three breakers from being in the "on" position at the same time.

Should a utility service experience an outage, the Qualified Electrical Worker opens the utility transformer main, opening the switch and "releasing" the captive key. This allows the Electrical

Worker to take the key to the tie-breaker, where inserting and turning the key into the mechanism allows the Electrical Worker to close the tie-breaker. When the tie-breaker is closed, the mechanism "captures" the key so that the key cannot be removed from the mechanism, assuring only two devices can be closed at any one time. These keying systems are a simple and cheap form of insurance against human error. **See Figure 2-4.**

Automatic Transfer of Utility Power Systems

Transfer from utility service to utility service using the main switches and tie-breakers can be accomplished without human intervention, using modern switching devices that communicate to one another and have the ability to act in concert. These automatic systems take human error out of the equation; however, they can create some issues as well.

When installed, these two services are 100% redundant. Each service is sized to carry the entire load of the health care facility and is designed to handle increased operational needs as the facility grows over time. Conversely, growth may impact a single service's ability to assume the entire health care facility's load. Should this occur, shedding of nonessential loads (such as some HVAC components) must occur before the transfer to a single service can occur. This kind of coordination can be programmed in an automatic transfer system, but only providing that all switching equipment, including previously installed equipment, can communicate together. A growing number of electrical power utilities require the health care facility to notify them before initiating a transfer to a single feeder. The idea is to protect utility infrastructure from overloads caused by significantly increased loads.

Additionally, automatic transfer schemes can cause issues with the timing of on-site generation start-up. These factors work against automatic

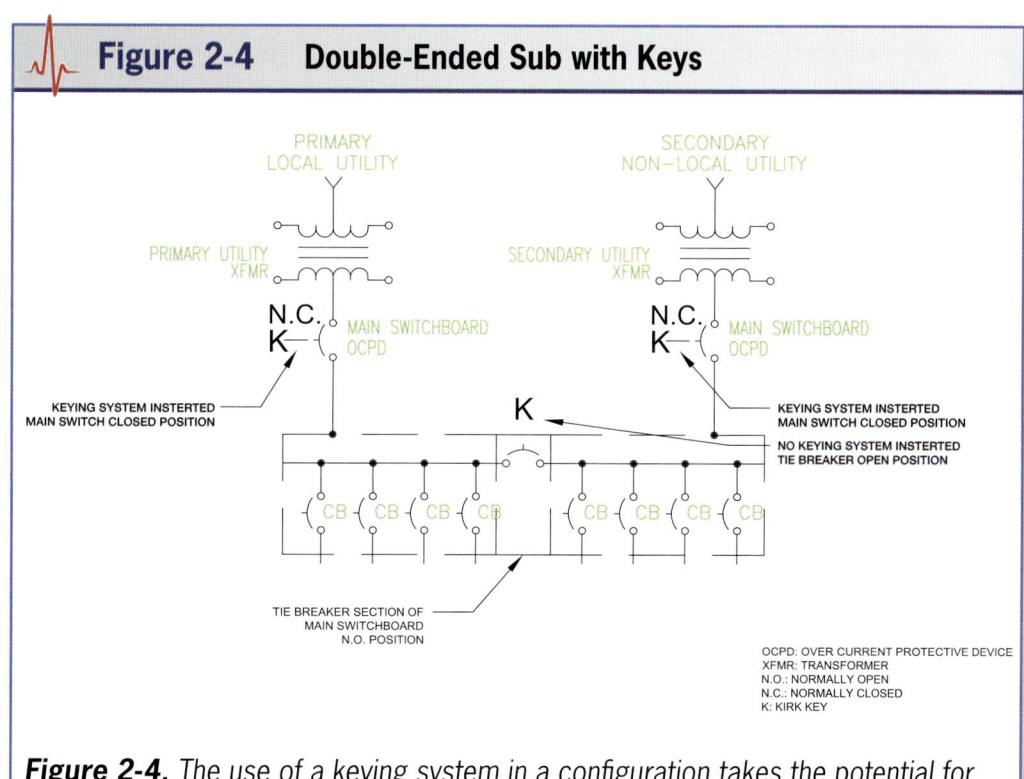

Figure 2-4   Double-Ended Sub with Keys

Figure 2-4. The use of a keying system in a configuration takes the potential for human error out of the equation.

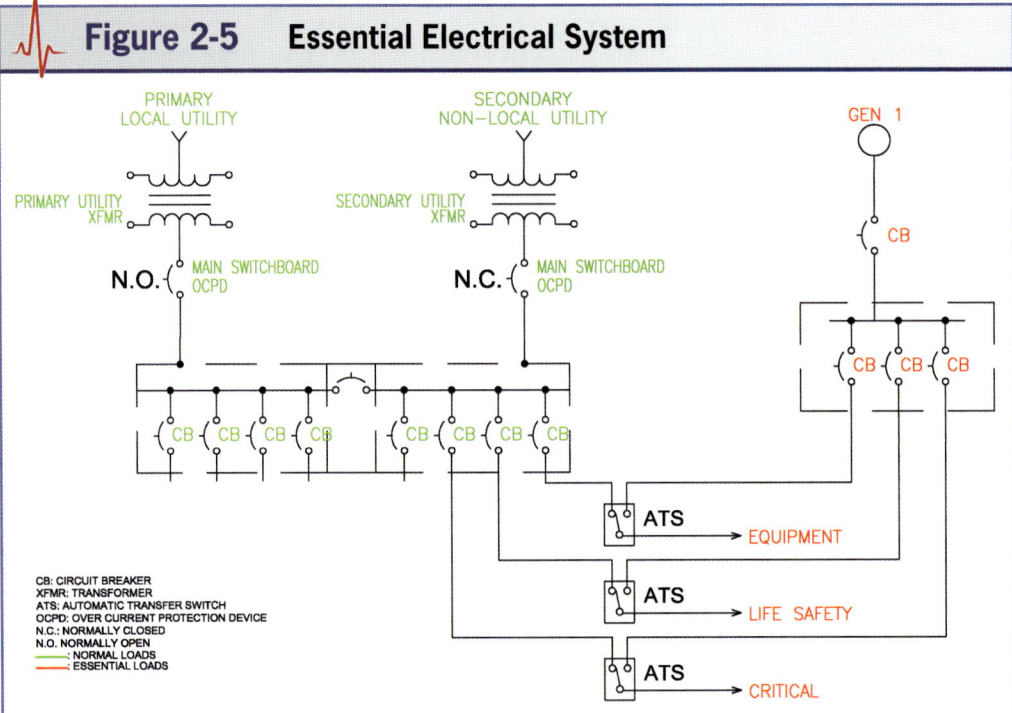

Figure 2-5   Essential Electrical System

Figure 2-5. A double-ended service includes the addition of the key elements of the health care facility's essential electrical system.

transfer between two utility services. **See Figure 2-5.**

Both *NFPA 99: Health Care Facilities Code* and *NFPA 110: Life Safety Code* require certain loads in health care facilities (namely elements of the life safety system and critical branches of the essential electrical system) to be brought online within 10 seconds of a power outage. None of the dual utility distribution systems outlined above will restore power to these essential loads in 10 seconds; they are not designed to. Additional redundant power supply systems are required by the *Code* for the essential electrical system loads. In the event of an outage, it is expected that the on-site generation system will start, come online, and assume the essential loads in the 10-second window, providing time for qualified persons to analyze the situation and make the appropriate shedding and transfer actions.

Essential Electrical System Connected Loads

The 2020 *National Electrical Code®* is very prescriptive as to the nature of the equipment that can be connected to the essential electrical systems life safety branch. The *Code* provides the design engineer a bit more flexibility when considering critical branch connected equipment, and while prescribing certain equipment to be connected to the equipment branch, the design engineer has the freedom to feed any load through the equipment branch. The connection for this branch to the generator is permitted to be delayed beyond the 10 seconds required of the life safety and critical branches.

Essential Electrical System Connected Loads (cont.)

Section 517.33 details the loads permitted to be served by the life safety branch of the essential electrical system. Only the following equipment can be served by this branch:

- Egress illumination
- Exit signs
- Alarm and alerting systems
  - Including the fire alarm system and medical gas alarms
- Communication systems (when used to issue instructions in the event of an emergency)
- Generator and Transfer Switch Locations
  - Includes illumination battery chargers, task illumination, and certain receptacles
- Generator Accessories
  - Loads designed to keep the generator performing. Includes equipment such as battery chargers, louver controls, fuel transfer pumps, and cooling fan motors
- Elevators
  - Car lighting, control, communication, and signaling systems only
- Automatic Doors (only when used for egress)

Section 517.34 details the equipment required to be connected to the critical branch of the essential electrical system. It should be noted that though the *Code* requires the following loads to be connected to the critical branch, it does not prohibit other loads from connection.

- Task illumination and selected receptacles in the following locations:
  - Critical care spaces
  - Nurseries
  - Pharmacies
  - Acute nursing locations
  - Treatment Areas
  - Nurses Stations
  - Angiographic Labs
  - Cardiac Catheterization Labs
  - Coronary Care Units
  - Hemodialysis Spaces
  - Selected Emergency Rooms
  - Human Physiology Labs
  - Intensive Care Units
  - Selected Post-Operative Recovery Spaces
- Isolated Power Systems
- Specialized Patient Care Equipment
- Critical Care Spaces
- General Care Spaces (at least one receptacle)
- Nurse Call Systems
- Blood, bone, and tissue banks
- Telephone and data equipment
- Other loads that are required for safe and efficient facility operation

Section 517.35 details the loads that must be connected to the equipment branch of the essential electrical system. This branch may be configured for delayed connection, and its loads are permitted to be shed in the event of an electrical emergency. These loads include:

- Vacuum Systems
- Sump Pumps
- Medical Compressed Air Systems
- Ventilating systems for operating rooms, delivery rooms, isolation rooms, labs, and other similar locations
- Ventilating systems for telephone and data equipment
- Heating equipment under certain conditions (may be manually connected)
- Elevators
- Hyperbaric Facilities
- Hypobaric Facilities
- Automatically Operated Doors
- Autoclaving Equipment
- Controls for all of the above
- Other loads required for a safe and efficient facility operation

NETWORK AND LOOP SERVICES

Network and loop service systems are expensive. Many engineers opt instead to use other utility service strategies and invest the savings in an additional on-site generation. These solutions use equipment that can synchronize phase relationships between different utility service conductors, essentially allowing the current from different utility service conductors to occupy the same service bus without issue. These systems also use network protector devices that open when a reverse current is detected, essentially isolating a service conductor experiencing an outage from the back-feed current. Because these systems synchronize the utility service conductors, any number of service conductors may be used for the common service. This creates multiple layers of redundancy. These networked systems are often paired with double-ended switchgear, offering additional redundancy. **See Figure 2-6.**

Loop fed distribution systems are popular in campus-style health care facilities, where the distribution voltage (utility) is fed from two distribution points to the entire campus. These systems use a single distribution system to provide redundant power to multiple locations on the loop. **It is very important to understand that loop distribution systems are intentionally back fed. Opening one device will not deenergize the distribution loop. See Figure 2-7.**

LEVEL OF SERVICE

The type of service the engineer chooses for the health care facility will depend largely on the level of care provided at the facility and on the existing utility assets available at the site. It stands to reason that a large multi-structure urban university medical center will have electrical service requirements quite different from a clinic in a rural county providing triage and first-level emergency care.

ON-SITE GENERATION

Despite the best intentions, utility electrical power can fail. No amount of redundancy can protect a health care

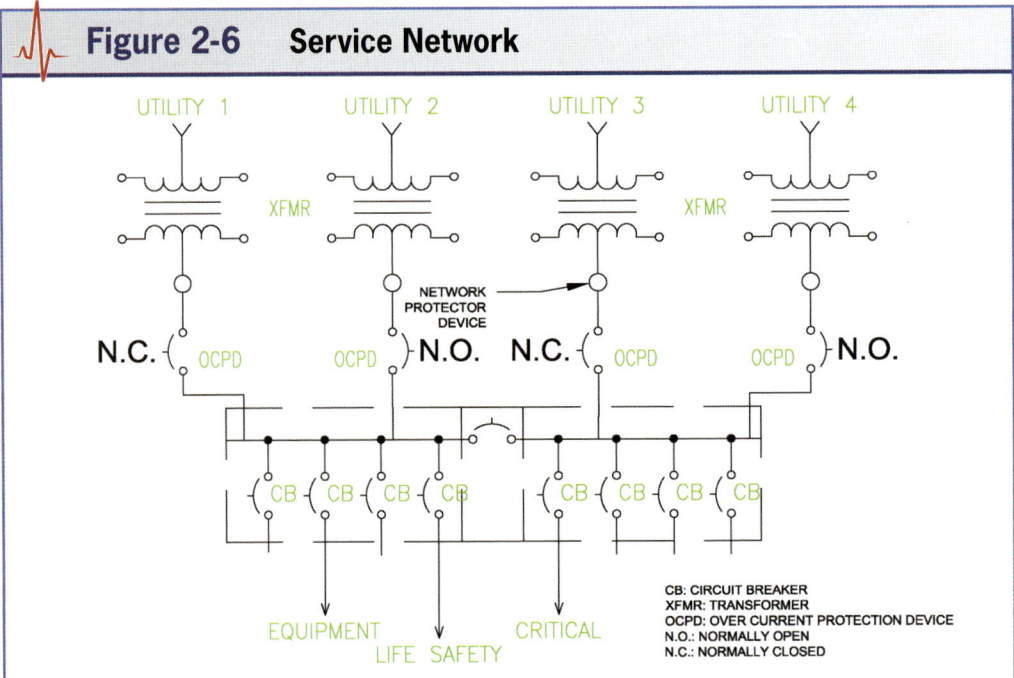

Figure 2-6   Service Network

Figure 2-6. *A health care facility can be served by multiple utility services, phase synchronized, and connected in a network configuration.*

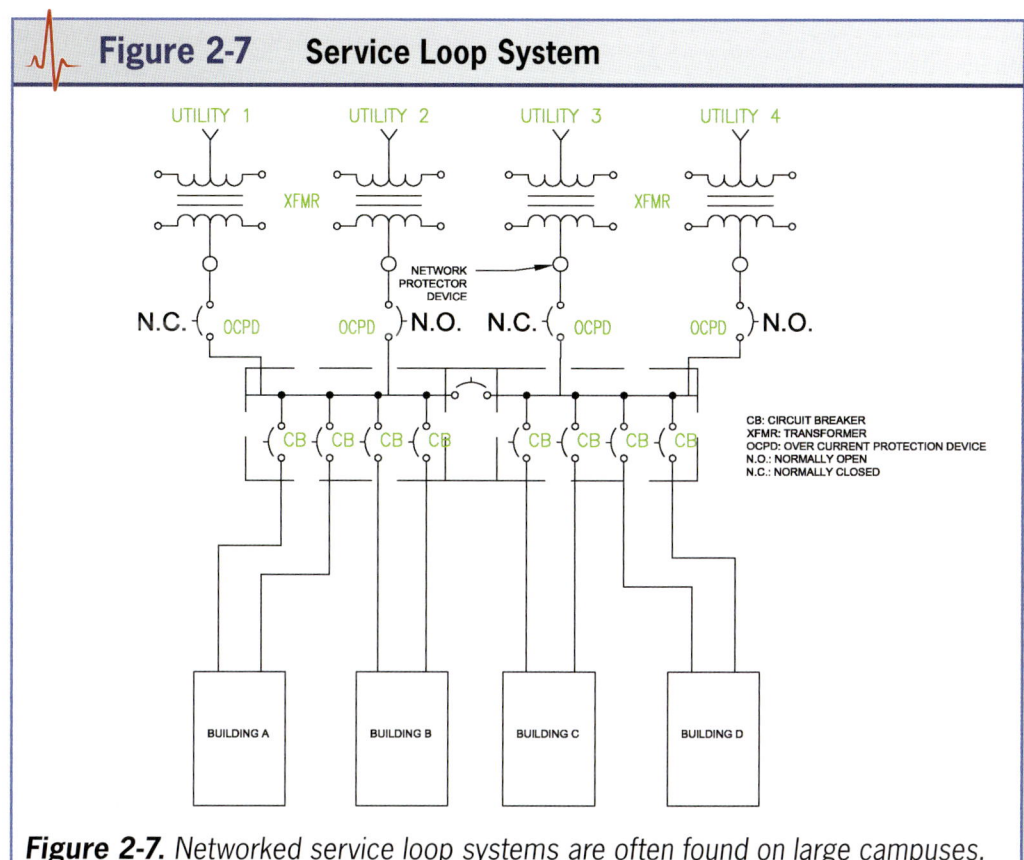

Figure 2-7   Service Loop System

Figure 2-7. Networked service loop systems are often found on large campuses.

facility from a utility power outage. This is why both *NFPA 99: Health Care Facilities Code* and *NFPA 110: Life Safety Code* require health care facilities to have on-site power generation capacity, properly sized to take on life safety, critical, and defined equipment loads during a utility power failure. These are the minimum required loads, and facilities and design engineers often opt to increase the size of the on-site power system to provide for increased load demands. It is permissible for the on-site generation to assume the entire load of the health care facility and not just essential electrical loads, but the codes require on-site generation be capable of supplying minimum power to the critical loads.

These codes also require on-site generation to assume the life safety and critical loads within 10 seconds of a normal power outage. This requirement is very important in maintaining power to life-preserving equipment. However, the 10-second requirement also limits the type of generator used to one that can start, come up to speed, go online, and power the life safety and critical loads in 10 seconds or less. Practically, this limits the generator selection to diesel or natural gas-fired reciprocating engines. Certain fuel requirements found in *NFPA 110* prohibit generator fuel such as natural gas, which is provided by an off-site utility, weighing the odds more heavily in favor of diesel generation.

A single skid-mounted diesel generator may be used in a smaller clinic. Note the louvers in the background to provide air flow.

An interesting change in the 2021 edition of *NFPA 99: Health Care Facilities Code* allows the use of micro-grid technology and structures to provide electrical power to the essential electrical system in place of or as a supplement to diesel generation. Micro-grid technology, in this application, uses a microprocessor-based load controller to pair loads with several sources of power, using a ring bus technology. For instance, during the day the load controller may have a majority of the health care facility load served by a large solar array. As the evening sets that load could be transferred to other power sources, such as a battery bank, or a natural gas fired turbine generator. These innovative systems are very new and remain largely in design phases, however, micro-grids bring a level of redundancy to the table that is quite attractive to both designers and health care organizations.

Perhaps the simplest and most cost-effective Type 1 Essential Electrical System uses a single diesel generator, that powers the essential electrical system with an emergency power supply to a health care facility using three automatic transfer switches (ATS) serving the life safety branch, critical branch, and equipment branch loads. Upon a normal power outage, the generator receives a signal from the automatic transfer switches and starts. Once the generator comes up to speed, matching the 60-hertz frequency of the normal supply, the life safety and critical branch automatic transfer switches transfer to the generator-powered feeder. A delay feature is often built into the equipment branch load transfer switch to allow the life safety and critical branches to become energized, also allowing the generator to stabilize before connecting the equipment load on the generator.

NFPA 99: Health Care Facility Code and *NFPA 70: National Electrical Code* allow generating systems to shed the equipment load (temporarily turning off some of the less critical systems) in

While life safety and critical loads are required to be reenergized in 10 seconds, the *Code* also requires certain equipment loads to be powered by the on-site generation system. The *Code* is silent on the timeframe required to assume the equipment loads, which, in theory, gives the design engineer some flexibility on generator design and selection of the methodology for powering these loads.

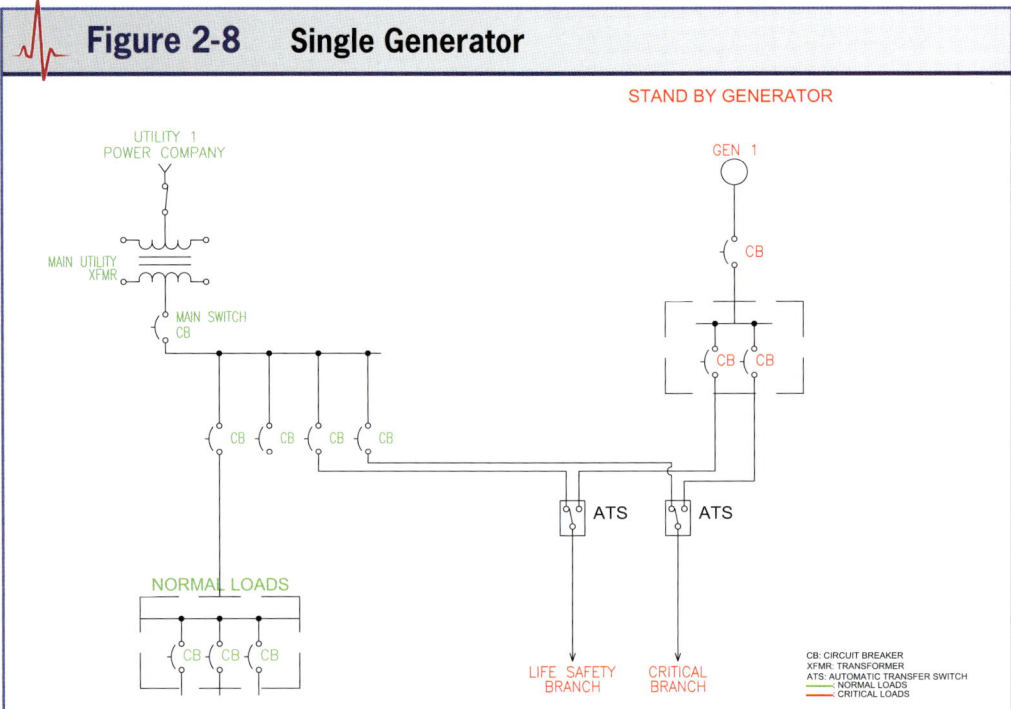

Figure 2-8   Single Generator

Figure 2-8. A typical Type 2 essential electrical system can be found in smaller health care facilities and nursing homes.

the event of a generator overload. Engineers need to be very careful when choosing loads to be shed. For example, a refrigerator in a pharmacy is used to keep lifesaving medication at a required temperature, and a simple air handler may be used to provide positive air flow in an infection control area. Both of these loads are considered equipment loads and could be shed, and yet both are still important critical loads used for protecting staff and patients. Load shedding always seems to be a choice between the lesser of two evils.

The single generator system is used quite extensively in small clinics. Larger facilities have larger loads and require multiple generators. **See Figure 2-8.**

Health care facilities tend to exponentially grow over time, which can pose a problem when a small facility outgrows its on-site generation capacity. The facility can either upsize and replace the existing generator, or it can install a second generator to pick up the additional load. Often the addition of a second generator will prove more cost-effective and provides an important layer of

A diesel generator may also be mounted on a raised pad. Note the control conduit and the fuel piping.

redundancy, as one generator will no longer be relied upon to carry the prescribed loads. In these cases, the existing generator is used to provide power to only the life safety and critical loads, while the new generator provides service to the equipment loads only. Should the original generator fail, a series of priority load switches change state, isolating the crippled generator and providing service to all three loads through the second, working, online generator. This system is a cost-effective solution to facility growth and brings the added benefit of generator redundancy. **See Figure 2-9.**

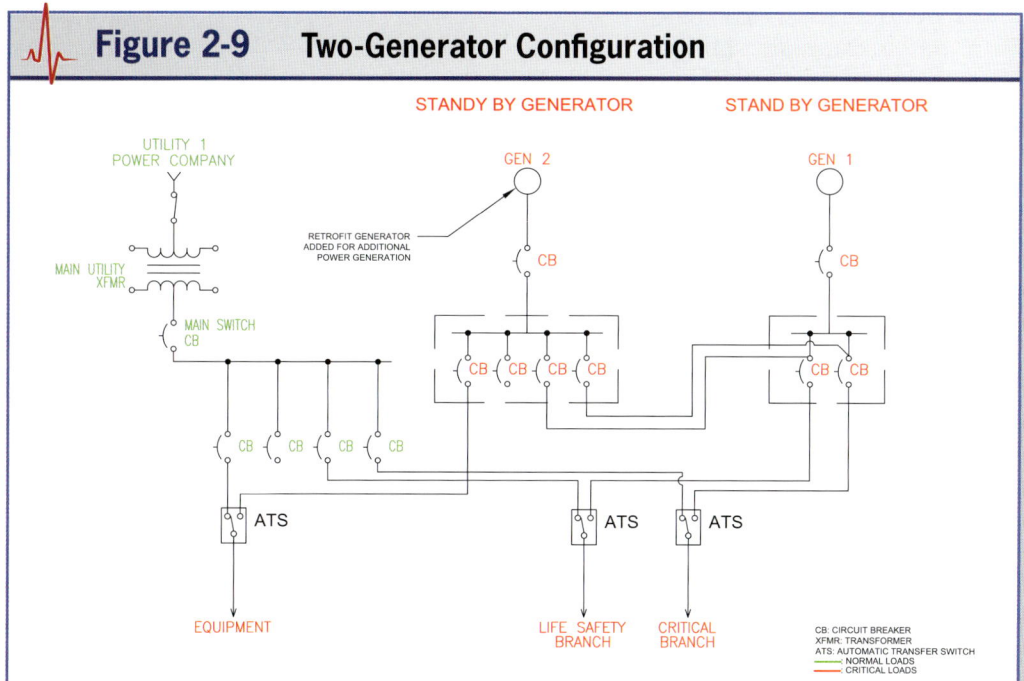

Figure 2-9 **Two-Generator Configuration**

Figure 2-9. A two-generator configuration is a common essential electrical configuration in small- to medium-sized health care facilities that have experienced growth in essential electrical system loads.

Figure 2-10   Two Parallel Generators

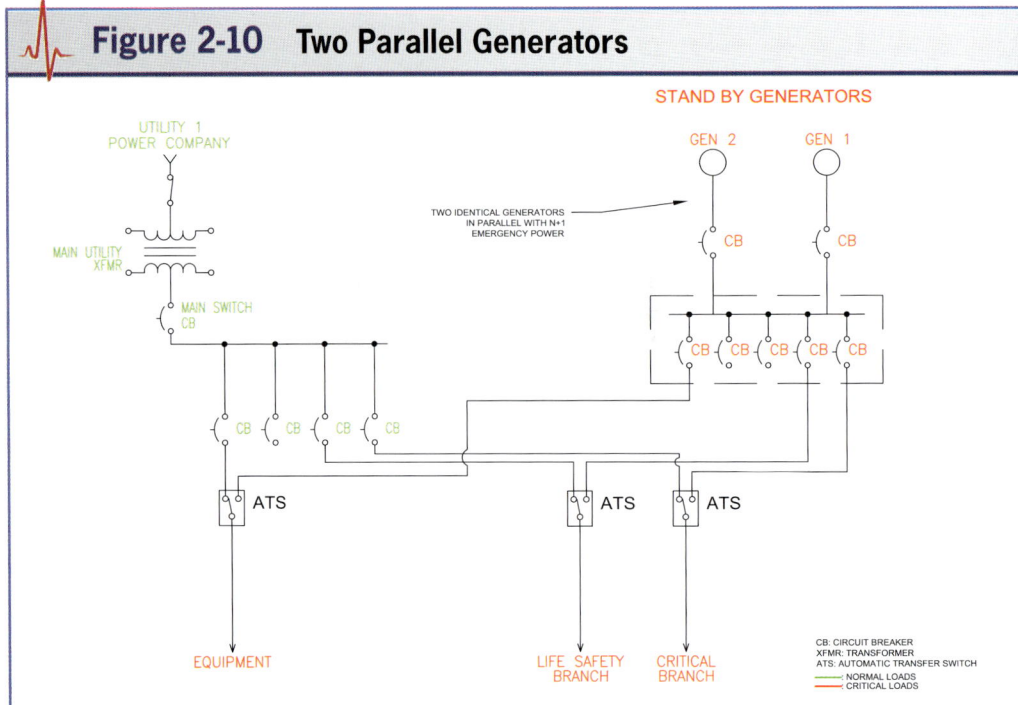

Figure 2-10. *A simple essential electrical configuration may include two generators in parallel feeding the three branches through automatic transfer equipment.*

While this solution makes much sense when retrofitting an existing facility, a new facility with large power and load demands may require more than one redundant stand-by system generator. There are solutions that provide greater redundancy and better control, improve generator wear and tear, and provide for periodic generator maintenance while assuring continued service. Systems that use multiple generators are attached to a common bus. Generator paralleling switchgear is used to assure each generator is synchronized or in-phase with every other generator and each generator frequency is a steady 60 hertz.

While paralleling switchgear is extremely expensive and may even cost as much as the generation equipment itself, paralleling systems provides the highest level of reliability and redundancy available today. Paralleling generators also allows design engineers to adopt an "N+1" strategy where "N" is the number of generators required to handle the calculated connected load; "+1" indicates that an additional unit is used to provide redundancy for both maintenance purposes, and in case a generator failure occurs while in service. Often generators in parallel service are matched—they have the same ratings, same manufacturer, and are essentially identical units—but to a certain extent, the design of modern paralleling equipment can handle mismatched generators.

Consider two matched generators placed on a common bus located in the paralleling gear. Upon a normal system outage, both generators start, and the first generator comes up to speed when the main circuit breaker closes, energizing the bus. The automatic transfer switches controlling the life safety branch, as well as the critical load branch, transfer to the generator feed.

As the second generator comes up to speed and comes into synchronization with the first generator, its main circuit breaker closes to the common bus. The automatic transfer switch controlling the equipment loads transfers to the generator feeder, bringing the equipment loads back online. At this point,

Figure 2-11   Multiple Paralleled Generators

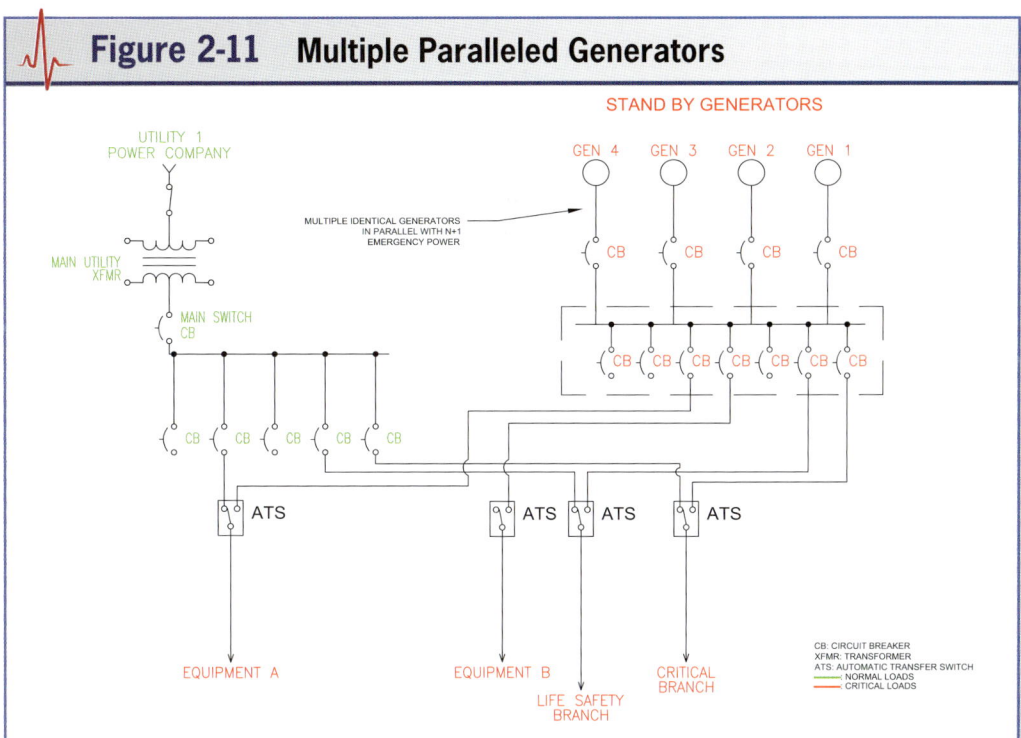

Figure 2-11. *A complex configuration may include multiple generators connected in parallel to serve large essential electrical system loads.*

both generators are equally sharing the fully connected load of the life safety, critical, and equipment branch circuit loads. These systems provide unmatched reliability, while keeping the wear and tear suffered by any single generator to a minimum. **See Figure 2-10.**

While the minimum number of paralleled generators is two, it should be noted that these systems can be designed to parallel any number of generators. The only restriction to the number of generating units is the budget and cost of the system. Over-building on paralleled generation systems is considered a good practice for future expansion, particularly in an area where utility power is not as reliable as desired. **See Figure 2-11.**

Health care facilities make an enormous investment in on-site generation; the proper operation of this equipment is dependent on precise installation in a proper environment. Because diesel generators are much more prevalent than natural gas-fired units, a focus on diesel units is likely. However, natural

gas-fired units share the same concerns attributed to diesel systems, such as heat distribution, fuel quality, starting systems, and mounting requirements.

A significant number of studies have been performed analyzing the failure of diesel drive generators in health care facilities. The top two issues reported are fuel system failures and cooling system failures.

Generator paralleling switchgear enables multiple generators to feed large loads. Courtesy of Lawson Electric Co., Chattanooga, TN

The proper operation of a large diesel generator line-up is dependent on the proper location of its installation.
Courtesy of Lawson Electric Co., Chattanooga, TN

This large diesel generator has a sophisticated fuel filtering system.

FUEL SYSTEMS

Diesel engines are particularly susceptible to fuel problems. Diesel engines employ precise fuel injectors to spray an exact pattern of carefully measured fuel into the engine's cylinder head. Any foreign material in the fuel will clog the injectors, rendering both the measurement and the pattern of fuel spray less than optimal. Clogged injectors usually cause the precision fuel system to dump more fuel into the injector, in an effort to keep the unit turning at the optimal level; this only dumps more contaminated fuel through the injector, further clogging the orifice. To combat this fuel issue, diesel generators employ very sophisticated fuel filtering systems, some of which can be changed while the engine is running. As with every filtering system, unless the filters are changed periodically, they are worthless.

Diesel fuel systems use a main storage tank, usually underground. However, in areas prone to flooding, they should be located above ground. Previous codes required at least 96 hours (four days) of fuel to be stored on site. These requirements have recently changed and are no longer in effect, although many facility specifications still call for at least 96 hours of fuel to be available on site under the assumption that fuel delivery services should be able to provide additional fuel in a 96-hour period. Particularly remote locations may have greater fuel storage requirements.

Figure 2-12   Day Tank Limit Switch Detail

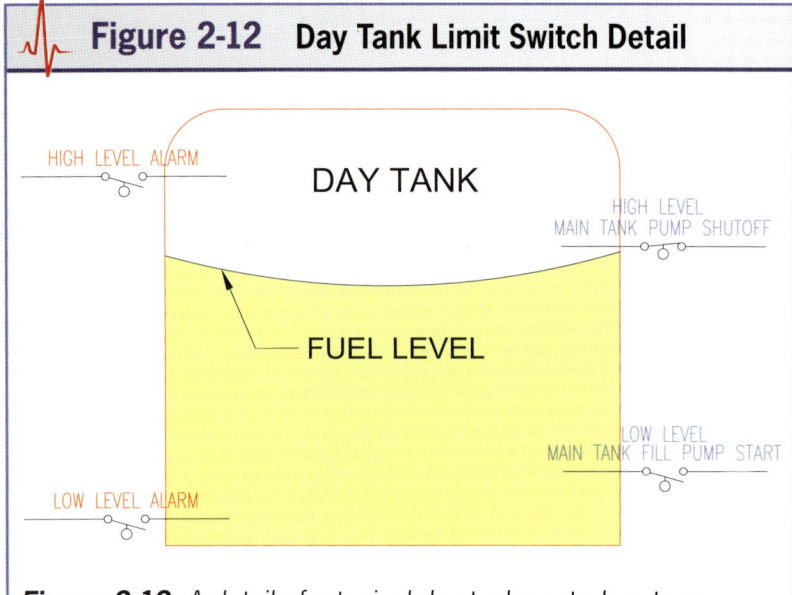

HIGH LEVEL ALARM

DAY TANK

HIGH LEVEL
MAIN TANK PUMP SHUTOFF

FUEL LEVEL

LOW LEVEL
MAIN TANK FILL PUMP START

LOW LEVEL ALARM

Figure 2-12. *A detail of a typical day tank control system includes high- and low-level alarms.*

An above ground diesel fuel storage tank provides fuel to a day tank, which in turn fuels the diesel prime mover.

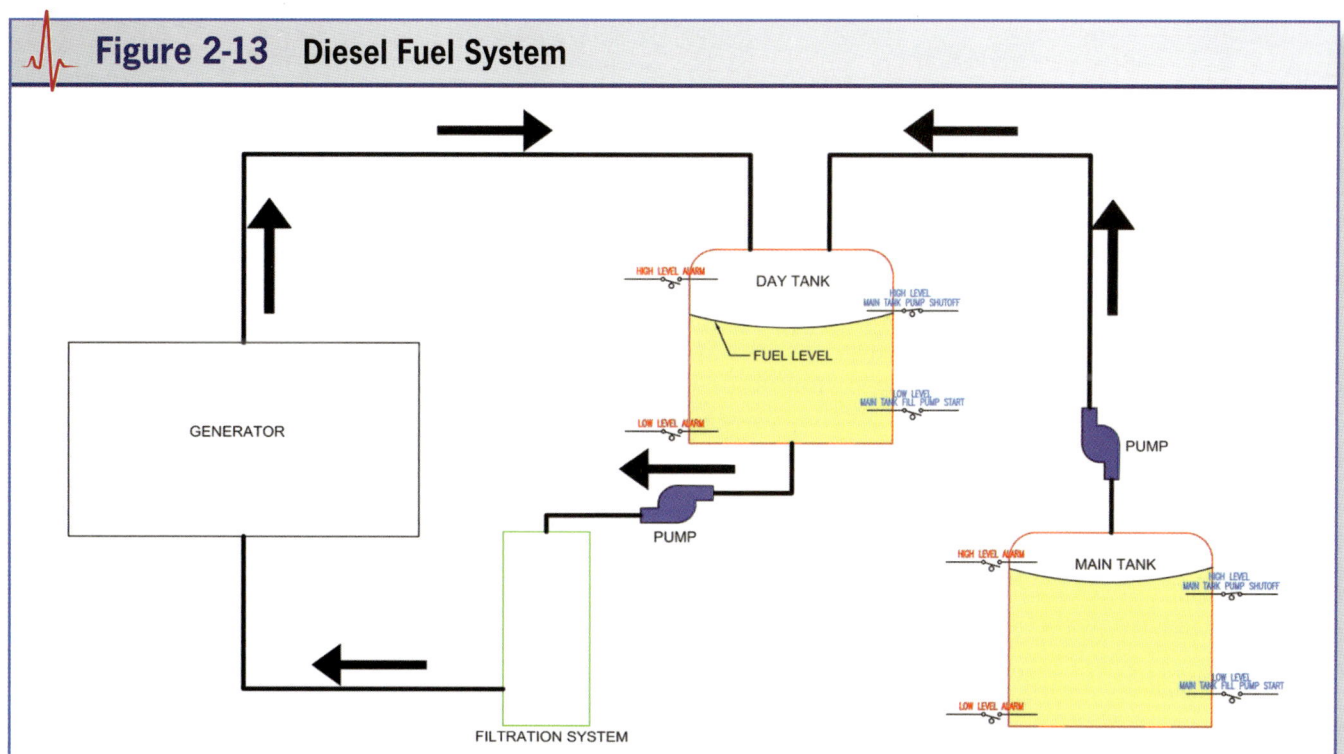

Figure 2-13   Diesel Fuel System

Figure 2-13. *A basic diagram of a generator fuel system shows a large holding tank, day tank, and filtration system. Note that the unused fuel sent to the generator is returned to the day tank.*

Fuel from the main tank is pumped to a day tank, sometimes called a transfer tank, located near the generator itself. It is recommended that each generator have its own day tank and that each day tank holds not less than one hour of fuel. Day tanks are equipped with certain fuel level sensors and a low fuel level alarm limit to alert personnel that something is wrong with the main tank pump. The low-level limit sensor is used to activate the main tank pump to fill the day tank. A high-level limit sensor is used to shut off the main tank pumping system when the day tank is full, and a high fuel level alarm limit is used to signal maintenance personnel that the day tank is about to overflow due to a main tank pump malfunction. **See Figure 2-12.**

The day tank, in turn, provides fuel via a filtration system to the diesel engine itself. Fuel is provided to the engine in a continuous loop, pumped from the day tank through the filtration system into the fuel management equipment on the engine. The engine uses about 30% of the fuel and returns the unused portion to the day tank. **See Figure 2-13.**

In addition to the filtration issue, these systems have many sensors, pumps and other potential failure points, any of which can cause the engine to fail. Additionally, diesel fuel deteriorates over time, making it difficult for facility managers to ensure their facility is protected by a proper supply of fresh diesel fuel. Some facilities in northern climates order oil-fired boilers to assure that diesel fuel can be properly rotated.

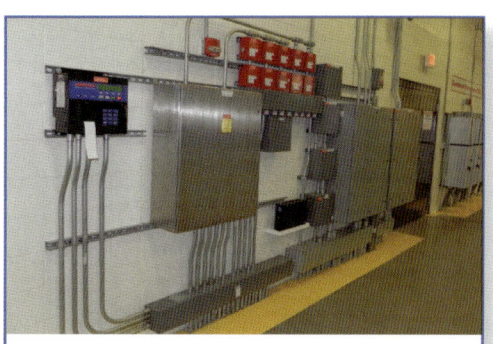

A sophisticated diesel fuel control system can be used to feed a large generator line up.

COOLING SYSTEMS

Reciprocating engines are very inefficient machines. About 33% of the energy released by burning fuel is turned into electrical energy. The rest of the wasted energy is released as heat through exhaust gases and through the engine's water jacket cooling system. An important negative aspect of reciprocating engines is the common practice among equipment manufacturers to increase fuel rates to a specific engine block in an effort to obtain more mechanical power from a particular engine. This practice is an effective means of increasing raw power, but it also increases the amount of waste heat, sometimes to the point that the cooling system of the machine is compromised and becomes too stressed to handle "normal" cycles of operation.

Heat exchangers are used to remove waste heat from the engine's water jacket cooling system, and in some cases, heat exchangers are used to convert waste heat found in exhaust gases to usable heat for health care facility operations such as laundry services. While converting waste exhaust gas heat is an environmentally responsible thing to do, it is important to note that the malfunction of an exhaust gas heat exchanger will not impact the performance of the generator. On the other hand, the malfunction of the water jacket cooling system will quickly cause the generating unit to overheat and go offline with the possibility of a major overhaul needed in the future.

Often, generator water jacket cooling systems are cooled using three basic schemes. The simplest plan uses a radiator physically attached to the frame of the generator unit itself. These radiator systems, both in appearance and design, work very much like the cooling system on a large truck. The radiator is made of steel, aluminum, copper or brass fins, or small tubes to form the core of the radiator. Tanks or tubes are sealed on both sides of the core. The inlet for the hot coolant is generally found on the upper left tank, while the cool water outlet is found on the bottom right tank. This flow pattern maximizes the coolants flow through the radiator core. Air is forced over the core via a large fan mounted on the engine block, which is usually belt driven. Air flow is usually controlled by a system of shutter dampers installed on the front of the radiator. These louvers are designed to be fail safe—that is, they will fail in the open position.

Just like cars and trucks, the coolant for these systems is a blend of soft water and ethylene glycol. This mixture provides very good thermal transfer properties while providing antifreeze protection for colder climates. These types of water jacket cooling systems are simple and reliable. However, they require a tremendous amount of supply and relief air to assure the generation units are being cooled properly. This can pose a problem for services in an urban environment, as well as units located in extreme environments.

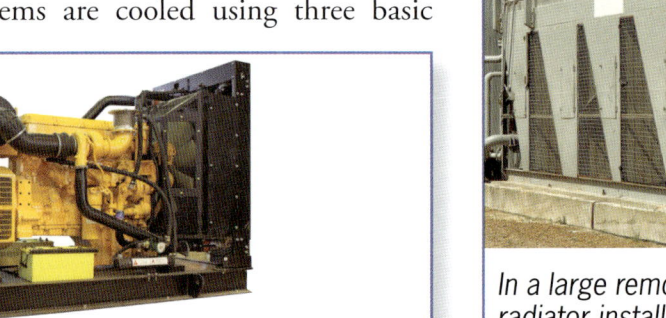

A skid-mounted diesel generator may have a premounted large cooling radiator.

In a large remote diesel generator radiator installation, coolant is cycled from the diesel to the radiators and back to assure proper operating temperature.

For generators installed in a more enclosed environment, remotely mounted radiators are a popular option. In these systems, the radiators are removed from the generator frame and placed in a remote location, such as a roof or a yard, where there is plenty of airflow. These remote radiator systems use electric pumps to move the hot coolant to the radiator. The radiator core is cooled by a large electric fan, and the cooled coolant flows back to the generator unit.

The biggest failures with radiator systems are coolant related. Coolant degrades over time, which can cause scale deposits to build up on the radiator core, severely limiting the core's ability to exchange heat with the surrounding air. In frame-mounted units, fan drive belts must be inspected and replaced periodically. Remotely-mounted radiators bring additional failure points with the use of electric pumps and fans and the systems that control them.

Installations with large banks of generators may opt to use a redundant cooling tower scheme to provide water jacket cooling for the entire generator system. In these systems, the water jacket coolant is cycled through a cooling tower and then back to the generation unit. These types of systems are very expensive and are only cost-effective for health care facilities with large generation capacity.

BATTERIES AND BATTERY CHARGERS

Health care facility generators must be able to start quickly to come up to speed and assume the essential electrical system load within 10 seconds. Sometimes failures do occur during the generation unit's starting sequence. Starting failures can generally be traced to one of two causes. The most common cause for starting failure lies with the generator starter motor batteries and the associated battery charging equipment. In cold climates, generators are fitted with block heaters that keep the engine block at the optimum temperature for quick starting, providing an additional point of failure regardless of the temperature of the surrounding environment.

Modern generator control equipment monitors the temperature of the engine block and will cause an alarm to sound if the block temperature falls below the optimum temperature. Older control systems did not monitor the block temperature, so a failure of the block heater or its control system often went unnoticed, causing difficult starting conditions that stressed both the engine and the starter motor battery system.

Batteries, which provide power for the engine's starter motor, and their associated charging equipment cause over one-half of engine starting related failures. Typically, generator starter motor batteries are lead-acid storage batteries, although some systems use nickel-cadmium batteries. The specific electrochemical nature of these batteries is complex enough to merit its own field of study; suffice to say, battery systems must be carefully matched to the current draw and duration of the individual engine's starting current and voltage.

A large roof-mounted cooling tower can be used to process diesel coolant from a large generator line-up.

Generator Codes and Standards

Electrical Generation Systems Association

- *ESGA 107T-1999, Test Methods for Engine Driven Generators*

National Electrical Contactor's Association together with the Electrical Generation Systems Association

- *NECA/EGSA 404-2014, Standard for Installing Generator Sets*

National Electrical Manufacturers Association

- *NEMA MG-2016, Standard and Guide for Selection, Installation, and Use of Electric Motors and Generators*

National Fire Protection Association

- *NFPA 37: Stationary Engines and Gas Turbines*
- *NFPA 70: National Electrical Code*
- *NFPA 99: Health Care Facility Code*
- *NFPA 101: Life Safety Code*
- *NFPA 110: Standard for Emergency Standby Power Systems*

UL

- *UL 2200, Stationary Engine Generator Assemblies*

As all batteries discharge over time, even when under no-load conditions, batteries must be provided with charging and conditioning equipment that ensures the batteries are in top condition when needed to start the engine. *NFPA 99: Health Care Facility Code* requires generator accessories such as battery charging equipment be installed on the life safety branch of the essential electrical system. The *Code* further states that these loads cannot be shed, providing the charging equipment with the most reliable source of electrical power.

The batteries themselves require periodic maintenance, inspection of electrical connections, and battery specific gravity levels. Moreover, batteries should be promptly replaced when not testing to the manufacturer's specification, or when they have reached the end of life, as determined by the manufacturer.

PEAK SHAVING

Health care facilities make an enormous investment in on-site generation equipment. A once-popular method for obtaining a return on this investment was a procedure known as peak shaving. During high-demand periods, such as summer afternoons when power demand use is at its peak due to

the use of air conditioning systems, power companies would offer health care facilities (and other customers with self-generation capabilities) a reduction in kilowatt-hour rates if the facility would self-generate power during the high demand periods. This was a double win for facilities, which ended up using less utility power during these high demand periods and paying reduced rates for utility power.

Many factors must be considered for these agreements to be beneficial to the health care organization. Some of the considerations are the price of utility power, the cost of fuel, as well as the cost of generator wear and tear. The United States Environmental Protection Agency has voiced concerns about diesel exhaust pollution, as well. While peak shaving agreements are not as popular as they once were, they do still exist in some areas.

ON-SITE POWER GENERATION FOR NON-ESSENTIAL LOADS

On-site power generation for the essential electrical system is a code-defined set of critical loads that serve patient and worker safety. No code or standard prohibits the use of on-site generation equipment for non-essential loads, and

Diesel Fuel Issues

Particulates

Simply called "dirt," particulates in diesel fuel cause problems due to excessive wear. Injectors, ball seat valves, and virtually every other element of the fuel system are damaged by particulates. Each time fuel is transferred from one container to another—from the refinery, to the pipeline, to the terminal holding facility, to the truck, to the generator storage tank—diesel fuel picks up particulates. They are in the atmosphere in the form of dust and grime, but more often, they occur from natural corrosion that happens in every vessel. Particulates can usually be removed by a good quality fuel filter.

Cold Weather

Diesel fuel contains hydrocarbons that have a relatively high freezing point. Like water, when these hydrocarbons freeze they turn solid; unlike water, they solidify not as hard ice, but as a thick waxy gel. This gel can clog fuel filters and starve a diesel engine into shutdown. Diesel fuel refiners include additives in their winter fuel blend to combat gelling, but if fuel is stored for long periods of time, the summer blend may mistakenly be used in the winter. Water in diesel fuel can also freeze, and the hard ice crystals can clog or damage fuel filters.

Additives

Additives placed into diesel fuel are generally beneficial, such as anti-gelling compounds. When additives are used improperly, however, the hydrocarbon compounds in the additive chemically bond with unintended compounds creating, a waxy substance that clogs fuel filters. This can ruin an entire storage tank of diesel fuel.

Water

Water is everywhere. Water in diesel fuel can cause excessive wear on ball valves and injectors, as well as accelerate fuel system corrosion creating particulate issues. In addition, water ice can cause fuel filter clogging and damage.

Microbes

When water is present in diesel fuel, microbes can live in the interface between diesel fuel and water. These microbes actually feed on the diesel fuel itself. Microbe colonies can consume as much as 1% of the capacity of the fuel tank and can foul the tank by creating acid which accelerates corrosion. The colonies themselves clog fuel filters, and over time the fuel becomes an unusable sludge.

Degradation Over Time

Diesel fuel has a shelf-life. Depending on the particular blend, that shelf-life can be as little as two months or as long as just under a year. In storage, diesel fuel oxidizes. The rate of oxidation depends on temperature, water intrusion, and the presence of contaminants. When diesel fuel begins to oxidize, degradation products such as gums, acids, sediments, and thickeners are formed. These products cause a loss of power by decreasing the energy level of the fuel. This causes increased fuel flow rates which can damage fuel system components. Predictably, oxidation by-products can also clog and damage fuel filters.

---

in some cases providing on-site generation for non-essential loads makes sense from several different perspectives. If the health care facility is in a remote location with questionable utility power, on-site generation for non-essential loads makes sense. Once freed of the 10-second start rule imposed for essential loads, other types of generator prime movers, namely gas turbines, become very attractive in consideration of powering non-essential loads.

Gas turbine engines are very different from reciprocating diesel and reciprocating natural gas engines. Turbine engines produce rotary motion on a continuous cycle by injecting hot combusted fuel and air through a series of bladed turbine vanes secured to a shaft. Because shaft rotation is continuous, turbines have considerably less vibration than reciprocating engines; they also have a much lower power-to-weight ratio than diesel.

Due to their relative simplicity, turbines have longer periodic maintenance time frames, which lowers costs. Turbines are also dual-fuel capable, have low emissions, and are considerably less noisy than reciprocating engines. Gas turbines can be a particularly good choice for on-site power generation for non-essential loads, particularly on loads greater than one megawatt.

While more efficient, gas turbine driven generators used as prime movers have trouble coming online in ten seconds.

SUMMARY

Health care facilities play such an important role in the communities they serve. As such, redundant electrical power must be supplied to ensure that they can function in the event of a service outage. Redundant power can be provided through multiple utility power sources and switchgear or with on-site power generation. It is important for Electrical Workers to understand how these systems work in order to install and maintain the most reliable electrical services possible.

REVIEW QUESTIONS

1. Power reliability in a health care facility equals distribution power __?__ .
    a. operational efficiency
    b. redundancy
    c. sequential starting plans
    d. utility quality

2. Before electrical power deregulation, a common method used by design engineers to provide backup power systems for health care facilities was to specify two utility services. One utility service fed from the local or primary power grid in the general location where the health care facility is located, and the other is fed from a separate, nearby nonlocal, secondary power grid.

    a. True   b. False

3. Which of the following statements best describes the advantages of using transfer of power for two utility services at a health care facility?
    a. Workers are always provided a system engineered to prevent shock and arc flash accidents.
    b. Workers can shut down either one of the utility transformers for testing, maintenance, repair, and replacement without deenergizing the entire distribution system.
    c. Workers can easily tie both power systems together for better power efficiency.
    d. Utility has complete control with regards to the loads used on their grid system.

REVIEW QUESTIONS

4. When a(n) __?__ system is used, the key cannot be removed while the breaker is in the "on" position and can only be removed when the breaker is in the "off" or deenergized position.

   a. individual safety management program design

   b. keying system

   c. lockout/tagout

   d. OSHA designed tagout system only

5. __?__ requires certain loads in health care facilities, namely elements of the life safety and critical branches of the essential electrical system, to be brought online within ten seconds of a power outage.

   a. NFPA 72: National Fire Alarm Code

   b. NFPA 99: Health Care Facilities Code

   c. NFPA 110: Life Safety Code

   d. Both b. and c.

6. One important concept for Electrical Workers to understand when using a "loop distribution system" is that they are intentionally back-fed, and opening one device will __?__ the distribution loop.

   a. damage

   b. deenergize

   c. energize

   d. not deenergize

7. Codes require health care facilities to have on-site power generation capacity properly sized to take on life safety, critical, and defined equipment loads during a utility power failure. All loads connected to the distribution system, including the normal power system, must be determined. The maximum demand is used by design engineers to size the on-site power system to provide for increased load demands.

   a. True   b. False

8. Life safety and critical branch loads are required to be reenergized in __?__ .

   a. 5 seconds

   b. 10 seconds

   c. 15 seconds

   d. 30 seconds

9. Specific codes allow generating systems to shed the __?__ load in the event of a generator overload.

   a. critical

   b. equipment

   c. life safety

   d. normal

10. Single generator systems are used quite extensively in small clinics, nursing homes, and small hospitals, whereas larger facilities that have larger demand loads require multiple generators.

    a. True   b. False

11. Systems that use multiple generators are attached to a common bus system and the generator must be connected in a parallel configuration using __?__ to ensure each generator is synchronized or in-phase with every other generator and each generator frequency is a steady 60 hertz.

    a. automatic transfer equipment

    b. manual transfer equipment

    c. paralleling switchgear

    d. phase-rotation indicating equipment

12. Which of the following are the top two issues for diesel generator failure?

    a. Automatic transfer equipment failure and generator overloads

    b. Clogged fuel filters and low oil pressure

    c. Contaminated fuel and dead batteries

    d. Cooling system failure and fuel system failure

13. Current codes required at least 96 hours (4 days) of fuel to be stored on-site in above ground or underground tanks.

    a. True   b. False

14. The most common cause of starting failure for hospital generator systems lies with __?__ .

    a. corroded contact and relay failure

    b. old fuel and improper equipment maintenance

    c. the generator starting motor batteries and the associated battery charging equipment

    d. transfer switch system failure

Distribution

T he principle of redundancy electrical power does not stop at the electrical utility and on-site generation. The overriding standard that the failure of one electrical system element will not significantly affect the safety and health of patients and staff is carried over to the health care facility's electrical distribution system as well. The layout of service equipment, generators and their switchgear, feeders, automatic transfer switches, and the entire essential electrical system load is critical to the overall success or failure of a health care facility's essential electrical system.

Objectives

» Describe the differences between normal electrical systems and essential electrical systems (Types 1 and 2).

» Define the different branch categories associated with each electrical system.

» Explain how transfer switches operate and how they are implemented in a health care environment.

» Analyze the different techniques used to distribute power within a health care facility.

Chapter 3

Table of Contents

FACILITY DISTRIBUTION SYSTEMS

The distribution of electrical power inside the property lines of the health care facility consists of the loads attached to the utility service(s), as well as the loads attached to the essential electrical system powered by standby generators or other alternate sources of power.

Previous discussions focused on common schemes to provide at least two sources of redundant, reliable electrical power to the health care facility. That commitment to redundancy does not stop at the service entrance equipment; many codes and standards, as well as good engineering practices, expand the concept of redundancy to encompass the premises distribution, feeder system, branch circuits, and utilization equipment earmarked for patient care. Every health care design and installation standard—*The Guidelines for Design and Construction of Hospitals, NFPA 70: National Electrical Code (NEC),* and *NFPA 99: Health Care Facilities Code*—requires health care facilities to have two premise power distribution systems: a "normal system" for non-essential loads and an "essential electrical system" for loads crucial to life safety. The essential electrical system provides power for critical services to both patients and staff, as well as specific equipment vital to safe facility operation.

NORMAL ELECTRICAL SYSTEM

There are reams and reams of monographs, papers, regulations, codes, and standards addressing the practical design, legal requirements, and construction and maintenance of essential electrical distribution systems. Other than the requirements found in Chapters 1 through 4 of the *NEC*, there are few specific regulations governing the normal electrical system in a health care facility. However, despite this lack of regulation, there are important practical considerations that come into play when installing normal distribution systems in health care facilities.

At their most basic element, normal electrical systems supply power to the distribution system for non-essential loads, such as waiting rooms, reception areas, business and office spaces, food services, irrigation equipment, and the like. While this is certainly true, consideration must also be given to the fact

Figure 3-1   Feeder Raceway

Figure 3-1. An essential electrical system feeder trench should be well-protected and physically remote from the normal system feeders.

that in a properly designed electrical system, normal system feeders powered from the utility with back-up power capabilities from the alternate power supply of the essential electrical system may be considered the preferred feeder wiring system for sophisticated power distribution equipment that may be located throughout the facility serving very critical patient care loads. For this reason, installers must appreciate the critical importance of physical separation between normal circuits and essential electrical system circuits.

While it may be convenient, and cost-effective, to run normal and essential electrical system feeders in the same trench or same corridor support rack, imagine the catastrophe that would occur should excavation equipment inadvertently damage both the normal and the essential feeders supplying power to a critical care cardiac unit. Patients would need to be evacuated to appropriate areas of the facility or moved to other health care facilities for proper care. The unit would then be offline for days as the repairs are made to both the normal and essential electrical system feeders. Normal and essential electrical system feeders should have as much physical separation as possible. For instance, one feeder could be located underground, and the other feeder located on a corridor support rack. The imperative concept of redundancy is destroyed if a single event disrupts service to both feeders. **See Figure 3-1.**

ESSENTIAL ELECTRICAL SYSTEMS (TYPE 1)

It is very important to understand that essential electrical systems required in health care facilities are not categorized as emergency standby systems as defined in Article 700 of the *NEC*. Strictly speaking, emergency systems do not exist in health care facilities, although essential electrical systems are often erroneously called *emergency systems* by installers. Health care facility essential electrical systems are much more complex and have more regulations than

the Article 700 emergency systems found in other occupancies.

Essential electrical systems in hospitals and other inpatient facilities (rated over 150 kVA in size) must be divided into three branches: the life safety branch, the critical branch, and the equipment branch. Each branch must be served by one or more dedicated transfer switch(es), identified for emergency use, and approved by the *authority having jurisdiction (AHJ)* that will transfer the load from the normal power feeder system to the essential electrical system feeder when power is lost to the normal feeder. Additionally, these transfer switches must be capable of sending a "start" signal to the standby generators during normal power outages, and the life safety and critical branches must come online and assume the loads in 10 seconds or less. The division of the life safety, critical, and equipment branches into their defined roles occurs at the individual branch system dedicated automatic transfer switch. **See Figure 3-2.**

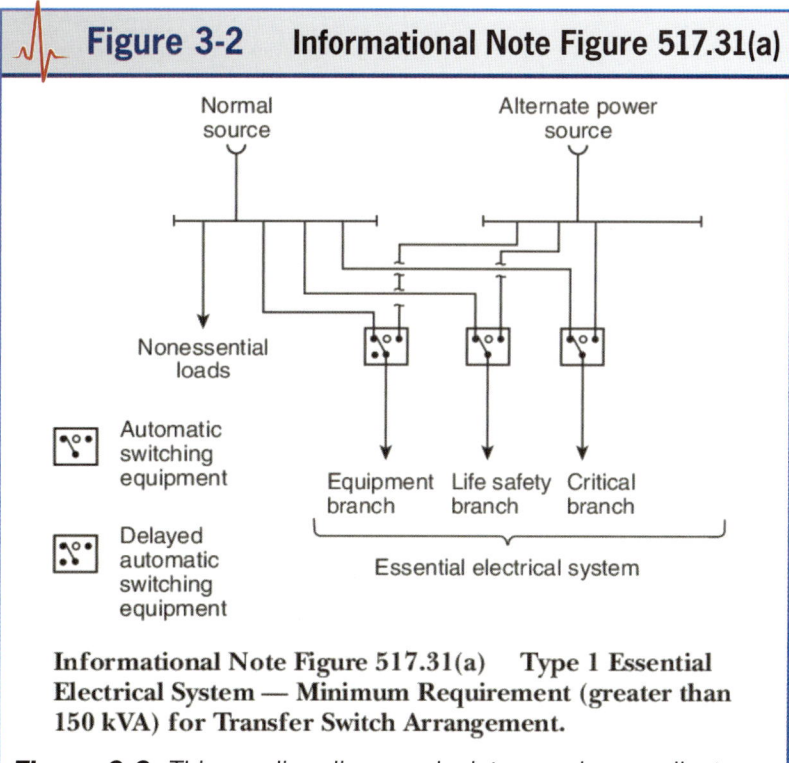

Figure 3-2   Informational Note Figure 517.31(a)

Informational Note Figure 517.31(a)   Type 1 Essential Electrical System — Minimum Requirement (greater than 150 kVA) for Transfer Switch Arrangement.

Figure 3-2. This one-line diagram depicts a code-compliant essential electrical system over 150 kVA.

Essential Electrical Systems Under 150 kVA

Type 1 essential electrical systems in health care facilities when the total connected essential electrical system load is under 150 kVA may employ one automatic transfer switch to serve the life safety, critical, and equipment branches simultaneously. Section 517.31(B) allows the use of one transfer switch under these conditions, provided the generator is capable of servicing the entire connected load and the automatic transfer switch is also rated for the connected load. This allowance acknowledges that not all health care is provided at large regional medical centers. In fact, the facilities served by these single transfer switch Type 1 systems are the largest growing segment of the health care industry. **See Figure 3-3.**

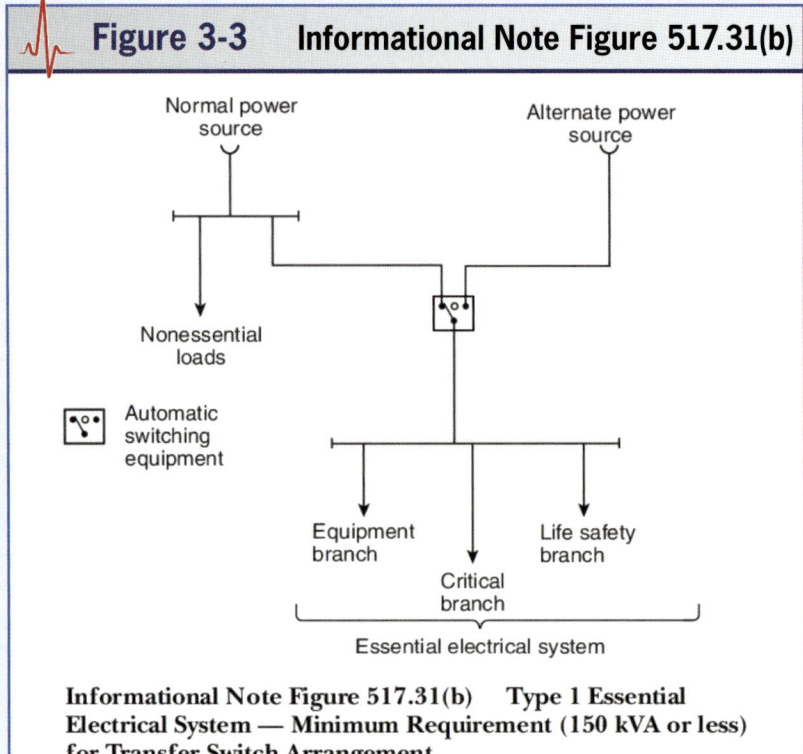

Figure 3-3   Informational Note Figure 517.31(b)

Informational Note Figure 517.31(b)   Type 1 Essential Electrical System — Minimum Requirement (150 kVA or less) for Transfer Switch Arrangement.

Figure 3-3. *This one-line diagram depicts a code-compliant essential electrical system at 150 kVA or less.*

Life Safety Branch

The life safety branch of the essential electrical system most closely resembles the emergency systems found in other occupancies as defined in Article 700. As the name suggests, the *life safety branch* feeds receptacles, illumination systems, and equipment that is required to "save lives" in the case of a normal power outage. Due to the extremely critical nature of these loads, both the *NEC* and *NFPA 99* have strict requirements limiting the type of loads served by the life safety branch. Only the following utilization equipment can be fed from the life safety branch of the essential electrical system:

- Means of egress illumination
- Exit signs
- Fire alarm systems, including HVAC equipment such as smoke dampers

- Other alarm systems including emergency communications equipment and medical gas alarms
- Elevator cab illumination, communications alarms, and controls
- Automatic doors used for building egress
- Task lighting, convenience receptacles, and battery chargers (for battery-powered lighting units) located at essential electrical system generator and transfer switch locations
- Generator accessories, including fuel transfer pumps, louver and ventilation controls, cooling system pumps and fans, battery charging equipment, and any other loads deemed necessary for operation

No other loads are permitted to be connected to the life safety branch. It should again be emphasized that the transfer switch serving the life safety branch must be capable of automatic connection to the essential electrical system in the event of a normal power outage, and the generator must start, come up to speed, and assume the life safety branch load within 10 seconds of normal system failure.

Because the nature of the life safety loads closely resembles those found in emergency systems as defined in Article 700, the requirements of Article 700 generally apply to the life safety branch as well, with some exceptions. In the *NEC*, Section 517.26 states the requirement of Article 700 shall apply to the life safety branch of the essential electrical system unless amended by Article 517. *NFPA 99: Health Care Facilities Code* goes even further by stating that the requirements of Article 700 apply only to the life safety branch of the essential electrical system as amended by 6.7.5.1.2.2, which calls out the following exceptions:

- *700.4 shall not apply*
  - o Emergency system capacity
- *700.10(D) 1 through 3 shall not apply*
  - o Feeders installed in two hour rated enclosures
- *700.17 Branch Circuits for Emergency Lighting.* Branch circuits that supply emergency lighting shall be installed to provide service from a source complying with 700.12 when the normal supply for lighting is interrupted or where single circuits supply luminaires containing secondary batteries.
- *700.32 shall not apply*
  - o Selective coordination

The life safety branch parallels that of emergency systems found in other occupancies; however, many of the occupants (patients) of health care facilities are incapable of self-preservation due to injury, illness, or anesthesia. Health care facilities employ emergency procedures known as defend-in-place strategies that are unique to health care. Whereas other occupancies stress the total evacuation of a structure in an emergency situation, defend-in-place strategies dictate that protective shelters be built into the structure, thereby providing protection to patients unable to move due to the nature of their illness, or incapable of self-preservation as a result of anesthesia or other infirmities. Furthermore, patients may require relocation from an area of danger to an adjacent area of the shelter when the wholesale evacuation of an entire structure is not possible. A defend-in-place strategy is a vitally important element of both health care design and construction.

Critical Branch

While the life safety branch is earmarked for defined loads required to keep building occupants safe in an emergency, the *critical branch* of the essential electrical system may be considered the branch that supplies essential power for life support and keeps patients and health care workers safe during the performance of everyday diagnostic, clinical, and treatment activities. The exponential growth of modern medicine has been driven by medical equipment fed by the critical branch, making this branch "critical" to sustaining human life in a health care facility. As with the life safety branch, both the *NEC* and *NFPA 99* have strict requirements for the loads permitted to be connected to the critical branch of the essential electrical system, although both codes permit a small degree of flexibility for the design engineer. Moreover, like the life safety branch, the transfer switch(es) feeding the critical branch must automatically connect to the essential electrical system feeder upon failure of the normal feeder. These automatic transfer switches must also be able to send a start signal to the generators, which are required to pick up the critical branch loads in 10 seconds or less. Prescribed critical branch loads include:

- Critical care spaces that utilize anesthetizing gases
- Isolated power systems
- Selected receptacles and task lighting in identified patient care spaces:

o Infant nurseries
o Medication preparation areas
o Pharmacy dispensing areas
o Select acute nursing areas
o Psychiatric bed areas (omit receptacles)
o Ward treatment areas
o Nurses' stations (unless lighted by corridor luminaires)
- Additional selected specialized patient care receptacles and task illumination where needed
- Nurse call systems
- Blood, bone, and tissue banks
- Telephone and data equipment rooms
- Task illumination, selected receptacles, and selected power circuits for:
  o General care beds
  o Angiographic labs
  o Cardiac catheterization labs
  o Coronary care units
  o Hemodialysis areas
  o Selected emergency room treatment areas
  o Human physiology labs
  o Intensive care areas
  o Selected postoperative recovery rooms
- Additional task illumination, receptacles, and selected power circuits needed for effective facility operation, including single-phase fractional horsepower motors

The critical branch is purposely limited to maintain as much reliability as possible while serving critical equipment in critical patient care spaces. Both the *NEC* and *NFPA 99* permit design engineers to subdivide the critical branch. Subdividing the critical branch into two or more automatic transfer switches, located as physically close to the critical loads as possible, makes sense from a reliability standpoint and is considered good practice in larger health care facilities. The addition of the final bullet point on the list allows the design engineer a great deal of latitude when selecting critical branch loads, although it is important to note that both the *NEC* and

Figure 3-4   ICU Space

Figure 3-4. *A typical intensive care unit (ICU) space would be served by the essential electrical system.*

NFPA 99 limit the motor loads to fractional horsepower only. It is also good practice for new building designs to add extra capacity into critical branches as future connected loads can be expected to significantly increase as technology drives medical improvements. **See Figure 3-4.**

Equipment Branch

As the name suggests, the *equipment branch* of the essential electrical system serves mechanical equipment that is important to the safety and health of both patients and staff. Because the continuous operation of this equipment is not critical to safety, the equipment branch of the essential electrical system is divided into two types of loads: those that are earmarked for delayed automatic connection, and those loads that may be manually transferred. Loads connected to the equipment branch are designed to be connected to the generators after the life safety and critical branches are transferred. This allows time for the generators to stabilize before assuming the equipment branch loads. As a result, the equipment branch loads can be immense. The *NEC* and *NFPA 99* allows time to lapse before assuming the automatically delayed connected loads, and allows additional time to lapse before the second-tier equipment branch loads are automatically or manually connected. These delays are in place to ensure that generators are not overloaded during the critical starting period. Equipment branch loads for delayed automatic connection include:

- Central suction systems
- Sump pumps and other similar equipment
- Medical compressed air systems and controls
- Smoke control and stair pressurization systems
- Kitchen hood supply and exhaust systems
- Supply, return, and exhaust ventilating systems for:
  - o Airborne infectious/isolation rooms
  - o Protective environment rooms
  - o Exhaust fans for lab fume hoods
  - o Nuclear medicine areas
  - o Ethylene oxide evacuation
  - o Anesthetic evacuation
  - o Operating and delivery rooms (*NFPA 70* only)
  - o Telephone and data equipment rooms and closets (*NFPA 70* only)

Equipment branch loads for delayed automatic or manual connection include:

- Heating equipment serving operating, delivery, labor, recovery, intensive care, coronary care, nurseries, infection/isolation rooms, and emergency treatment spaces
- Heating equipment serving general care areas (only if the outside design temperature meets certain parameters)
- Water-based fire protection system pressure maintenance pumps (jockey or make-up pumps)
- Selected elevators
- Hyperbaric facilities
- Hypobaric facilities
- Autoclaving equipment
- Controls for connected equipment branch loads
- Other selected equipment
- Automatically operated doors (*NFPA 70* only)
- Supply, return and exhaust ventilating systems serving surgical, obstetrical, intensive care, coronary care, nurseries, and emergency treatment spaces (*NFPA 99* only)

The equipment branch of the essential electrical system becomes the "catch-all" for all other loads not specifically assigned to the life safety and critical branch. With the addition of "other selected equipment" in both the *NEC* and *NFPA 99*, the design engineer has the freedom to consider any load for the equipment branch. While both *NFPA 70* and *NFPA 99* focus on health care electrical systems, they do not always agree on the nature of the equipment branch connected loads. Though this is unfortunate, it is not particularly problematic when one considers the "other selected equipment" clause in both codes. **See Figure 3-5.**

Once more, it is important to note that the essential electrical system is not an emergency system as defined in Article 700. The life safety branch of the essential electrical system comes closest to the function of an emergency system described in Article 700, but must include several exceptions for health care facilities. The remaining two branches, the critical branch and the equipment branch, have totally different functions than the life safety branch and have unique requirements outside of the requirements of Article 700. Despite common installer jargon, health care facility essential electrical systems are not emergency systems.

ESSENTIAL ELECTRICAL SYSTEMS (TYPE 2)

Both the *NEC* and *NFPA 99* recognize that essential electrical systems designed for inpatient care hospitals are not appropriate or cost-effective for nursing homes and other limited care facilities where policies preclude the use of life-sustaining equipment. Most nursing homes and limited care facilities do not provide critical care services to patients; therefore, the critical branch of the essential electrical system is not installed. Both codes prescribe a limited essential electrical system for these facilities, known as a Type 2 essential electrical system. These systems have the same on-site generation requirements as Type 1 systems; however, rather than three branches, Type 2 systems employ only two branches: a life safety branch and an equipment branch.

The loads for the life safety branch are exactly the same as those permitted in Type 1 essential electrical systems. The life safety branch serves the same function as in Type 1 systems, and falls under the requirements of Article 700 with the same exceptions.

The equipment branch of Type 2 essential electrical systems is a hybrid of both the critical and equipment branches found in Type 1 systems. Loads are specified for three categories of connection periods: non-delayed automatic, delayed automatic, or delayed automatic or manual connection. Specific performance requirements for Type 2 essential electrical systems can be found in 6.5.2 in *NFPA 99*, and specific installation requirements for Type 2 essential electrical systems can be found in Section 517.40 in *NFPA 70*. **See Figure 3-6.**

Figure 3-5   Communications Space

Figure 3-5. A health care facility's essential electrical system would serve communications spaces.

Health Care Facility Business Office – Article 700 Applies

While the requirements of Article 700 do not apply to health care facilities as defined in Article 517, the portions of a building not used for health care, such as a hospital's business office, by definition are not considered health care facilities. The provisions of Article 700 still apply to that specific space.

TRANSFER SWITCHES

Transfer switches are designed to move power sources between different loads. Some transfer switches are manually operated. As used in a health care environment, most, if not all, transfer switches are automatically controlled. *Automatic transfer switches* are self-acting equipment for transferring one or more load connections from one power source to another. Transfer switches are typically installed with backup generators so that temporary electrical power can be provided in the event a utility power source fails.

Transfer switches are an important element in any essential electrical system; unfortunately, they are also a proven point of essential electrical system failure. Studies commissioned by ASCO, a subsidiary of Emerson Electric, and *Building Operating Management* magazine show 20% of responders reported at least one automatic transfer switch failure in a five-year period.

This extraordinary failure rate can be contributed to a number of factors. For instance, modern automatic transfer switch controls can be microprocessor driven and quite complex. More

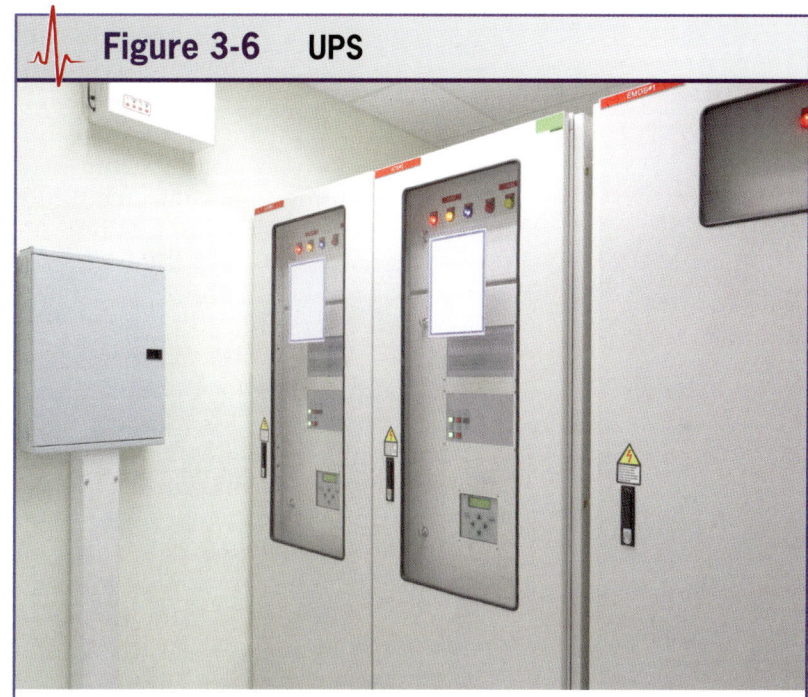

Figure 3-6   UPS

Figure 3-6. *While not required by code, uninterruptable power supply (UPS) systems can bring a high level of redundancy to critical essential electrical systems elements, such as operating room lighting.*

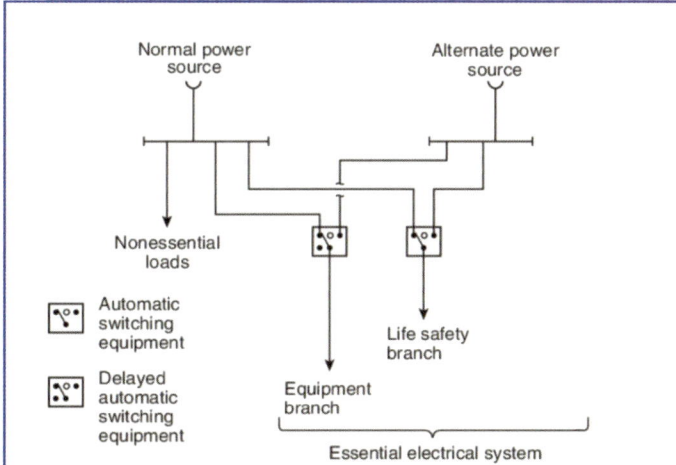

Informational Note Figure 517.42(a)   Type 2 Essential Electrical Systems (Nursing Home and Limited Health Care Facilities) — Minimum Requirement (greater than 150 kVA) for Transfer Switch Arrangement.

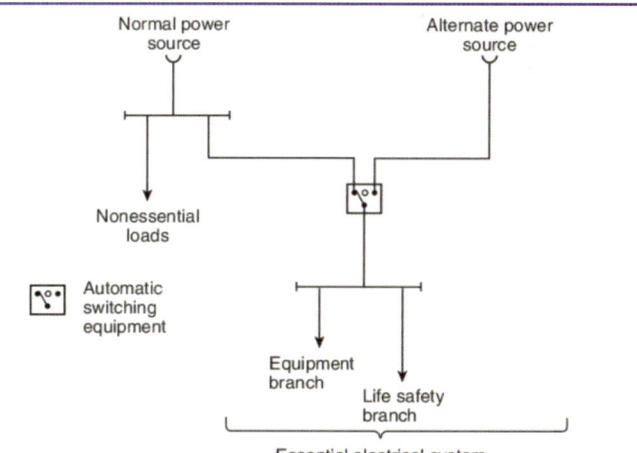

Informational Note Figure 517.42(b)   Type 2 Essential Electrical Systems (Nursing Home and Limited Health Care Facilities) — Minimum Requirement (150 kVA or less) for Transfer Switch Arrangement.

A Type 2 code-compliant essential electrical system (left: over 150 kVA; right: 150 kVA or less) combines the critical and equipment branches.

importantly, transfer switches operate under continuous duty conditions. Even when the essential electrical system is being fed from "normal" utility power, the switch is under full-load current conditions and subjected to the stresses of transformer and motor inrush currents; as well as the high currents associated with short circuit and other fault currents.

These stresses have been compounded by the lack of selective coordination on transfer switches in essential electrical systems, which further exposes them to high fault currents that, in a properly coordinated system, would have been controlled or mitigated by a downstream overcurrent protective device. For this reason, in 2014 UL LLC updated its *UL 1008* "Standard for Transfer Switch Equipment" to provide more robust testing methodologies for transfer switch short circuit rating, among other revisions. Hopefully, this will have a positive impact on the number of future transfer switch failures. **See Figure 3-7.**

Transfer switches are devices that connect a specific load from one source to another. This equipment is divided into two main categories: automatic transfer switches and nonautomatic or manual transfer switches. IEEE documents and some other NFPA documents use the term *nonautomatic transfer switches*, while the *NEC* and *NFPA 99* use the term *manual transfer switches*. Both terms apply to the same equipment.

Manual transfer switches require human interaction to transfer the power connection to the essential electrical system. This power connection transfer can happen via an operator pushing a button on a control panel or physically operating a handle that causes the switching mechanism to connect to the alternate power source. In health care facilities, manual transfer switches are only permitted on some low priority equipment branch loads.

Automatic transfer switches are self-acting devices that are capable of transferring a specific load from one connection to another without human interaction. Automatic transfer switches are required on the life branch, the critical branch, and any high priority equipment branch loads in health care facilities.

Automatic transfer switches can generally be divided into two categories based on their construction. Contactor automatic transfer switches employ a system of contacts, similar to a motor starter, to transfer the load connection from one source to another. **See Figure 3-8.**

Molded case transfer switches employ interlocked molded case circuit breakers that enable the automatic transfer of the load to either source. **See Figure 3-9.**

Both types have their advantages and disadvantages; it is up to the design engineer to make the right choice for the unique role the automatic transfer switch will play in the essential electrical system.

Figure 3-7　**ATS**

Figure 3-7. An automatic transfer switch (ATS) switches the load from normal to essential power when normal power fails.

Operation

In health care facilities, automatic transfer switches have an order of operation that is defined in *NFPA 99: Health Care Facilities Code*, Section 6.7.2.1.2. Automatic transfer switches monitor the voltage and frequency of the current on the normal connection. In the event either factor falls below a pre-determined level, the automatic transfer switch sends a start signal to the generator. Depending on the circumstances, the start signal can be delayed as much as one second to allow for voltage sags that may be a regular occurrence for normal utility power in a location.

Once the start signal is sent, the generator starts and comes up to speed. Once the minimum voltage and frequency factors are met, the generator's main circuit breaker closes, energizing the essential electrical system bus. The automatic transfer switch senses the essential electrical source is now "hot" and within voltage and frequency parameters. The automatic transfer switch then automatically transfers the load to the energized essential electrical system contacts, energizing the load. At this

Transfer Switch Definitions

Article 100 provides the following definitions that may prove helpful when studying transfer switches:

- **Switch, Transfer.** An automatic or nonautomatic device for transferring one or more load conductor connections from one power source to another.

- **Automatic.** Performing a function without the necessity of human intervention.

- **Nonautomatic.** Requiring human intervention to perform a function.

Figure 3-8   Contactor ATS

Figure 3-8. A large 1,600-ampere contactor type ATS uses a system of contacts to transfer the load connection.

Figure 3-9   Molded Case Switch – Type ATS

Figure 3-9. Some ATS use molded case switches and microprocessors to transfer essential loads. *Courtesy of Eaton*

point, the generator is assuming the entire load served by the transfer switch. In the event the generator fails and is no longer producing power, the automatic transfer switch, by default, transfers to the normal utility power position, even though that position is not energized. This default allows the generators to restart under a no-load condition.

Once normal utility power is returned to the automatic transfer switch, several actions can be programmed into the equipment. After a short delay (two to three seconds) to examine the stability of the power source, the automatic transfer switch can transfer the load to the normal power source, essentially relieving the generator of the load.

Under certain circumstances, it may be advisable to delay transfer from the essential electrical system to the normal system for several minutes to ensure the normal system has regained stability. This delay is significant for critical loads in areas where the reliability of the utility may be in question.

Finally, the load may be programmed to re-transfer to the normal source for a period of up to thirty minutes to allow for the cool-down period sometimes recommended by generator manufacturers. All transfer switches have a "push to test" feature that simulates a normal power outage for testing purposes. *NFPA 110: Standard for Emergency and Standby Power Systems* requires that essential electrical systems be tested monthly; this also requires testing transfer equipment, meaning that automatic transfer equipment will change states at least once a month.

The action of the automatic transfer switch contacts can be configured in two schemes: open transition and closed transition. An open transition design is a "break before make" arrangement where the load is not attached to a source for a short period of time as the contacts physically move from one source to another. The open transition scheme is more cost-effective, and is acceptable for certain equipment branch loads that can ride through the momentary power interruption.

Closed transition automatic transfer switches use a "make before break" arrangement where the load is connected to both sources of power for a period in the 100- to 200-millisecond range. These automatic transfer switches have phase sensors that determine when the two power sources are in-phase and synchronized before initiating the transfer of power. Closed transition automatic transfer switches are more costly than open transition models but provide a truly seamless transition of power for critical loads. Considering that a transfer switch requires monthly testing during its life cycle, installing a closed transition automatic transfer switch may be the best option.

Bypass/Isolation Units

Because automatic transfer switches are complex and a known source of failure, periodic maintenance becomes very important. The use of an automatic transfer switch with a built-in bypass switch simplifies the maintenance procedures required to maintain critical equipment that is constantly under load.

Bypass switches isolate the automatic transfer switch from the circuit and allow maintenance to be performed safely without interrupting power to the loads connected to the essential electrical system. They shunt the circuit around the automatic transfer switch, which enables personnel to work and test the equipment without interrupting service downstream. Some manufacturers provide a "draw out" feature to simplify the work. It is important that the bypass switch has the capability to manually transfer from one source to the other in the event of a normal power outage while the automatic transfer switch is isolated by the bypass device. Bypass switches add cost to the automatic transfer switch assembly, but considering the importance of maintenance, bypass switches are among the most cost-effective options.

Neither the *NEC* nor *NFPA 99* require automatic transfer switches with *bypass/isolation switches*. However, *NFPA 99* Section 6.7.2.1.2.8 requires that if automatic transfer switches with bypass switches are used, the bypass switch assembly must be able to transfer between the normal and essential electrical system sources manually. **See Figure 3-10.**

Location

Years ago, before the advent of microprocessor controls, it was considered good engineering practice to have all facility transfer switches in one location, preferably in close proximity to the generation equipment. Facility managers preferred this practice because it meant that all of the equipment to be monitored was in one location; contractors and installers liked it because everything was in one place and a single feeder could be run to equipment in outlying areas.

Modern engineering practices, however, employ the opposite strategy: moving the automatic transfer switches out of the powerhouse or electrical equipment room and placing them as close to the loads they serve as possible. This arrangement provides the most protection for the loads, as two feeders are available at the utilization equipment, and moves the transfer equipment across the entire health care facility, eliminating the danger of having all transfer equipment in one location. The movement to local transfer locations adds additional benefit in that the installer maintains as much physical separation of the normal and essential system feeders as possible. As discussed, no matter its physical location, the automatic transfer switch is rendered useless if both feeders are taken out of service. **See Figure 3-11.**

UPS SYSTEMS

An uninterruptible power supply (UPS) is an electrical apparatus that utilizes a back-up DC-voltage system (batteries) or a flywheel (dynamic generation), and provides emergency power to specific loads or systems when a power source or main power fails. While technically not an automatic transfer switch, UPS systems have

Figure 3-10 ATS with Bypass Feature

Figure 3-10. A contactor type ATS with a bypass allows essential electrical system loads to remain energized while maintenance can safely be performed on the deenergized ATS. *Courtesy of Eaton*

Figure 3-11 Small Contactor Type ATS

Figure 3-11. A small contactor type ATS may also include a bypass feature.

become a popular option of choice for health care facility critical and sensitive loads such as operating room lighting, sensitive laboratory equipment, delicate diagnostic equipment, critical life support equipment, and data processing operations.

UPS systems are always in "transfer" mode; that is, they provide conditioned power to their critical loads through a normal system feeder, an essential electrical system feeder, or in the event that both systems are deenergized, a battery bank. Automatic transfer switches, by their very operation, can introduce power quality issues for sensitive electronic equipment in the form of a destructive voltage spike or voltage sags as loads transfer from normal power system to the alternate or back-up electrical system.

UPS systems solve power quality issues by delivering clean conditioned power to their sensitive loads, no matter the upstream power source. Ironically, UPS systems, especially older systems, are often a source of triplen harmonics and can cause power quality issues for upstream equipment. Although not required by any code or standard, UPS systems have gained a

solid presence in the essential electrical systems of many health care facilities. **See Figure 3-12.**

DISTRIBUTION ARRANGEMENT OPTIONS

While the design of a health care facility electrical distribution system is the responsibility of the design engineer, an understanding of basic distribution design principles aids the installer in the performance of his or her duties, particularly during remodel, retrofit, and service call activities. The overriding principle of health care electrical system design is reliability, which can be accomplished using many different arrangements. The intended use, size, and electrical load of the facility are all important elements design engineers consider when crafting a distribution system. These distribution arrangements, starting with those found in smaller facilities and moving to more complex schemes found in larger hospitals and campus type medical centers, will briefly be examined.

Radial Systems

Radial systems are generally found in smaller health care facilities such as nursing homes, storefront clinics, and boutique surgeries. These systems employ a single distribution switchgear close to the normal service entrance. The switchgear serves feeders that provide power to panelboards, motor control centers, and all other normal loads throughout the structure.

The essential system is served in a similar manner. Switchgear or smaller distribution equipment is located close to the transfer equipment, and this distribution equipment serves feeders and perhaps branch circuits that power the life safety branch loads; a second transfer switch and distribution equipment serves the equipment branch loads. If the level of care provided by the facility requires a Type 1 essential electrical system, a third transfer switch and associated distribution equipment will be used for the critical branch loads.

Figure 3-12   UPS Systems

Figure 3-12. While not required by code, UPS systems can bring a high level of redundancy to critical essential electrical system elements, such as operating room lighting.

Figure 3-13   Radial Systems

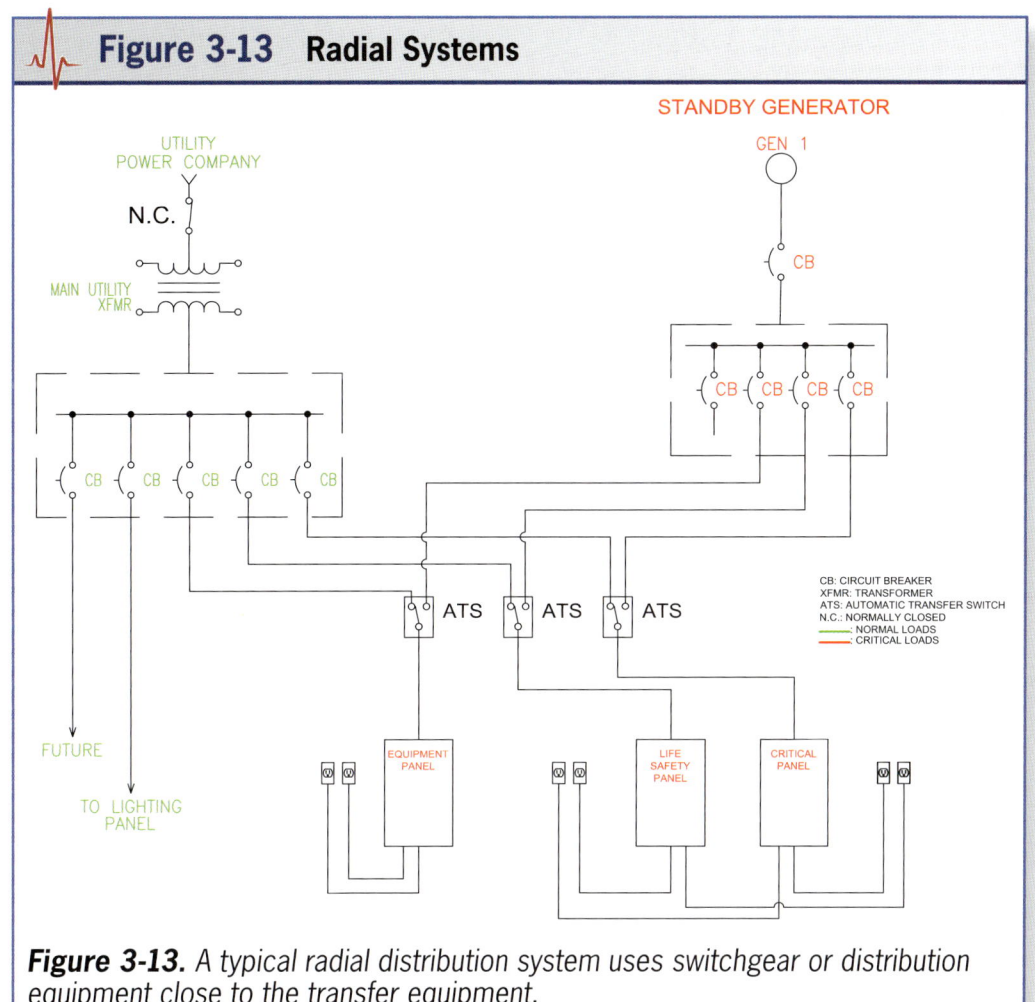

Figure 3-13. *A typical radial distribution system uses switchgear or distribution equipment close to the transfer equipment.*

These distribution arrangements are relatively cost-effective, are code-compliant, and are typically used when one generator is sufficient to carry the essential system loads. The main drawback of these distribution arrangments is that they have a limited capacity for future growth and expansion, which may not be an issue in the smaller types of occupancies served by these distribution arrangements. **See Figure 3-13.**

Double-Ended Gear Systems

Double-ended gear systems are used in medium to large health care facilities that employ two normal services and two sets of service entrance conductors. The double-ended gear arrangement is duplicated throughout the facility, providing a high degree of normal system reliability as well as a means to isolate certain sections of the distribution system for maintenance and inspection

Delay Functions in Equipment Branch Motor Control Circuits

Many years ago, large 3-phase loads such as chillers, large air handlers, compressors, and other mechanical equipment proved difficult to connect to generation equipment in the event of an outage. The across the line, series-parallel, and reduced voltage starting equipment used at the time subjected the generation and transfer equipment to enormous inrush currents that stressed the equipment. Modern motor starting equipment, specifically variable frequency drives, has come a long way in reducing the dangerous inrush currents. Furthermore, motor controls that take advantage of network capabilities assure that large inrush current equipment will not start concurrently.

without impacting the remaining loads. Multiple transfer switches are located close to the essential loads they serve and also provide a high degree of reliability. These systems are expensive; however, if designed properly, they provide a high capacity for future growth and expansion. These distribution arrangements are ideal for a health care facility that provides critical care and has the potential for growth. **See Figure 3-14.**

Loop Systems

Loop systems are used in large multi-structure campus type medical centers. Normal power from two normal sources is distributed through a double-ended switchgear and a loop feeder arrangement to various distribution points. At each distribution point, the downstream equipment is served by a series of loop feed switches as well as an overcurrent protection device that can be opened to completely isolate the distribution point from the remainder of the system. It is important to note, just like the loop systems described previously, these systems are intentionally back-fed; opening one device will not deenergize the loop

circuit. Loop systems provide an almost unlimited capacity for growth, which is very desirable in a campus situation. **See Figure 3-15.**

Overcurrent Protection

Properly sized overcurrent protection, installed as detailed in drawings and specifications, is the most important element in any electrical distribution system. Due to the complex nature of these systems in health care facilities, overcurrent protection in both the normal and essential electrical systems becomes extremely important. Basically, overcurrent protection can be divided into two categories: fuses and circuit breakers.

Fuses have the ability to open quickly and limit fault current; except for the fuse clips and holders, they do not require maintenance or regular exercising. Modern fuses are current limiting, have outstanding interrupting ratings, and are easily designed for selective coordination throughout the distribution system. Adversely, they must be replaced when subjected to a fault current, which means keeping an extensive inventory of spare fuses in stock and readily available for quick replacement.

Circuit breakers, on the other hand, are resettable after a fault and do not require equipment to be opened, potentially exposing workers to live voltages. Circuit breakers are mechanical devices that must be maintained periodically according to the manufacturer installation and maintenance instructions, including operation testing (opening/closing) at least once per year, thermal image testing, and torque tightening conductor connections. Circuit breaker operation during a fault current at or near its maximum interrupting rating can damage the device and will require replacement. Circuit breakers tend to be slower-acting than fuses, which increases the amount of fault current impressed on the fault, although recent developments in microprocessor-based circuit breakers have considerably narrowed the reaction time gap. Microprocessor-based circuit breakers also have the ability to communicate and act in

Figure 3-14 Double-Ended Switchgear

LOCAL UTILITY PRIMARY NON-LOCAL UTILITY SECONDARY ON-SITE GENERATION

TIE BREAKER

CB CB CB   CB CB CB   CB CB CB

NORMAL LOADS

ATS → LIFE SAFETY

ATS → CRITICAL

ATS → EQUIPMENT

CB: CIRCUIT BREAKER
ATS: AUTOMATIC TRANSFER SWITCH

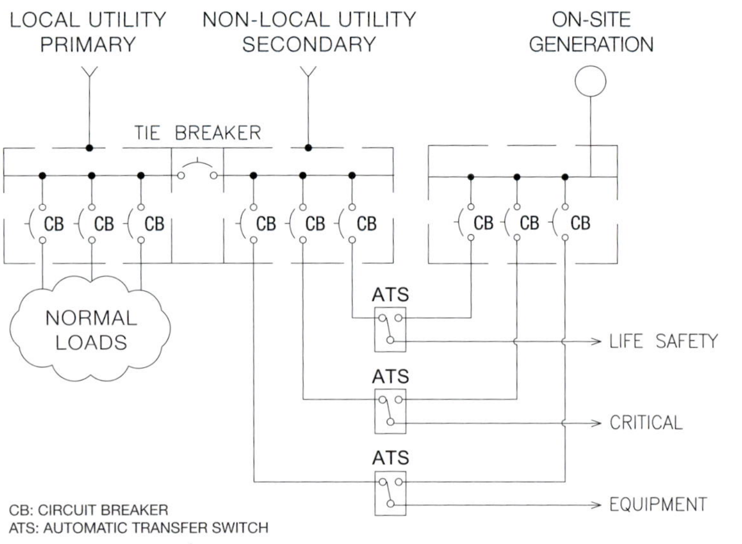

Figure 3-14. A double-ended main switchgear configuration provides a high degree of reliability as well as the ability to isolate parts of the system.

concert with one another, which has great benefits when coordinating the pick-up or shedding of loads on the essential electrical systems equipment branch. However, circuit breakers, especially those that are microprocessor-based, are considerably more expensive than fuses. **See Figure 3-16.**

Selective Coordination

The 2005 revision of the *National Electrical Code* added the following:

700.27 Coordination. Emergency system(s) overcurrent devices shall be selectively coordinated with all supply side overcurrent protective devices.

This addition mandated that the overcurrent protective devices used in emergency systems as defined in Article 700 be selectively coordinated. *Selective coordination* is defined in the 2020 *National Electrical Code* in Article 100.

Coordination, Selective (Selective Coordination). Localization of an overcurrent condition to restrict outages to the circuit or equipment affected, accomplished by the selection and installation of overcurrent protective devices and their ratings or settings for the full range of available overcurrents, from overload to the maximum available fault current, and for the full range of overcurrent protective device opening times associated with those overcurrents.

Simply put, selective coordination means the overcurrent device electrically closest to the fault should open to clear the fault. In 2005, this rather simple engineering principle proved difficult, especially in regard to complex distribution systems. At the time, the requirements of Article 700 applied to the essential electrical systems found in health care facilities.

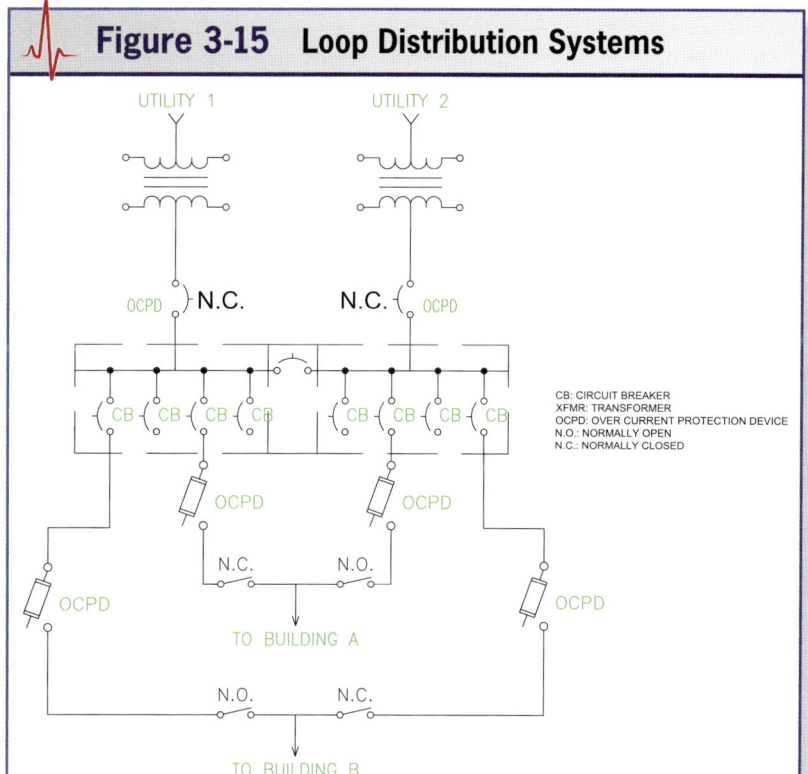

Figure 3-15   Loop Distribution Systems

Figure 3-15. *A loop distribution system is often used in campus environments.*

Figure 3-16   Microprocessor Circuit Breaker

Figure 3-16. *Some circuit breakers have a microprocessor control that provides a very high level of communication and coordination with other distribution system equipment.*

Design engineers were challenged to design health care essential electrical systems with overcurrent protection that was selectively coordinated using the standard catalog devices on the market in 2005. Many design engineers thought they were being forced to use fuse type (rather than circuit breaker type) overcurrent protection, which was not acceptable to them or to the facility managers and owners. The ensuing editions of the *National Electrical Code* and *NFPA 99: Health Care Facilities Code* saw the applicability of Article 700 reduced to only the life safety branch of the essential electrical system and even then, modified by amendment.

Despite this reaction from the health care community, selective coordination remains a hallmark of a reliable and safe essential electrical system, although no longer mandated by Article 517 or *NFPA 99*. Modern microprocessor-based circuit breakers that can communicate across the distribution system spectrum can go a long way to selectively coordinate faults.

Ground-Fault Protection of Equipment

In the 2020 edition of the *NEC*, Sections 210.13, Branch Circuits, 215.10, Feeders, 230.95, Services, and 240.13,

Ground-Fault Protection of Equipment, require ground-fault protection for distribution systems over 1,000 amperes serving a 480/277-volt grounded wye configuration. These requirements were additions to the *National Electrical Code* in the 1970s. Section 517.17 modifies this requirement to require second level ground-fault protection on feeders and/or branch circuits that are downstream of the ground-fault protection required in Article 230. The purpose of this second level of protection is to limit the ground-fault outage to the feeder experiencing the fault, rather than disturbing the entire electrical system.

Obviously, the trip and duration settings on both microprocessor-based and programmable circuit breakers are extremely critical to the proper function of the entire electrical system and should not be changed or modified in any manner, unless under the direct supervision of a facility or design engineer. The interaction between overcurrent protection devices is a complex equation.

Furthermore, in order to assure low-impedance equipment grounds are in place in complex feeder systems, Article 517 requires the use of bonding bushings, threaded hubs, or grounding locknuts in feeder conduit or cable.

ENERGIZED WORK IN A HEALTH CARE FACILITY

Along with the general safety hazards associated with the use of electricity in an occupancy, redundant power systems in health care facilities create additional safety concerns for Electrical Workers. Hospitals and ambulatory care centers can have up to three, and sometimes four, back-up power systems. For example, a hospital may use a utility power source for main power; a generator to provide back-up power for the critical, life-safety, and equipment branches upon failure of the utility system; and an uninterruptible power system (UPS) to provide constant current flow for surgery units, ICUs, emergency rooms, and trauma treatment

---

517.19(E) Equipment Grounding and Bonding. Where a grounded electrical distribution system is used and metal feeder raceway or Type MC or MI cable that qualifies as an equipment grounding conductor in accordance with 250.118 is installed, grounding of enclosures and equipment, such as panelboards, switchboards, and switchgear, shall be ensured by one of the following bonding means at each termination or junction point of the metal raceway or Type MC or MI cable:

(1) A grounding bushing and a continuous copper bonding jumper, sized in accordance with 250.122, with the bonding jumper connected to the junction enclosure or the ground bus of the panel

(2) Connection of feeder raceways or Type MC or MI cable to threaded hubs or bosses on terminating enclosures

(3) Other approved devices such as bonding-type locknuts or bushings. Standard locknuts shall not be used for bonding.

Qualified Person

A *qualified person* is defined in *NFPA 70E: Standard for Electrical Safety in the Workplace—2021* as "One who has demonstrated skills and knowledge related to the construction and operation of electrical equipment and installations and has received safety training to identify the hazards and reduce the associated risk." In part, a qualified person is specifically trained and has demonstrated skills and techniques to determine nominal voltage levels, distinguish energized live circuit conductors and parts, and establish approach boundaries. It is possible for a person to be considered a "qualified person" for some types of equipment or aspects of the work, but unqualified for other types of equipment or work.

A worker may be considered a qualified person if they have received on-the-job training and have demonstrated the ability to perform work safely when under direct supervision of a qualifed worker as part of qualified person training. A qualified worker must also demonstrate to their employer the special skills necessary to perform job safety planning, identify electrical hazards and associated risks, and implement a hierarchy of safety controls, including selecting the proper personal protective equipment as part of their qualified person training. Refer to *NFPA 70E* in its entirety.

Reproduced with permission of NFPA from NFPA 70E®, *Standard for Electrical Safety in the Workplace*®, 2021 edition. Copyright© 2020, National Fire Protection Association. For a full copy of the NFPA 70E®, please go to www.nfpa.org.

areas. *NFPA 99*, 2021 edition allows the use of multi-source health care microgrid systems in health care facilities.

It is vital for Electrical Workers to understand the dynamics of a building electrical distribution system and the location of all power sources, including all redundant sources used to energize the system, before proceeding with any work. The Occupational Safety and Health Administration (OSHA) and *NFPA 70E: Standard for Safety in the Workplace* require electrical systems to be deenergized, locked out and tagged, and put in an electrically safe work condition before work begins on electrical systems. OSHA allows energized work in health care facilities where shutting down an essential electrical system may create additional or increased life safety hazards to patients and staff, or where infeasible for workers performing diagnostic testing, start-up of equipment, maintenance, or repairs. Many times, energized work is the rule rather than the exception in health care facilities. Workers must constantly be vigilant in protecting patients, staff, visitors, and themselves when considering live work on electrical systems.

OSHA puts the responsibility on the employer to determine when employees work on energized equipment.

Generally, journeyman and apprentice workers are not allowed to make the decision to work on energized equipment and circuit parts. While the employer may designate a lead employee as a "qualified person" to make live-work decisions as to when rank and file workers are allowed to preform energized work, only employers that have documentation of demonstration of proficiency for workers that have received the extensive training and who have demonstrated they understand shock and arc flash risk assessment, the hierarchy of risk control methods, safe work practices (including selecting appropriate PPE and insulated tools) are qualified to work on energized electrical systems. See *NFPA 70E* 110.6(A)(1) for example.

The *NEC* is considered a safety document addressing the performance and prescriptive requirements for installations of electrical systems. The *NEC* typically does not directly address safe work practices; however, the *Code* does provide performance requirements that relate directly to worker safety. For Example, 110.16 addresses arc-flash warning and applicable marking on warning labels, 110.21 addresses equipment marking, 110.24 addresses available fault current, 110.25 addresses lockable disconnecting means, 110.26 addresses spaces about electrical equipment, and 240.67 and 240.87 address arc energy reduction. These general installation rules help save lives and provide the owner of the equipment reasonable protection against damaging accidents to the electrical distribution system causing power disruption and loss of production.

OSHA requirements address faulty electrical equipment, damaged receptacles and equipment, and unsafe work practices. OSHA also addresses performance requirements ("shall comply") for electrical safety, and when combined with the prescriptive requirements ("how to comply") of *NFPA 70E*, employers can create a safe work environment for their employees during periods of construction, repairs, and maintenance. At a minimum, workers should obtain OSHA 10-Hour Training and supervisors should have OSHA 30-Hour Training with all workers trained in aspects of *NFPA 70E*.

Review all of the *NFPA 70E*, including The Risk Assessment Procedure outlined in *NFPA 70E* 110.5(H) which addresses requirements such as the need for employees to be trained to recognize exposure to electrical hazards and to identify the process used to identify electrical hazards, assess risks, and implement a risk control procedure according the hierarchy of risk control methods.

Also review *NFPA 70E* Article 120. Per *NFPA 70E* 110.2, in part, all of Article 120 must be met in addition to following the eight steps of *NFPA 70E* 120.5 to achieve and verify an electrically safe work condition. Be sure to include OSHA's rules for de-energizing electrical systems; including the lockout/tagout procedure, as well as verifying the absence of voltage on the equipment, among other requirements.

Follow OSHA requirements as supplemented by *NFPA 70E* standards in an effort to provide the safest possible work environment for Electrical Workers. Employers that establish an electrical safety program and provide and document training that relies on employee participation, demonstration of safe work practices, identifying hazards, assessing risks, and implementing a hierarchy of risk control method strategy minimize worker injury, are taking steps that are among those that strive to provide their employees with the safest possible work environment.

SUMMARY

At their most basic element, normal electrical systems supply power to the distribution system for non-essential loads, such as waiting rooms, reception areas, business and office spaces, food services, and irrigation equipment. Essential electrical systems shall be connected to both the normal power system and an alternate power supply system, typically a fuel-driven generator system. Consideration must also be given to the fact that in a properly-designed electrical system, normal system feeders powered from the utility with back-up power capabilities from the essential electrical system may be considered the preferred feeder wiring system for sophisticated double-ended switchgear located throughout the facility serving critical patient care loads.

It is important to understand essential electrical systems required in health care facilities are not categorized as emergency standby systems as defined in Article 700 of *NFPA 70: National Electrical Code*. Strictly speaking, emergency systems do not exist in health care facilities, although essential electrical systems are erroneously often called emergency systems by installers.

Essential electrical systems in hospitals and other inpatient facilities (rated over 150 kVA in size) must be divided into three branches: the life safety branch, the critical branch, and the equipment branch. Each branch must be served by one or more dedicated transfer switch(es) that will transfer the load from the normal power feeder system to the essential electrical system feeder when power is lost to the normal feeder. The life safety branch of the essential electrical system most closely resembles the emergency systems found in other occupancies as defined in Article 700. As the name suggests, the life safety branch feeds equipment that is required to "save lives" in the case of a normal power outage. While the life safety branch is earmarked for defined loads required to keep building occupants safe in an emergency, the critical branch of the essential electrical system may be considered the branch that keeps patients and health care workers safe during the performance of everyday diagnostic, clinical, and treatment activities. Like the life safety branch, the transfer switch(es) feeding the critical branch must automatically connect to the essential electrical system feeder upon failure of the normal feeder. The equipment branch of the essential electrical system serves mechanical equipment that is important to the safety and health of both patients and staff.

During an emergency, health care facilities will use "defend-in-place" strategies to protect patients rather than a mass evacuation.

The intended use, size, and electrical load of the facility are all important elements design engineers consider when crafting a distribution system. These systems include radial systems, double-ended gear systems, and loop systems.

Selective coordination means the overcurrent device located closest to the fault should open to clear the fault. Selective coordination remains a hallmark of a reliable and safe essential electrical system, although no longer mandated by Article 517 or *NFPA 99*. Modern microprocessor-based circuit breakers that can communicate across the distribution system spectrum can go a long way to selectively coordinate faults.

REVIEW QUESTIONS

1. Essential electrical systems required in health care facilities, categorized as emergency standby systems, are defined in Article 700 of *NFPA 70*.

   a. True   b. False

2. Essential electrical systems in hospitals and other inpatient facilities (rated over 150 kVA in size) consist of the __?__ .

   a. critical branch
   b. equipment branch
   c. life safety branch
   d. all the above

3. Each branch must be served by one or more dedicated transfer switch(es) __?__ and approved by the authority having jurisdiction (AHJ) that will transfer the load from the normal power feeder system to the essential electrical system feeder when power is lost to the normal feeder.

   a. acceptable
   b. identified for emergency use
   c. listed, labeled
   d. selected by

4. The life safety branch of the essential electrical system most closely resembles the emergency systems found in other occupancies as defined in Article 700 and includes equipment relating to installations of egress illumination, exit signs, alarm and communication equipment, elevator cab lighting, automatic doors, task lighting, generator accessories, and other such equipment; no other loads are permitted to be connected to the life safety branch.

   a. True   b. False

5. The critical branch of the essential electrical system may be considered the branch that is used to __?__ and keeps patients and health care workers safe during the performance of everyday diagnostic, clinical, and treatment activities.

   a. provide emergency lighting
   b. provide power for heating and air conditioning systems
   c. provide power waiting areas, cafeterias and hallways
   d. sustain human life

6. The equipment branch includes equipment designed to be connected to the generators after the life safety and critical branches are transferred and includes such equipment as central suction systems, sump pumps and similar equipment, medical compressed air, smoke and stairway control systems, supply, return and exhaust ventilation systems, telephone and data equipment rooms, and other delayed or manually connected equipment systems.

   a. True   b. False

7. Based on the limited level of care, the critical branch of the essential electrical system is required for installation in a nursing home.

   a. True   b. False

8. Transfer switches are devices that connect a specific load from one source to another. This equipment is divided into two main categories: automatic transfer switches and nonautomatic or manual transfer switches. Transfer switches are typically installed with __?__ so that temporary electrical power may be provided in the event that the utility power source fails.

   a. backup generators
   b. battery exit and emergency lighting systems
   c. dual-fed switchgear
   d. normal utility power systems

REVIEW QUESTIONS

9. Automatic transfer switches are __?__ that are capable of transferring a specific load from one connection to another without human intervention. Automatic transfer switches are required on the life branch, the critical branch, and any high priority equipment branch loads in health care facilities.

   a. categorized as alternative power devices

   b. manually operated devices

   c. power consumption devices

   d. self-acting devices

10. While the design of a health care facility's electrical distribution system is the responsibility of the __?__, an understanding of basic distribution design principles aids the installer in the performance of their duties, particularly during remodel, retrofit, and service call activities.

    a. design engineer

    b. general contractor

    c. governing body of the health care facility

    d. local government AHJ

11. Which type of overcurrent devices will open quickly and limit fault-current and do not require maintenance or periodic exercising?

    a. Circuit breakers

    b. Fuses

    c. Motor circuit protectors

    d. Supplementary overcurrent devices

12. What type of additional protection for distribution systems does the *NEC* require for distribution service, feeder, and branch circuit equipment disconnecting means rated over 1,000 amperes serving a 480/277-volt grounded wye configuration?

    a. Ground-fault circuit interrupters

    b. Ground-fault protection of equipment

    c. Microprocessor overcurrent monitoring

    d. Standard circuit breakers and/or fuses

13. When performing maintenance work on a system, it is not necessary for Electrical Workers to understand the dynamics of a building electrical distribution system and to locate all power sources, including all redundant sources used to energize the system before proceeding with any work.

    a. True   b. False

14. OSHA allows energized work in health care facilities where shutting down an essential electrical system may create additional or increased life safety hazards to patients and staff, or where infeasible for Electrical Workers performing diagnostic testing, start-up of equipment, maintenance, or repairs.

    a. True   b. False

15. Only Electrical Workers that receive extensive training and demonstrate that they understand __?__ and safe work practices are qualified to work on energized electrical systems.

    a. electrical power generator systems

    b. how to use insulated tools

    c. the operational requirements of the electrical equipment

    d. shock and arc flash risk assessment

Patient Care Spaces

Careful essential electrical system design and installation is meaningless if safe and redundant electrical power is not consistently delivered to patients. Proper performance is critical for patient care spaces. The areas in health care facilities where patients receive treatment and care are known as *patient care spaces*. The provisions of both *NFPA 99: The Health Care Facilities Code* and *NFPA 70: National Electrical Code* are quite specific and detailed regarding both the design and installation of both essential and normal electrical systems in patient care spaces.

Objectives

» Define risk assessment as it applies to health care facilities and explain the different classifications as they apply to patient care spaces.

» Apply the *NEC* guidelines found in Article 517, Part II, to the enhanced wiring methods rules used in health care facilities.

» Describe both the mandatory and optional systems used to protect patients, staff, and visitors in Category 1 (Critical Care) and Category 2 (General Care) spaces, and how they are utilized.

» Analyze operating rooms and the rules that guide electrical installations in them.

Chapter 4

Table of Contents

RISK ASSESSMENT VS. OCCUPANCY

Health care electrical systems have thus far been discussed in terms of reliability and the critical importance of maintaining electrical service to health care facilities in all situations. The importance of how this critical power is used in patient care spaces and the regulations in place to ensure patient safety is pertinent in health care. Patients are particularly susceptible to electrical shock. Through the years, both *NFPA 99: The Health Care Facilities Code* and *NFPA 70: National Electrical Code (NEC)* have adopted many requirements designed specifically to keep patients, health care workers, and visitors safe from stray electrical current.

RISK ASSESSMENT

In 2005, *NFPA 99* began a revolutionary process that moved the document from a traditional, occupancy-based standard founded on the type of care to a code-based document. The basis for the code document is risk assessment,

or category level, where activities, systems, or equipment failure are likely to cause injury or death to a patient, staff member, or visitor. Article 517 of the *NEC* also followed this move from occupancy designation to health or hazard risk assessment beginning with the 2011 edition.

Occupancy-based regulations simply detail the requirements for a space or area in accordance with the use of the space. For example, patient care areas (later changed to patient care spaces) in 2011 were required to have at least one circuit supplied from the critical branch and one circuit supplied from the normal branch, in addition to six receptacles, at least one or more supplied from a critical branch circuit. Every electrical circuit in the patient care space (except for some lighting circuits) are required to be redundantly grounded to provide two different effective ground fault pathways. Each circuit is required to have two intact equipment grounding conductors: one supplied by a metal raceway or a cable having a listed metallic armor of sheath assembly, and one additional path that is required to

CODE vs. STANDARD

What is a STANDARD?

A standard is a document that contains mandatory provisions using the word *shall* to indicate requirements and is written in a form generally suitable for mandatory reference by another code or standard. If adopted, it can be used as established law.

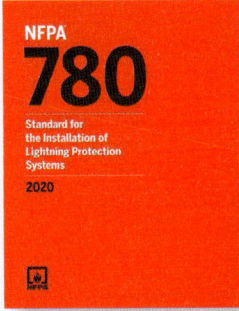

What is a CODE?

A code is suitable for adoption into law independently of other codes or standards. The decision to designate a standard as a code is based on the size and scope of the document and its intended use as suitable for enforcement and administration provisions.

be a green insulated copper wire. These are just two examples of multiple special installation requirements required for patient care areas.

By 2005, the pace of technology and rapidly escalating care began eclipsing the occupancy requirements found in codes and standards. The industry needed a more open process to detail electrical requirements required for patient and worker safety while providing a degree of flexibility for the changing nature of patient care. Therefore, in 2005, in a bold move, *NFPA 99* started looking at health care facilities differently and began to scrap the traditional occupancy model, instead instituting requirements based solely on risk assessment.

Although a new concept to codes and standards, risk assessment is a very normal human activity; as rational beings, people consciously (and unconsciously) perform risk assessments all the time. *Shall I cross the street mid-block or continue to the corner and use the crosswalk? Shall I join the crew for a beer after work, or meet my spouse as promised?* Humans perform hundreds of these risk assessments every day.

Risk assessment in a health care environment is the process designed to place a specific facility space in a defined designated risk category. *NFPA 99* defines four risk categories: Categories 1, 2, 3, and 4, where Category 1 indicates procedures that create the possibility of the most danger of patient injury or death and Category 4 has the least opportunity for patient injury.

Surprisingly, *NFPA 99* is particularly silent on how the risk assessment is performed by the governing body of the facility, only stating in Section 4.2 that "Categories shall be defined by following and documenting a defined risk assessment procedure." The annex material in *NFPA 99* for this section provides some additional guidance directing the user to several documents that can be used for model risk assessment, and strongly suggests that the procedure be documented and the records retained.

The governing body of the health care facility has ultimate responsibility for the facility risk assessment, which is performed on a system-by-system basis. A defined space may have a Category 1 electrical system and a Category 3 mechanical system depending on the risk assessment results for the individual systems serving a particular space.

NFPA 99 details four risk categories in which a risk assessment may place a particular electrical or mechanical system serving a particular space. In the 2021 edition of *NFPA 99*, Section 4.1 defines these categories as follows:

> **4.1.1 Category 1.** Activities, systems, or equipment whose failure is likely to cause major injury or death of patients, staff or visitors shall be designed to meet Category 1 requirements, as detailed in this code.
>
> **4.1.2 Category 2.** Activities, systems, or equipment whose failure is likely to cause minor injury of patients, staff or visitors shall be designed to meet Category 2 requirements, as detailed in this code.
>
> **4.1.3 Category 3.** Activities, systems, or equipment whose failure is not likely to cause injury to patients, staff or visitors, but can cause discomfort, shall be designed to meet Category 3 requirements, as detailed in this code.
>
> **4.1.4 Category 4.** Activities, systems, or equipment whose failure would have no impact on patient care shall be designed to meet Category 4 requirements, as detailed in this code.

Taking the Section 4.1 definitions at face value, the performance of a risk assessment answering a series of simple but highly significant questions.

Should the electrical or mechanical system serving a particular space fail, various outcomes occur:

- *Will patients or staff die or become injured?*
  - o *Yes – Category 1*
  - o *No –*
- *Will the patient or staff suffer minor injuries?*
  - o *Yes – Category 2*
  - o *No –*
- *Will the patient or staff suffer discomfort?*
  - o *Yes – Category 3*
  - o *No –*
- *Will the outage impact care?*
  - o *Yes – review assessment*
  - o *No – Category 4*

Once a system is assigned a risk category, the requirements for that particular system will be found in the *NFPA 99* chapter relevant to that system. For example, the details of gas and vacuum systems are in Chapter 5, electrical systems in Chapter 6, telecommunications systems in Chapter 7, and plumbing systems in Chapter 8.

To aid the *Code* user, annex material in *NFPA 99* (A4.1) helpfully provides examples of occupancies and their likely risk category assignment:

- Ambulatory surgical center, two patients with full OR services: Category 1
- Reconstructive surgeons office with general anesthesia: Category 1
- Procedural sedation suite for outpatient services: Category 2
- Cooling Towers in Houston, TX: Category 2
- Cooling Towers in Seattle, WA: Category 3
- Dentist office, no general anesthesia: Category 3
- Typical doctor's office/exam room: Category 4
- Lawn sprinkler system: Category 4

Risk assessments, by their very nature, are always performed in the design stage of a new build, remodel, or renovation. The real impact for an electrical installer lies in the fact that the assigned risk category for a particular space determines the type of essential electrical system (EES) serving that space. Chapter 6 of *NFPA 99* requires risk Category 1 spaces to be served only by a Type 1 EES; risk Category 2 spaces shall be permitted to be served by a Type 1 EES or a Type 2 EES; and risk Category 3 and 4 spaces shall not be required to be served by an EES, as normal electrical service is considered adequate for these spaces. Contiguous spaces required to provide life safety and equipment branches are permitted to rely on a Type 1 EES. Although risk assessment and risk category assignments are performed long before an electrical installer is on the job, the impact of risk category assignment is evident throughout not only the installation but the working life of the health care facility.

OCCUPANCY

Risk assessment is all well and good for *NFPA 99*; however, other safety codes, including the *NEC*, are occupancy-based documents. The article most associated with health care facilities, Article 517, is found in the *NEC* Chapter 5, Special Occupancies. With each revision cycle, the risk assessment criteria currently found in *NFPA 99* will continue to be a resource in Article 517 as code-making panels and technical committees work to coordinate the two NFPA documents. However, it is unlikely that the occupancy-based elements of Article 517 will be replaced by a pure risk-assessment criteria because the two have slightly differing missions. *NFPA 99* is a performance and design document, and *NFPA 70* is an installation document. In other words, the regulations governing the installation of electrical systems will remain occupancy-based because the document is designed in that manner. Article 517 contains many occupancy-based rules, beginning with Part II, Wiring and Protection.

Patient Care Spaces

NFPA 99 defines patient care spaces in 3.3.136 as, "any space of a health care facility wherein patients are intended to be examined or treated." This includes hospitals, ambulatory surgical centers, nursing homes, and medical and dental offices. The governing board of the health care facility determines the level of infrastructure required to safely care for patients by preforming a risk assessment analysis of the spaces before construction begins. The board assigns designated category levels based on the results of the risk assessment analysis.

The requirements of *NEC* Article 517 become relevant via 517.10(A), which states that all requirements of Part II, Wiring and Protection, apply to patient care spaces as defined in *NFPA 99*. It is worthwhile to study the requirements found in *NEC* Article 517, Part II, that apply to all patient care spaces, regardless of their designated category.

Common Criteria
All branch circuits serving patient care spaces shall be run in a metal raceway system or cable having a metallic armor or sheath assembly. The metal raceway system, metallic cable armor, or sheath assembly shall itself qualify as an equipment grounding conductor as found in Section 250.118. Additionally, the raceway or cable assembly must have a green insulated copper conductor installed in the raceway or within the cable jacket with the current-carrying conductors sized per 250.122. This copper equipment grounding conductor must be insulated and green in color through-out its entire length, and must be terminated to: metal boxes and metal enclosures, surfaces of fixed electrical equipment that may become energized, and device equipment grounding terminals.

These requirements create a classic redundant equipment grounding conductor installation, which provides an additional level of protection to patients and staff. These installations provide a secondary pathway to ground should the primary pathway become compromised in any way. These dual equipment grounding conductors

assure a low impedance ground pathway for stray electrical currents protecting the patient in the event of an electrical fault. This type of installation is considered the keystone element in protecting patient care spaces.

Panelboard Bonding
It is critical that the equipment grounding conductors serving patient care space be on the same electrical plane, so that there is no difference in potential between equipment grounding conductors from different panelboards or systems. Section 517.14 requires that panelboards serving a particular patient care vicinity be bonded together with at least a 10 AWG insulated copper conductor. This special bonding conductor shall be terminated on the equipment grounding bus found in each panel. This common bonding conductor provision applies to both normal and essential electrical systems.

Isolated Ground Receptacles
Isolated ground receptacles used to provide power to sensitive electronic equipment limits the amount of electrical "noise" sometimes found on ground paths. When wired properly, isolated ground receptacles cannot provide the redundant ground pathways required in patient care spaces.

Recognizing the importance of clean power to some sensitive medical equipment the *NEC* does allow an exception to allow isolated ground receptacles in patient care spaces provided they are wired to the requirements of 250.146(D) and the isolated equipment grounding conductor is green with a yellow stripe along its entire length. Isolated ground receptacles are prohibited in patient care vicinities were the danger to the exposure of stray electrical currents is deemed too important to override the redundant ground provisions noted above.

Patient care vicinities are defined in *NFPA 99* as, "a space within a location intended for the examination and treatment of patients, extending 1.8 m (six feet) beyond the normal locations from

Pediatric Locations

The 1981 edition of the *National Electrical Code* was the first time the *NEC* required then "Tamperproof," now "Tamper-resistant," receptacles in pediatric wards, now locations, in 517.90(b). The modern requirement can be found in 517.18(C), which requires receptacles found in "patient rooms, bathrooms, playrooms, and activity rooms of pediatric units or similar spaces…shall be listed and identified as tamper-resistant…" Interestingly, because these spaces are considered as Category 2 patient care spaces, the receptacles must also be listed as hospital grade. This requirement was adopted to assure curious children who are undergoing care will not come to harm "exploring" receptacles. Through the years much antidotal testimony heard and code-making panel meetings suggests young siblings visiting brother or sister in hospital may benefit from this requirement more so than young patients. In any case, the protection offered by tamper-resistant receptacles is well proven.

the bed, chair, table, treadmill, or other device that supports the patient during examination and treatment and extending vertically to seven feet six inches above the floor. Essentially, a patient care vicinity in a subset of a patient care space."

CATEGORY 1 SPACES

NFPA 99 defines Category 1 spaces as, "a space in which failure of equipment or a system is likely to cause major injury or death of patients, staff, or visitors," per 99:3.3.136.1. These spaces have patients and personnel that are heavily dependent on safe and reliable electrical power. Patients in these spaces are undergoing invasive treatment or are so compromised that the loss of electrical power, beyond the ten-second EES assumption, may cause death. Operating rooms, induction rooms, intensive care units, neonatal care units, trauma centers, and cardiac catheterization labs are all considered Category 1 spaces.

Both the *National Electrical Code* and the *Health Care Facilities Code* require Category 1 spaces to be served by a Type 1 EES. Type 1 EES are covered extensively in Chapter 3, Distribution. Life safety and critical branch Type 1 EES circuits are required to be physically separated from all other wiring and equipment including the normal system circuits; the idea being accidental damage to a normal (or EES) circuit will not completely leave a Category 1 space without electrical service. This provision also applies to installations were Category 1 spaces are served entirely by the EES with circuits behind two separately subdivided EES transfer switches.

The intermingling of these circuits is permitted in a few well-defined locations, including transfer equipment, exit lights, and their junction boxes served from two sources. EES circuits behind the same transfer switch are permitted to share raceways and enclosures. The raceways, cables, enclosures, and equipment (including transfer equipment) carrying life safety and critical branch circuits shall be marked and identified as part of the EES. Additionally, raceways and cable assemblies must be marked as EES components at least every seven feet; markings may be field or factory installed.

Because of the acute nature of their service, life safety and critical circuits serving patient care spaces are required to be mechanically protected by using raceways. Only the following optional wiring methods are permitted.

- Nonflexible metallic raceways, nonmetallic systems shall not be used to supply branch circuits in patient care spaces
- Type MI cable
- Schedule 80 PVC, nonmetallic systems shall not be used to supply branch circuits in patient care spaces
- Type RTRC-XW, nonmetallic systems shall not be used to supply branch circuits in patient care spaces
- Where encased in at least two inches of concrete:
  o Schedule 40 PVC
  o Jacketed metallic flexible raceways approved for concrete installations
  o Jacketed metallic cable assemblies approved for concrete installations

- Listed flexible metal raceways and listed metal sheathed cable under the following conditions:
    - Prefabricated headwalls
    - Listed office equipment
    - Fished in existing walls and/or ceilings
    - When required for flexible connection to equipment
    - When required for flexible connection to equipment due to vibration, movement, or operation.
    - Luminaires installed in ceiling structures

Category 1 Patient Bed Locations

An occupancy found in Category 1 spaces are patient bed locations. These occupancies are defined in *NFPA 99* as, "the location of a patient sleeping bed, or the bed or procedure table of a Category 1 space." A simple and to the point definition. Patient bed locations must be served by at least two circuits, neither of which can be part of a multiwire branch-circuit system. One circuit must be from the EES critical branch and must be dedicated to that location. The other circuit may originate from the normal electrical system or it may originate a second EES critical branch panel served by a different transfer switch from the other circuit.

All receptacles or cover plates of receptacles originating from a critical branch must have a distinctive color and must be marked as to the panelboard and circuit number. There must be at least 14 receptacles at each patient bed location and these receptacles must be listed hospital grade. **See Figure 4-1.**

In an unusual twist, the *NEC* permits two optional installations in patient bed locations; neither of which are required. If the designer choses to use them, these installations must conform to specific provisions in Article 517. *NEC* 517.19(D) allows the use of grounding points in patient bed locations to provide an extra level of protection from stray electrical currents by providing listed grounding and bonding jacks and jumpers that would connect to mobile surfaces that may become energized. This assembly must be connected by a 10 AWG copper conductor to the grounding terminal of all receptacles in the patient bed location. *NEC* 517.19(F) permits the use of

Hospital Grade Receptacles

Hospital grade receptacles must meet the performance and construction requirements of general use receptacles. The provisions of a *Hospital Grade* designation adds additional requirements to ensure good electrical contact between the male attachment plug and the receptacle contact blades, as well as increased grounding reliability, face strength, and overall durability.

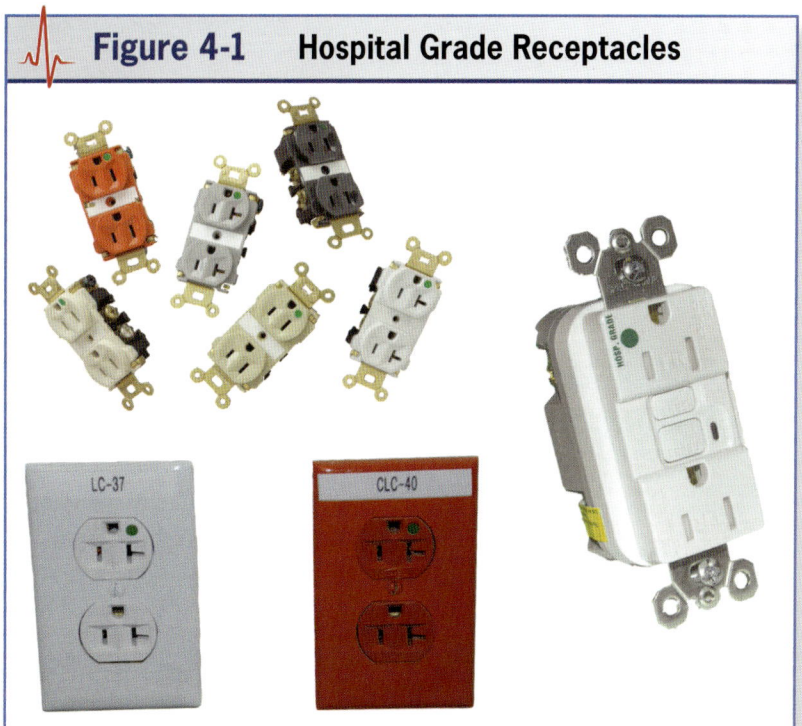

Figure 4-1 **Hospital Grade Receptacles**

Figure 4-1. Hospital grade receptacles are identifiable by their green dot.

Hospital Grade Mounting

Hospital grade receptacles require very low contact resistance between the male attachment plug and the receptacle wiping blades. The contact pressure between the two is higher than a general duty receptacle. Hospital grade receptacles are periodically tested for pull-out strength as a means to ensure good electrical connection.

Due to this increased contact tension, placing a male attachment plug into a hospital grade receptacle requires more force than that of a general duty receptacle. If a box for a hospital grade receptacle is mounted using a standard catalog or on-site bracket, after several years of continuous use the mounting bracket may fail and the entire receptacle/box assembly will become recessed into the wall. Using special care to secure rough-in hospital grade receptacle boxes goes a long way to ensure decades of trouble-free operation. Understanding these special situations is a trademark of a true crafts worker.

Figure 4-2   Patient Equipment Grounding Point

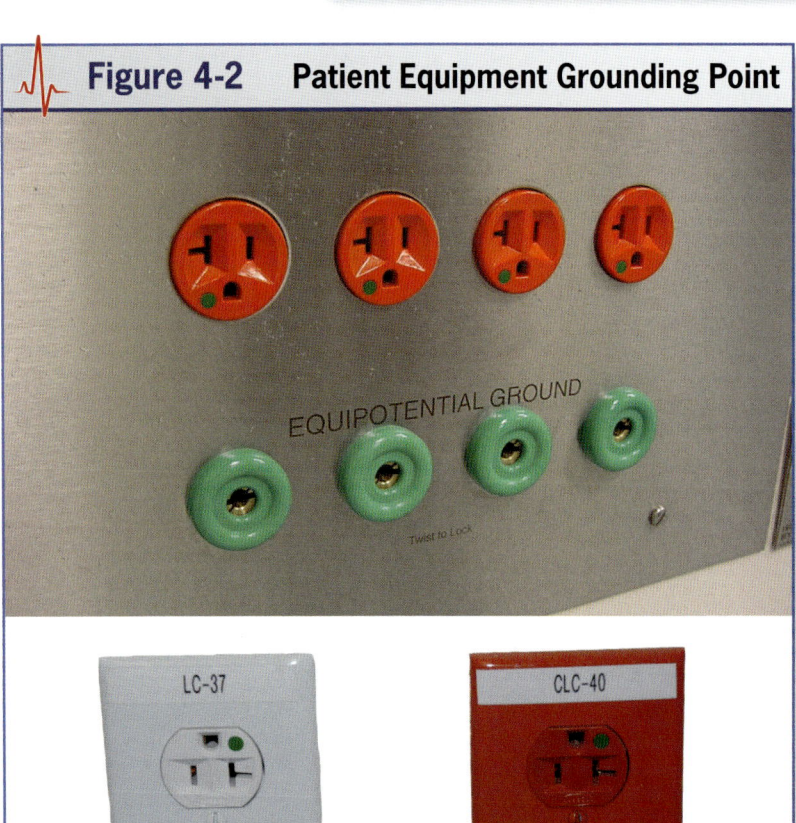

Figure 4-2. *Listed grounding and bonding jacks are specially manufactured to serve as patient equipment grounding points.*

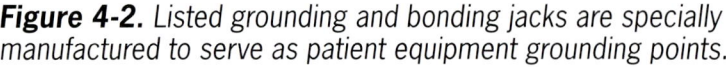

isolated ungrounded power source in patient bed locations listed as isolated power equipment and details that if these systems are designed and installed, they must conform to Section 517.160. **See Figure 4-2.**

CATEGORY 1 OCCUPANCIES

Category 1 Occupancy requirements include wet procedure locations, operating rooms, and isolated power systems.

Wet Procedure Locations

Not to be confused with "wet locations" found elsewhere in the *NEC*, *wet procedure locations* are defined in *NFPA 99* as, "the area in a patient care space where a procedure is performed that is normally subject to wet conditions while patients are present, including standing fluids on the floor or drenching of the work area, either of which condition is intimate to the patient or staff." Annex material in *NFPA 99* goes on to detail that routine housekeeping procedures do not create a wet procedure location. The very nature of these occupancies creates an environment that exposes patients and staff to additional risks when using electrical power.

In recognition of these hazards, both *NFPA 70* and *NFPA 99* require wet procedure locations to be classified as Category 1 spaces, furthermore both code documents require that conductive surfaces are connected to an insulated copper equipment grounding conductor. As an additional layer of protection, fixed electrical equipment and receptacles serving wet procedure locations shall be protected by one of the following methods:

- An isolated power system installed to the requirements of Section 517.160
- The use of Class A GFCI devices that are not connected to life-support equipment circuits

Operating Rooms

Interestingly, the phrase "operating room" is not defined in either *NFPA 99* or *NFPA 70*, although *anesthetizing location* is defined in Section 517.2 as, "any area of a facility that has been designated to be used for the administration of any flammable or nonflammable inhalation anesthetic agent in the course of examination or treatment including the use of such agents for relative analgesia." This unhelpful definition points to Part VI of Article 517, which details requirements for obsolete medical procedures.

Through the years the phrase *operating room*, from a code and standard prospective, has come to mean the spaces where surgical procedures are undertaken, induction rooms where patients are prepared for surgery, as well as associated clean and soiled storage rooms. Operating rooms are the epitome of Category 1 locations and have many additional requirements that exceed basic Category 1 conditions.

NFPA 99 6.3.2.3.4 states that, by default, operating rooms are considered wet procedure locations. This provision brings the requirements for wet procedure locations into play in an operating room environment. *NFPA 99* 6.3.2.3.4 also provides a mechanism for the governing body of the health care facility to exempt themselves from the wet procedure location default by performing a risk assessment analysis indicating that patients and staff will not be exposed to the conditions defined as a wet procedure location during the working life of specific occupancy. Most health care facilities forgo the risk assessment analysis, unwilling to limit the use of the operating room as the future of surgical treatment is ever changing.

In addition to providing isolated ground systems or GFCI protection, operating rooms are required to have at least 36 receptacles, at least 12, but not more than 24 on a normal system – or a critical branch system served from separate transfer equipment than the other circuit(s) in the space. All conductive surfaces shall be connected to an equipment grounding conductor. Finally, battery powered lighting units, much like those used for egress lighting, shall be installed in the surgery area to provide illumination to "ride through" the ten-second dark period as the EES generating equipment starts and comes on-line. It is important to note that these requirements are the minimum, many designers go above and beyond these requirements, and, of course, installed or mobile medical equipment will have separate exacting electrical requirements.

Isolated Power Systems

Isolated power systems provide an extremely high level of safety for patients and staff in health care facilities. Isolated power systems intentionally have no reference to ground and therefore no stray electrical currents can have a ground path through a patient or health care provider. Isolated power systems use line monitors to assure electrical currents are staying on intended pathways. Should currents stray from the normal path, line isolation monitors pick up the difference in outgoing and incoming current and sound an alarm, notifying staff that the currents are unbalanced. Because these circuits are isolated from ground, the affected circuit can remain energized and in-service allowing health care providers to continue procedures while the trouble is identified and resolved. The continuity of service isolated power systems inherently provide is a big advantage these systems have over the alternative GFCI protection, which, of course, interrupts all electrical current when stray currents are detected.

Due to the critical nature of these systems, Section 517.160 provides very specific installation regulations for branch circuits served by isolated power systems. Because neither conductor is intentionally grounded, both conductors are considered current-carrying conductors and must be protected by an overcurrent protective device that opens both conductors simultaneously: using a double pole circuit breaker. These conductors must be installed independently of conductors of other systems. *NEC* 517.160(A)(5) requires isolated circuit conductors to be identified in the following manner:

- Orange with a distinctive colored stripe (not green, white, or gray) along the entire length, for conductor one.
- Orange with a distinctive colored stripe (not green, white, or gray) along the entire length, for conductor two.
- Yellow with a distinctive colored stripe (not green, white, or gray)

along the entire length, for 3-phase systems third conductor.

To reduce the leakage current to ground found in normal service conditions, 517.160(A)(6) forbids the use of wire pulling compounds and suggests the length of these conductors be kept to a minimum. *NFPA 99* also has strict requirements as to the impedance of these circuits, which are echoed in manufacturer's requirements that branch-circuit conductors have very high dielectric rating. Practically, for Electrical Workers, this means that isolated power system conductors will have type XHHW insulation, which can be a bit of a challenge both to pull and to terminate when compared to type THHN or THWN.

Isolated power systems provide power continuity by operating ungrounded. This means that a phase-to-ground fault condition on any of the ungrounded conductors supplied by the system will not trip an overcurrent device; it will only trigger an audible and visible signal. It is the responsibility of the trained hospital staff to understand the proper response to these conditions. Isolated power systems are designed to monitor leakage current levels and provide annunciation when the leakage level of the circuits supplied by this system reach levels higher than five milliamperes. This level is very similar to the shock protection thresholds of a Class A type ground-fault circuit interrupter. When leakage current exceeds five milliamperes, the shock hazard increases. Reducing leakage current levels from line-to-ground reduces the hazard current for patients and facility personnel.

Leakage is controlled by insulation type and the length of the circuit. Minimizing the length of branch-circuit conductors and using conductor insulation types with a dielectric constant less than 3.5 and an insulation resistance constant greater than 20,000 megohm-feet (6,100 megohm-meters) at 60°F (16°C) reduces leakage from line-to-ground, which reduces the hazard current.

Working Isolated Power Systems

The color code for isolated circuit systems—brown, orange, and yellow with a distinctive stripe—may seem a little odd. Isolated power systems are one of the few places in the *NEC* that require conductors to be a specific color. This unusual color requirement was put in place to protect workers who may have trouble checking or pulling maintenance on an isolated power system. The color code is there to remind workers that the system is ungrounded and any voltage verification test to ground will show a false deenergized reading. Since the system is purposefully ungrounded, any check to ground will give an erroneous reading. The Electrical Worker must check for voltage between the two conductions secured to the device, and not rely on phase-to-ground readings.

Although the isolated power systems are ungrounded, the equipment grounding rules in Parts VI and VII of Article 250 must be satisfied. For circuits supplied by isolated power systems, an equipment grounding conductor is required on each outlet. When isolated power systems are installed, a reference to ground (the earth) is still necessary for the equipment supplied by such systems. As a result of the system being ungrounded, there is no solid grounding reference to the secondary side of the isolated power systems. The equipment grounding requirements are satisfied by connection to an equipment grounding conductor that terminates on a reference grounding bus terminal bar located within the isolated power system equipment.

The general requirements for sizing and installation of equipment grounding conductors as presented in Article 250 are to be applied to circuits supplied by isolated power systems. For example, if the circuits supplied by an isolated power system are rated at 20 amperes, the minimum size equipment grounding conductor required by Table 250.122 must be no smaller than 12 AWG copper. The general requirements for equipment grounding serving patient care areas contained in *NEC* 517.13(A) and (B) are also applied to these branch circuits. This means that redundant equipment grounding conductors are required for all branch circuits that serve patient care locations, even branch circuits supplied by isolated power systems.

An isolated system can easily become unintentionally grounded without giving any indication to the user. Therefore, a line isolation monitor must automatically and continuously check the integrity of the isolation of the system and activate an alarm should leakage current rise above the five-milliampere threshold without interrupting the electrical service.

Line isolation monitors include two signal lamps; one is green, and when lit, indicates that the system is adequately isolated from ground. The

---

Medical Equipment

NFPA 99: Health Care Facilities Code is a comprehensive document covering all aspects of health care facilities. Chapter 6 regulates electrical systems and equipment that is integral to delivering safe electrical power throughout the facility. Chapter 10 discusses the performance, testing, and use of electrical medical equipment by the patient.

Perhaps the easiest way to draw the distinction is that Chapter 6 covers the facility electrical system from utility/generation to the receptacle on the wall and Chapter 10 covers the medical equipment that attaches to the receptacle.

---

green lamp must be visible to people located in each area served by the isolated power system. Next to the green lamp is a red one that illuminates only when the total hazard current (consisting of possible resistive and capacitive leakage currents) from either isolated conductor to ground reaches a threshold of five milliamperes under nominal line voltage conditions. At the same time the red light becomes energized, an audible warning signal (remote if desired) sounds. An ammeter calibrated to the preset total hazard current is mounted in an obvious location on the line isolation monitor with the "alarm on" zone at approximately the center of the scale if the display is analog.

CATEGORY 2 SPACES

Category 2 spaces are defined by *NFPA 99* 3.3.136.2 as, "a space in which failure of equipment or a system is likely to cause minor injury to patients, staff, or visitors." These spaces are not as critical as Category 1 spaces but a level of risk is present for both patients and health care providers. These spaces may be served by either a Type 1 or Type 2 EES.

There are many common installation requirements between Category 1 and 2 spaces. EES circuits are required to be physically separated from normal system circuits. Just as with Category 1 EES, the combination of these circuits is permitted in a few well-defined locations: transfer equipment and exit lights and their junction boxes served from two sources. EES circuits behind the same transfer switch are permitted to share raceways and enclosures. The raceways, cables, enclosures, and equipment (including transfer equipment) carrying Category 2 EES circuits shall be marked and identified as part of the EES. As with Category 1 EES, these raceways and cable assemblies must be marked as EES components at least every seven feet; markings may be field or factory installed.

Category 2 EES circuits serving patient care spaces are required to be mechanically protected by metal raceways, the same wiring methods permitted by Category 1 EES namely:

- Nonflexible Metallic Raceways, nonmetallic systems shall not be used to supply branch circuits in patient care spaces
    o Type MI cable
- Schedule 80 PVC, nonmetallic systems shall not be used to supply branch circuits in patient care spaces
- Type RTRC-XW, nonmetallic systems shall not be used to supply branch circuits in patient care spaces
- Where encased in at least two inches of concrete:
    o Schedule 40 PVC
    o Jacketed metallic flexible raceways approved for concrete installations
    o Jacketed metallic cable assemblies approved for concrete installations

Receptacle Requirement Exceptions

NEC 517.18(2) Exceptions 1 and 2 exempt *NEC* receptacle requirements from "psychiatric, substance abuse, and rehabilitation hospitals," as well as "psychiatric security rooms," in order to remove a potential means from those who may self-harm.

- Listed metallic cable assemblies and listed flexible metallic raceways under the following conditions:
    o Prefabricated headwalls
    o Listed office equipment
    o Fished in existing walls and/or ceilings
    o When required for flexible connection to equipment
    o When required for flexible connection to equipment due to vibration, movement, or operation
    o Luminaires installed in ceiling structures

Category 2 Patient Bed Locations

Patient bed locations are often found in Category 2 spaces. Just like their Category 1 counterparts, patient bed locations must be served by at least two circuits, neither of which can be part of a multiwire branch-circuit system. One circuit must be from the EES and the receptacle itself or the coverplate must be a distinctive color and marked as to panelboard location and circuit number.

The other circuit may originate from the normal electrical system or it may originate at second EES branch panel served by a different transfer switch from the other circuit. Spaces served by a Type 2 EES may have these circuits served by the equipment branch of the Type 2 EES, as critical branches do not exist in Type 2 EES. There must be at least eight receptacles at each patient bed location and these receptacles must be listed hospital grade.

CATEGORY 3 AND 4 SPACES

NFPA 99 defines Category 3 spaces as, "activities, systems, or equipment whose failure is not likely to cause injury to patients, staff or visitors, but can cause discomfort." In Category 4 spaces, patient care will not be affected should activities, systems, or equipment fail. Other than the Section 517.2 definitions, Category 3 and 4 spaces are not mentioned in the *NEC*, and are barely mentioned in *NFPA 99*.

NFPA 99 6.6.1 simply states that Category 3 and 4 spaces shall not be required to have an EES.

The clear implication of this vast silence is that Category 3 and 4 spaces need only to comply with the first four chapters of the *NEC* and 517.13(A) and (B), as would any other installation. It may be important to note that neither code prohibits Category 3 and 4 spaces from being provided an EES, *NFPA 99* simply states it is not required. As health care facilities continue to adapt to unforeseen stresses, it will be interesting to see if this non-requirement is modified in future editions.

SUMMARY

The purpose of the *NEC* is to safeguard people and property from the use of electricity. Elements to eliminate shock hazard to patients, staff, and visitors in a health care facility are paramount to safety. In recent years, the NFPA documents relating to health care have addressed several important changes for evaluation and installation of electrical systems in patient care spaces. Risk assessment is the process that the governing body of a hospital uses to categorize areas of a health care facility regarding the type of treatment and the resulting relative harm that treatment places on a patient. Article 517, Part II provides special occupancy installation rules designed to reduce hazardous elements of shock from capacitive affects and direct contact with deadly currents. Included are special grounding and bonding techniques designed to reduce or eliminate touch potential from various treatments and procedures.

It is important to have reliable electrical service provided to all health care facilities. The different classifications of spaces in these facilities and the related wiring methods are used to ensure all power consuming devices are safely supplied with the critical energy needed to maintain optimal health care services.

REVIEW QUESTIONS

1. In __?__, health care facility documents began to change from a traditional occupancy-based standard, founded on the type of care or the type of procedure room, to code documents based on risk assessment or category level where activities, systems, or equipment failure is likely to cause minor injury, major injury, or death to a patient, staff member, or visitor.

   a. 1980
   b. 1985
   c. 1995
   d. 2005

2. Risk assessment in a health care environment is the process that is designed to place a specific facility space in a defined designated risk Category 1, 2, 3, or 4, ranging from __?__, where procedures create the most patient danger of injury or death, to __?__, which has the least opportunity for patient injury.

   a. Category 1 / Category 2
   b. Category 1 / Category 4
   c. Category 2 / Category 3
   d. Category 3 / Category 4

REVIEW QUESTIONS

3. The __?__ has the ultimate responsibility for the facility risk assessment, which is performed on a system-by-system basis.
   a. governing body of the health care facility
   b. government AHJ
   c. hospital administration
   d. hospital governing body and local AHJ

4. In the *NEC*, __?__ applies to all patient care spaces of all health care facilities as designated by the facility governing body.
   a. Article 517, Part II
   b. Article 700, Part I
   c. Article 701, Part II
   d. Article 702, Part II

5. The general purpose of Article 517, Part II in the *NEC* is to specify the wiring methods and installation requirements that will minimize electrical hazards by reducing exposure to conductive surfaces that are likely to become energized with a voltage potential that may cause a patient harm or death.
   a. True   b. False

6. Match the following risk assessment category with the proper category number.

   I.   Category 1

   II. Category 2

   III. Category 3

   IV. Category 4

   a. __?__ Activities, systems, or equipment whose failure is likely to cause major injury or death of patients, staff or visitor
   b. __?__ Activities, systems, or equipment whose failure is likely to cause minor injury of patients, staff, or visitors.
   c. __?__ Activities, systems, or equipment whose failure is not likely to cause injury to patients, staff, or visitors, but can cause discomfort.
   d. __?__ Activities, systems, or equipment whose failure would have no impact on patient care.

7. An important provision found in Section 517.13 specifies that all branch circuits serving patient care areas shall provide __?__ different effective ground-fault current pathway(s).
   a. 1
   b. 2
   c. 3
   d. 4

8. The concept of ground path redundancy includes patient rooms, examining rooms, therapy spaces, and anywhere a patient may receive treatment or care, providing alternate ground paths that protect __?__ from stray electrical currents should a single ground path become compromised.
   a. patients
   b. staff
   c. visitors
   d. all the above

9. Isolated power systems __?__ .
   a. are voltage specific
   b. shall not be grounded
   c. shall only be required in general care areas
   d. none of the above

10. Which of the following items regarding the second ground-fault current conductor are required in *NEC* 571.13(B)?

   I.   The conductor must be an insulated copper conductor with green-colored insulation.

   II. The conductor must be connected to all conductive surfaces that are accessible to patients and staff and are likely to become energized in the event of a fault.

   III. The conductor must be connected to the branch-circuit panel ground bus.

   IV. The conductor must be installed with the branch-circuit conductors and must be directly terminated to the grounding terminals from the device and all metal junction or outlet boxes.

   V.   Luminaires and lighting devices located more than 7.5 feet above the finish floor along with switches serving those fixtures that are located outside of the patient care vicinity are permitted to have one grounding path: either an armor shield or metallic conduit or a copper equipment grounding conductor.

   VI. Metal faceplates are permitted to be grounded through the metal mounting screw.

   VII. The use of a green-colored insulated equipment bonding jumper is permitted between the metallic box termination and the device terminal.

   a. I., II., III., and IV.
   b. I., II., III., IV., V., VI., and VII.
   c. I., II., IV., V., and VII.
   d. III., IV., VI., and VII.

REVIEW QUESTIONS

11. Which *NEC* section requires the wiring methods used for the life safety and critical branch of the essential electrical system to be kept entirely separate and independent of all other wiring, equipment, enclosures, raceways, cabinets, etc.?

    a. Section 517.15
    b. Section 517.19
    c. Section 517.26
    d. Section 517.31

12. Section 517.14 requires rules that keep the electrical systems serving patient care spaces on a single-ground plane, thus reducing the possibility of a harmful voltage differential to the patient, and requires all panelboards, regardless of system, or voltage, serving a patient care space to be bonded together by a continuous insulated copper conductor not smaller than __?__. This wire must be terminated to the __?__ conductor bus of each panelboard serving that particular patient care space.

    a. 10 AWG / equipment grounding
    b. 10 AWG / grounded
    c. 8 AWG / ungrounded
    d. 6 AWG / neutral

13. Additional wiring method rules on essential electrical systems can be found in *NEC* Article 517, __?__.

    a. Part I
    b. Part II
    c. Part III
    d. Part IV

14. Important regulations on __?__ of the essential system branch circuits that serve patient care spaces are detailed in *NEC* 517.31(C)(3).

    a. combination wiring methods
    b. mechanical protection
    c. operational isolation with aluminum products
    d. separate isolated distribution

15. *NEC* 517.160(A)(5) requires the circuit conductors be identified using the color orange for isolated circuit conductor number 1 and the color brown for isolated circuit conductor number 2. In addition to the specific colors (orange and brown), these conductors are also required to be identified with a distinctive colored stripe other than white, green, or gray, which must extend along the entire length of the conductor.

    a. True   b. False

16. __?__ that increase(s) the dielectric constant must not be used on the secondary conductors of the isolated power supply.

    a. Cable armor
    b. Conductor insulations
    c. Metallic raceways
    d. Wire-pulling compounds

17. A __?__ is an area where a procedure is performed that is normally subject to wet conditions, including standing fluids on the floor or drenching of the work area, while patients are present.

    a. critical care area
    b. general care area
    c. storage (housekeeping) space
    d. wet procedure location

18. "Inhalation anesthetizing locations" are always classified as hazardous-flammable spaces.

    a. True   b. False

Facility Electrical Equipment Maintenance

An Electrical Worker's job is not done after a proper code-compliant installation is complete. Federal and state regulations, as well as good practices, require regular maintenance on both normal and essential electrical systems, especially on generation and distribution equipment. Essential electrical systems must be able to perform as designed under any emergency. Maintenance and testing are critical to achieving those goals.

Objectives

» Apply all the codes, standards, and related documents that regulate maintenance in health care facilities.

» Understand the general scope of maintenance procedures for electrical equipment and the problems Electrical Workers encounter performing maintenance protocols.

» Explain a number of the safe work practices that must be followed when working with energized conductors and equipment.

» Describe the most common maintenance procedures used for electrical equipment.

Chapter 5

Table of Contents

WHY PERFORM MAINTENANCE?

In order to be eligible to receive Medicare and Medicaid payments from the United States Department of Health and Human Services, health care facilities must conform to the Centers for Medicare and Medicaid Services (CMS) conditions of participation. One of the conditions of participation requires that health care facilities "…maintain adequate facilities for its services." A related subsection [42 CFR 482.41(a)] states: "The condition of the physical plant and the overall hospital environment must be developed and maintained in such a manner that the safety and well-being of patients are assured." In this manner, proper maintenance of health care facilities, supplies, and equipment become incorporated into federal law.

In health care, the term "maintenance" is far-reaching, covering topics from floor care to landscaping to diagnostic equipment. CMS makes a hard distinction between "facility equipment" used to support the physical environment of the health care facility; and "medical equipment" used for diagnostic, therapeutic, or monitoring care provided to a patient.

It may be useful to narrow the scope of discussion to the maintenance of fixed electrical distribution equipment and other work that a health care facility's governing body would contract with an electrical contractor to perform rather than relying on in-house maintenance personnel. **See Figure 5-1.**

Maintenance Activities

Maintaining the electrical system generation and distribution equipment in a health care facility is the kind of work a facility would most likely contract out to an electrical contractor. There are quite a few everyday maintenance activities not usually farmed out, such as the monthly testing of the essential electrical systems (EES), monthly battery operated lighting unit testing, periodic ground integrity testing, and periodic receptacle pull-out testing, to name a few. The majority of these maintenance tasks are performed by health care facility staff.

The CMS requires regular maintenance of facility electrical distribution equipment, which makes a lot of sense from a simple "return on investment" standpoint. Essential electrical systems alone represent a significant investment in a health care facility's infrastructure. The proper regular maintenance of that equipment can easily be justified by increased reliability, performance, and increased lifespan. Regular maintenance and testing allows a facility to identify a failing distribution component and schedule an outage for repair or replacement before the equipment fails during an emergency.

Figure 5-1   Switchgear Installation

Figure 5-1. Once placed into service at a health care facility, a typical switchgear installation requires regular maintenance.
Courtesy of Hatzel & Buehler, Inc., Circleville, OH

The CMS requirements for facility electrical equipment maintenance are very simple and straightforward: "Maintenance shall be performed in accordance with the equipment manufacturers' recommendation." Realizing that electrical equipment is an integral part of a critical system, CMS allows health care facilities to develop alternative equipment maintenance (AEM) programs that may increase or decrease the intervals between the manufacturer's recommended maintenance periods, depending on the requirements of the electrical system taken as a whole. AEM programs must be in writing and must detail not only the rationale for the program but must also provide past data justifying the adoption of the AEM program. These programs should be published for maintenance personnel or contractors who should become familiar with the programs. This documentation will be one of the first things a CMS auditor will ask to see.

Documentation does not end at the written maintenance program; each piece of electrical distribution equipment undergoing maintenance and testing should be documented also. Photographs should be taken of dirt and grime build-up, contact carbon deposits, and any discoloration of electrical

Maintenance Can Be Risky

According to hospital engineering legend Hugh Nash, "Every maintenance procedure carries with it an inherent risk."

Electrical Workers must be able to balance the reward of a properly performed maintenance procedure with the very real fact that the piece of equipment could become damaged during the procedure and may not be able to be put back into service. This damage can be caused by something as simple as a careless worker leaving a wrench across phases upon reenergization and damaging a bus, insulators, and the enclosure.

Damage can also be caused by age and negligence. Would it be a good thing to perform maintenance on a 50-year-old main switch that has never been opened, let alone maintained? The answer is emphatically *no*. The risk of severe damage in trying to open the switch would far exceed the reward of long overdue maintenance.

Elements in an Electrical System Maintenance Program

The Centers of Medicare and Medicaid Services outline the requirements for electrical system maintenance in their Environment of Care standards. These standards essentially prescribe that health care facilities conform to the requirements of *NFPA 99: Health Care Facilities Code, NFPA: 101 Life Safety Code*, and *NFPA 110: Standard for Emergency and Stand-by Power Systems*, among other codes and standards. Most importantly, the CMS requires that electrical distribution equipment be strictly maintained to manufacturer's recommendations.

The CMS does allow the health care facility to adopt an AEM program that can supersede the manufacturer's recommendations under the following conditions:

- The AEM program must be based on accepted practices and not reduce the safety of the equipment in any manner.

- A written documented record of substantial past maintenance activities must be available. The data from this documentation must be used to justify an AEM.

  - If the equipment is new or detailed records do not exist, manufacturer's recommendations must be used.

- A written record has been provided of how the equipment is used during normal operation and the harm that can occur should the equipment go offline.

- A written record of incidence events is available.

- Alternative or back-up equipment is available in the event the equipment goes offline.

connections before and after maintenance procedures. Infrared thermography should be taken as a matter of course as well. Insulation resistance readings, contact resistance tests, withstand voltage tests, and any other tests required by the facility should be done in a manner consistent with past testing procedures. Instrument readings should be carefully notated over time, providing the facility the best possible data for engineering evaluation. Equipment maintenance and testing may seem like just a nice break from the construction site; however, it is critical that maintenance and testing be accomplished in a professional, meaningful manner to ensure the health care facility is consistently receiving the best data.

Generally, each health care facility will create a chart of values or equipment information and maintenance log for each major element in an electrical distribution system. This chart will detail the expected lifespan of the particular equipment: 30 years for a generator; 30 years for paralleling gear; 20 years for a draw-out circuit breaker; 25 years, or "x" number of operations, for an automatic transfer switch; and so on. The data gathered during maintenance testing, both numerical and photographic, is added to the chart. Analysis done on the actual condition of the equipment is then graded out in value from A to F. An "A" indicates that the equipment is early in its lifespan and is in excellent condition; an "F" indicates that the equipment is severely degraded and in need of swift replacement. These sophisticated tracking systems allow health care facilities to stay ahead of any potential issues and responsibly budget for electrical system component repair or replacement. However, all of this fails if the testing data is flawed. **See Figure 5-2.**

CODES AND STANDARDS

CMS specifically points to two NFPA codes—*NFPA 99: Health Care Facilities Code* and *NFPA 101: Life Safety Code*—and requires compliance with each. From an electrical standpoint, the *Life Safety Code* speaks to the testing of egress lighting and exit signs, while the *Health Care Facilities Code* goes into greater detail regarding the maintenance and testing of electrical distribution equipment. The *Health Care Facilities Code* specifically requires essential electrical system generation equipment be maintained to come online in 10 seconds upon a power outage. It also requires that generator sets be tested 12 times a year in intervals of not less than 20, but no more than 40 days, as well as specific main and feeder circuit breaker inspection and exercise requirements. *NFPA 110: Standard for Emergency and Standby Power Systems* is under the jurisdiction of the Correlating Committee on *National Electrical Code*—the same people who develop *NFPA 70: National Electrical Code*. This document does not specifically reference health care facility essential electrical systems. However, both

Figure 5-2   ATS with Bypass

Figure 5-2. Some automatic transfer switch (ATS) equipment incorporates a bypass feature that would enable the load to remain energized during maintenance activities. *Courtesy of Hatzel & Buehler, Inc., Circleville, OH*

NFPA 70 and *NFPA 99*, as well as other non-NFPA codes and standards, specifically refer to *NFPA 110* requirements for essential electrical systems, the one case where requirements for "emergency systems" do, in fact, apply to health care.

Revisions to the 2021 edition of *NFPA 99* provide helpful guidance for health care facilities when considering electrical equipment maintenance. *NFPA 99* 6.9 requires all components of an essential electrical system serving Category 1 and 2 spaces, to be part of an electrical preventative maintenance program. The section then goes on to define what elements must be part of an electrical preventive maintenance program:

- An inventory of all equipment and systems included in the electrical preventative maintenance program
- Schedule of inspection, testing, and servicing (maintenance) of equipment
- Survey and analysis of electrical equipment and systems, to determine maintenance requirements and priorities
- Scheduled routine inspections and tests
- Review of inspection and test reports so that proper corrective measures can be prescribed
- Performance of necessary work
- Complete records

The Section 6.9 revision includes a new Table 6.9.4.1, which provides maintenance intervals for 19 elements found in an essential electrical system. This table is designed to supplement manufacturer's recommendations. It is important to note that this table does differentiate between inspection, testing, and maintenance.

N   **Table 6.9.4.1 Electrical Preventive Maintenance (EPM) Intervals**

Item	Inspection Period	Testing Period	Maintenance Period
Medium-voltage switchgear	Every 3 months	Every 3 years	Every 3 years
Power distribution transformers (≥ 750 kVA)	Monthly	Every 3 years	Every 3 years
Generator (alternate source)	*(See Chapter 8 of NFPA 110.)*	*(See Chapter 8 of NFPA 110.)*	*(See Chapter 8 of NFPA 110.)*
Generator paralleling switchgear	Monthly	Annually	Every 3 years
Low-voltage switchgear/switchboards	Every 3 years	Every 3 years	Every 3 years
Overcurrent Protective Devices			
Fuses (≥ 400 A)	Every 3 years	Every 3 years	Every 3 years
Low-voltage power circuit breakers (≥ 400 A)	Every 3 years	Every 3 years	Every 3 years
Low-voltage molded-case circuit breakers (≥ 400 A)	Every 3 years	Every 3 years	Every 3 years
Medium-voltage circuit breakers	Every 3 years	Every 3 years	Every 3 years
Relays (including polyphase ground-fault equipment protection)	Every 3 years	Every 3 years	Every 3 years
Transfer equipment	Monthly	Every 3 years	Every 3 years
Bus duct	Every 3 years	Every 3 years	Every 3 years
Uninterruptible power supplies (≥ 100 kW)	Every 3 months	Every 6 months	Every 6 months
Isolated power panels	*(See 6.3.3.3.3.)*	*(See 6.3.3.3.3.)*	*(See 6.3.3.3.3.)*
Motor control equipment	Annually	Every 3 years	Every 3 years
Branch-circuit panelboards	Annually	Every 3 years	N/A
Wiring devices	*(See 6.3.3.2.)*	*(See 6.3.3.2.)*	*(See 6.3.3.2.)*
Battery-powered lighting units	*(See 6.3.2.6.8.)*	*(See 6.3.2.6.8.)*	*(See 6.3.2.6.8.)*

N/A: not applicable.

Following the lead of the CMS, the 2021 revision of *NFPA 99* Section 6.9.4.2 permits health care facilities to produce and implement alternative equipment maintenance programs based on careful analysis of past inspection, test and maintenance data gathered for the unique essential electrical system serving one facility.

NFPA 110 Chapter 8 is focused only on essential electrical systems, although the health care facility is free to voluntarily use the requirements of *NFPA 110* for the normal electrical system as well. Maintenance is defined as the periodic inspection of connections, contacts, dirt and grime build-up, and any evidence of overheating and corrosion. *NFPA 110* also demands that findings be documented as part of the essential electrical systems maintenance plan. It requires that corrective action is taken where needed: connections tightened to specifications, pitted and eroded contacts replaced, equipment cleaned of dirt and grime, and moving parts lubricated as per the manufacturer's specifications. This document also details the regular operational testing of the essential electrical system. The system is to be exercised, under load, once a month and the test is to be initiated by

Figure 5-3 2019 NFPA 70B

Figure 5-3. NFPA 70B *is as important to electrical equipment maintenance as the* National Electrical Code *is to electrical installations.*

an automatic transfer switch, simulating a power outage. Of course, all of the critical elements of the test—time to come online, current load, and any load shedding—should be well documented as part of the essential electrical system maintenance plan.

In the event the health care facility uses stored energy, usually a battery bank as part of an uninterruptable power supply system to provide energy for an element of an essential electrical system, *NFPA 111: Standard on Stored Electrical Energy Emergency and Standby Power Systems* Chapter 8 provides guidance on the maintenance and operational testing of these systems as well. As is the case with *NFPA 110*, *NFPA 111* is also under the purview of the Correlating Committee on the *National Electrical Code*.

The most valuable NFPA document covering electrical systems maintenance is not a code or standard. It is *NFPA 70B: Recommended Practice for Electrical Equipment Maintenance*, also under the jurisdiction of the Correlating Committee on the *National Electrical Code*. Responding to requests from the electrical industry to place maintenance practices in the *NEC*, in 1968, the NFPA created a Committee on Electrical Equipment Maintenance which was charged with compiling generally accepted practices for equipment maintenance in a single set of guidelines. In 1973, the Committee published the fruits of its labors as *NFPA 70T: Tentative Recommended Practice for Electrical Equipment Maintenance*, which, after a revision cycle, became *NFPA 70B: Recommended Practice for Electrical Equipment Maintenance*. Over the years, *NFPA 70B* has changed and grown with technology, and the current edition has chapters detailing the maintenance of photovoltaic systems, electrical vehicle charging stations, wind power systems, and electrical disaster recovery. Although not a standard or code, and therefore not enforceable by an authority having jurisdiction (AHJ), when considering maintenance and testing, *NFPA 70B* is just as important to an Electrical Worker as *NFPA 70* when installing electrical systems. **See Figure 5-3.** However, *NFPA 70B* is under revision and was moved from the Fall 2021 to a custom Fall 2022 revision cycle. Importantly, *NFPA 70B* is being rewritten from a recommended practice to a standard. This shift from "should" to "shall" as it evolves from a document containing recommendations to mandatory requirements is scheduled to become effective sometime in 2022 as the 2023 edition of *NFPA 70B*.

TESTING ASSOCIATIONS

Legitimate schools and colleges are accredited by a third-party organization that periodically reviews the educational institution's policies, procedures, course(s) of study, and outcomes to ensure students, graduates, and society are fully benefiting from the educational institution. In short, accreditation organizations ensure that the educational institutions are performing as advertised. In 1972, the InterNational Electrical Testing Association (NETA) was founded to provide facility owners with a third-party accreditation agency certifying that both electrical testing firms and technicians employed by these firms meet minimum standards—in short, to ensure testing firms and their employees are performing as advertised. As part of its mission to provide electrical testing consistency and accuracy, NETA produces four ANSI standards: acceptance testing, maintenance testing, commissioning specifications, and technician certification. Firms must meet certain criteria to become a NETA Accredited Company. Per the NETA website, "NETA Certified Technicians have earned a Level 2, Level 3 or 4 NETA Certification in electrical power systems testing and bring the knowledge and field experience necessary to perform testing according to industry standards." Many NETA firms are affiliated with NECA and employ IBEW workers.

MAINTENANCE ELECTRICAL CONTRACTORS IN HEALTH CARE FACILITIES

When health care facilities engage outside electrical contractors to perform maintenance on the facility's electrical system, it is generally to perform specific preventive maintenance procedures on specific electrical equipment or perhaps an entire branch of an essential electrical system. Because these procedures are dependent on the equipment manufacturers' recommendations as well as the facility's required unique preventive maintenance program, a generic maintenance procedure guideline is difficult to provide; however, basic maintenance protocols and procedures should be reviewed, utilized, and evaluated. These are the basic building blocks of any maintenance job.

The ability to examine an equipment maintenance project and to walk through each step of the process in a pre-job setting is absolutely critical to the overall success of the activity. For example, a relatively simple deenergized annual switchgear inspection and cleaning pre-job questionnaire may consist of questions such as:

- Is the work scheduled for after hours? If so, have arrangements been made for feeding the crew? Are restroom facilities available, or should other arrangements be made? Is there a source of drinking water on site? (If not, arrangements should be made.) Does the job require any special skills? Does the job require any special equipment or test instruments? Will the job require any wire or cable terminations that are not in stock on site? Does the site require any special personal protective equipment (PPE) or other safety equipment (such as ventilators) for worker safety?
- Has the one-line diagram been studied to obtain an understanding of how the proposed work affects the entire electrical system? Is the facility's standard electrical

systems placarding up to date? Are the placards easily understood by the average worker? Has a contingency plan been formulated in the event that the out-of-service equipment cannot be brought online in the required time frame?

- How many Electrical Workers can efficiently work in the switchgear location? Does the location allow for the ready movement of materials and workers? Are there a sufficient number of receptacles available to do the job? Is the lighting level appropriate for the work to be performed? Will the lighting and power remain energized once the switchgear is deenergized? Should arrangements be made for back-up power and lighting? Will the environmental air be active once the switchgear is deenergized, or should arrangements be made for portable fans? Is an emergency/evacuation plan in place for the protection of Electrical Workers?

- Has a written scope of work been created in concert with the health care facility? Does each Electrical Worker know his or her role on the project? Are the proper forms in place to document every activity for every piece of equipment? Is there a checklist protocol in place to ensure every tool, part, or item that goes into a switchgear enclosure comes back out upon completion of the work? Are there any special-order parts or items that should be acquired before work begins? Is there a specific protocol that should be followed when deenergizing equipment fed from the switchgear?

- Are switchgear panels to be removed? If so, what kind of machine screw is used? Can a battery drill or driver be used to remove and install fasteners? How many will be needed and used? How many spare bits should be on hand in case a fastener bit fractures? How many spare, charged batteries should be on hand to ensure the job gets done efficiently? Are there any door panels to be removed? Are there special tools required to remove the doors? Is there a means to ensure any wired devices installed on the door will be correctly returned to service? Is there a safe, close, out-of-the-way place to store the panels and doors while the work is being done? Are small sealed containers available to securely hold the panel/door fasteners while work is being performed, or are the fasteners captive?

- Who has the responsibility to perform a phase rotation test and document the results? What are the means to check for live voltage? Are the proper instruments available? Is the proper PPE available? Has the proper lockout/tagout protocol been used? Are safety grounds installed, and has the proper signage been temporarily installed? Are all Electrical Workers aware of the deenergization and subsequent equipment reenergization procedures?

- Are there a proper number of vacuums in good condition available to do the cleaning job efficiently? Are the vacuum filters new? Are all the required accessories in place? Are the proper numbers of lint-proof rags available? Is the proper solvent in the proper quantities available? Are there means for safe rag disposal available on site? Do Electrical Workers know how to use and dispose of the solvent and rags correctly? Is there a protocol for any Electrical Worker to document a perceived abnormality?

- Are the proper number of torque wrenches available? Have they been calibrated? Are the appropriate number and size of sockets available? Are spare sockets needed? Are the proper number and size of open-end, box-end, or combination wrenches to hold the bolt end of the fastener available?

Are the torque values for each type of fastener known and published to the Electrical Workers? Is there a means available to uniquely mark or otherwise identify each checked fastener? Are spare fasteners, washers, and other accessories on hand in case of breakage? Who needs to approve a replacement of a fastener—crew foreman, or facilities engineer? Is there a protocol in place where any Electrical Worker can document a perceived abnormality?

- Is every termination tight? Are any wire or cable terminations discolored? (Discolored terminations should be closely examined to determine if heating has damaged the cable, the terminal, or both. If the cable is damaged, the damaged portion of the cable should be cut away and the cable re-terminated (care should be taken with conductors in parallel). If the terminal is damaged, it should be removed and replaced with an approved terminal. If an aluminum cable is present, it is critically important that terminations be closely inspected.)

- Are there any special lubrication tasks to be performed, and is the proper equipment and lubrication available to complete the job? Are there any specific elements, such as contact surfaces, that need to be inspected? Are the renewal parts on-site? Do they require replacement? Who has the authority to order a part replaced—crew foreman, or health care facility engineer?

- Are there any special retrofits to be performed, such as the installation of infrared thermography windows indoors or panels? If so, are the tools available to perform the installations safely and efficiently? Are installation instructions available to the Electrical Workers, and is a means present to make sure the instructions are being followed?

- When tasks are completed, who makes the final inspection? Who has the authority to order that the panels and doors be installed? Is there a protocol in place to account for every tool that went into the enclosure and to confirm that they have all come back out? Are multiple people looking at the in/out checklist?

- When the equipment is placed back in ready condition, who has the authority to order the safety grounds be removed? Who has the responsibility to confirm that the safety grounds have been removed? Who will order a megohmmeter test to confirm that the phases are isolated from ground and each other? Who has the authority to order the lockout/tagout equipment be removed and the equipment energized? What process is in place to ensure the equipment is energized on all three phases, and the phase rotation is the same as before it was taken out of service? Is the proper PPE available to perform these tests? Is there a specific protocol to be followed when equipment fed by the switchgear is energized? Is there a procedure in place where equipment fed from the switchgear is checked for voltage and perhaps phase rotation if the feeders have been disturbed?

- Is there a procedure to meaningfully compile and deliver data and other reports to the owner in a timely manner? Is there a protocol in place to assess the job from the health care facility's management, contractor supervision, and workers' perspectives toward the goal of improving efficiency and safety in future activities?

The pre-job questionnaire is merely a very basic list of questions that should be considered when involved in a general shut-down. For more information on performing maintenance on specific equipment, review *NFPA 70B* (2019 edition) Chapters 13 through 29.

Figure 5-4   Switchboard

Figure 5-4. *A switchboard is an important element of a health care facility's regular maintenance program. Courtesy of Hatzel & Buehler, Inc., Circleville, OH*

Furthermore, Annex H of *NFPA 70B* provides 54 different forms—everything from work orders, to air breaker tests, to uninterruptible power supply surveys. These forms provide a great starting point for proper professional documentation. **See Figure 5-4.**

PROTOCOLS AND PROCEDURES

Maintenance work is risky. There is a risk to the Electrical Worker who may be exposed, knowingly or unknowingly,

Use All Your Senses

It is a good professional practice for an Electrical Worker to use his or her eyes, ears and nose every time he or she enters a switchgear room. Look for discolored enclosures indicating a hot spot, or clutter that may impede a quick exit. Listen for crackling or any other "off" sounds outside of the normal 60 cycle hum. Smell the air for any signs of ozone or metallic smell of excessive heat.

to electrical hazards. There is also a risk to the health care facility that may have a critical piece of equipment go offline for a prolonged period due to a tired Electrical Worker leaving a torque wrench lying across busses in a high current switchgear compartment, for example. It is necessary to minimize this risk by adopting a series of procedures and protocols designed to make sure work is done as safely and efficiently as possible.

Protocols

Refer to *NFPA 70E* in its entirety. However, among the most important protocol in all safety discussions is worker knowledge and skills necessary to identify hazards and reduce associated risk as addressed in the *NFPA 70E* Article 100 definition of a qualified person, in part. Among other things:

- Qualified workers must be trained by their employer about the construction and operation of systems and equipment, identification, and avoidance of electrical hazards per 110.6(A)(1), in part.
- Employees must also be trained to have the self-awareness and self-discipline to follow safety procedures per 110.5(D), in part.
- It is vital for workers to be trained in special precautionary techniques to turn off the power source, use of PPE, use of insulating tools, shields, and other insulating materials, and use of proper voltage testing instruments per 110.6(A)(1), in part.

Risk assessment procedures are covered in *NFPA 70E* 110.5(H) and shall address employee exposure to electrical hazards and shall identify the process used by the employee before work is started. *NFPA 70E: Standard for Electrical Safety in the Workplace* requires preventive and protective risk control methods to be implemented in accordance with the hierarchy of risk control methods in 110.5(H)(3). Elimination is the highest order of risk control. This step requires the employer to put conductors and circuit parts into an electrically safe work condition before work is started as a nonmandatory example of elimination as illustrated in Table F.3 in Informative Annex F. Also, see *NFPA 70E* Section 110.1. Compliance with all of Article 120 is an example of how to verify OSHA's lockout/tagout procedure has been followed and that all conductors and circuit parts are both locked out and tagged out and in an electrically safe work condition. Note that deenergizing is one step in lockout/tagout and establishing an electrically safe work condition. This is reinforced in OSHA's requirements. For example, per 1910.333(b)(1), conductors and parts of electric equipment that have been deenergized but have not been locked out or tagged in accordance with paragraph (b) of this section shall be treated as energized parts, and paragraph (c) of this section applies to work on or near them. This is essentially saying that anything that is deenergized must still be treated as being energized.

It is important to note that before a qualified Electrical Worker proceeds executing the lockout/tagout procedure, the employer must provide the Electrical Worker with risk assessment evaluation information. This information identifies information such as the results of the shock and arc flash risk assessments and results such as the shock and arc flash boundaries and the PPE required for use by the employee to protect against shock and arc flash. After donning the proper PPE, the qualified Electrical Worker must follow all of Article 120 per 110.2, including following the steps to verify and establish an electrically safe work condition as shown in the following abbreviated requirements list of 120.5:

1. Determine all possible sources of the electrical supply.
2. After interrupting any loads, open all applicable disconnecting means.
3. If possible, visually verify that all blades or cutout devices are open or fully drawn out.
4. Release stored electrical energy.
5. Release or block stored mechanical energy.

6. Apply proper lockout/tagout devices in accordance with the employer's written policy.
7. Using an adequately rated test instrument, verify that the conductors or circuit parts are deenergized. Test each phase conductor or circuit part to verify it is deenergized. Test each phase conductor or circuit part both phase-to-phase and phase-to-ground. Before and after each test, determine the test instrument is operating satisfactorily through verification on any know live circuit.
8. Where induced voltages or stored energy exists, ground the phase conductors or circuit parts.

Again, while a number of OSHA and *70E* requirements were mentioned in part or in an abbreviated manner as examples of things to consider, be sure to refer to and comply with all OSHA and *NFPA 70E* requirements in their entirety.

OSHA Part 1910 allows work on energized conductors and equipment under certain conditions. 29 CFR 1910.333(a)(1) essentially states, in part, that energized work is justified when exposed live parts are not deenergized for reasons of **increased or additional hazards**, or when it is **infeasible** to turn off the power, as is the case for most essential electrical systems. It is widely believed that more energized work occurs in health care facilities than any other occupancy, for obvious reasons. When energized work is justified, the employer is responsible for protecting employees, and must provide all effective safework practices necessary. OSHA documents generally do not provide specific information detailing safe-work practices other than stating that qualified persons may work on energized circuits, and require lockout/tagout devices and other safety procedures. *NFPA 70E* has developed detailed suggestions for several safety-related work practices the employer must use before authorizing work on energized circuits. The following safety criteria should be implemented if maintenance work is required on energized electrical equipment:

- **Qualified Person.** Only those persons that have demonstrated the skills and knowledge related to the construction and operation of electrical equipment and installations can perform work on or near energized equipment. An important part of becoming a qualified person is for the employer to provide safety training to each employee that instills the employee with the self-discipline to identify and avoid all hazards involved in the work process. If unqualified persons are involved in any aspects of the work, they too shall be trained in, and become familiar with, all safety-related work practices necessary for the work. See the *NFPA 70E* Article 100 definition of *qualified person* and the 110.6 training requirements, for example.

- **Approach Boundaries and Shock and Arc Flash Risk Assessment.** A shock risk assessment per 130.4 determines, among other things, the voltage to which Electrical Workers will be exposed. Shock protection approach boundaries, identified as the limited approach boundary and the restricted approach boundary, are established in Table 130.4(E)(a) for AC system voltage. Unqualified Electrical Workers are not allowed to work within the restricted approach boundary, but can work within the limited approach boundary under limited circumstances. Refer to 130.4 for these requirements in their entirety. An arc flash risk assessment per 130.5 is performed to determine, among other things, whether an arc flash hazard exists. If one does exist, then determination of additional protective measures is required. Refer to 130.5 for these requirements in their entirety.

- **Energized Electrical Work Permit.** An energized work permit is required in accordance with 130.2(A) including, in part, when hot work is performed within the restricted approach boundary, and when energized equipment, conductors, or circuit parts are not exposed but an increased likelihood of injury from arc flash exposure exists, which often occurs in maintenance work. An important part of the energized electrical work permit is the use of a pretask or job briefing safety form as described in 130.2(B)(8) and 110.5(I). This one element of the hot work planning process has limitless opportunities for both supervisor and Electrical Workers to discover unique unsafe conditions and prevent any accidents that are waiting to happen. Refer to 130.2 for these requirements in their entirety, including the minimum required elements of the energized electrical work permit are found in *NFPA 70E*, Section 130.2(B) and an example permit is found in Figure J.1 in Informative Annex J.

- **Safety-Related Work Practices.** An important part of live work is that safety-related work practices must be developed and implemented. A critical part of a safe work procedure is completing a job briefing or "pre-task" report before beginning the work. Nonmandatory example of job briefings and planning checklists can be found in Informative Annex I in *NFPA 70E*. Refer to 110.5(I) for the related requirements which require that, before starting each job that involves exposure to electrical hazards, the employee in charge shall complete a job safety plan and conduct a job briefing with the employees involved. The job safety planning and job briefing requirements in 110.5(I)(1) and (2) are vital in preventing accidents and is a critical element of the safety process. Other safety-related work practices include donning and doffing all required shock and arc flash protective clothing; using insulated tools and equipment; installing signs, barricades, and/or safety watch personnel; ensuring proper illumination of the work area; removal of all conductive jewelry and clothing; and ensuring employees are not impaired by drugs, alcohol, or lack of sleep. See 130.7(C), 130.130.7(D)(1), 130.7(E), and 130.8, for example. Be sure to refer to *NFPA 70E* in its entirety.

Another important protocol is the documentation of every item, including tools, that goes into, and out of, an electrical equipment enclosure. It is critical that every item that goes in comes out, unless it is a renewal or replacement part of some kind (and if that is the case, the old part being replaced should be documented as coming out). The inventory sheet/checklist needs to balance—everything taken into an enclosure should come out.

Procedures

Due to the unique nature of health care facility electrical systems, the exact procedures used in maintenance activities are difficult to generalize. However, when considering pre-job questionnaires, there are a series of general procedures that can come into play in any maintenance activity:

- Infrared thermographic scans, taken before the scheduled maintenance session, should be consulted for abnormal hot spots or any area showing overheating. Depending on the magnitude of the readings, the identified part or parts should be replaced or thoroughly examined to determine the cause of the problem. For example, if a hot spot is caused by the intrusion of water into disconnect switches, it can make or break the contact area. The contacts should be cleaned or replaced depending on the amount of damage, and the defect in the enclosure should be repaired to ensure water is kept out of the enclosure.

Bolted Pressure Switches

Bolted pressure switches are a direct descendant of the old open knife switches used at the turn of the last century. Bolted pressure switches are a cost-effective means to provide under 1,000 volts electrical isolation in the 800 to 4,000-ampere range. These switches use a series of springs and levers to operate the switch blades, which enter a set of contacts that are then mechanically "bolted" in place to ensure optimum contact. These switches are manually operated, but often have electrical shut-trip capability. Bolted pressure switches can provide decades of steady service if maintained properly. These switches require routine maintenance which requires the cleaning of the operating mechanism and contacts and the application of a specified lubricant in a manner described by the manufacturer. The more popular trade names for these switches are Bolt-Loc, Pringle, Boltswitch, BP Switch, or a THPC Switch.

Too often this required maintenance goes by the wayside, and due to the nature of the service environment, the lubrication becomes thick and almost glue-like. This condition has been known to prohibit switch knives from completely disengaging from the contacts during opening, or not allowing the bolting mechanism to completely engage the knives during a closing operation. This causes a very dangerous situation where one or two phases are energized. It is critical that when working on a bolted pressure switch, the Electrical Worker visually checks the position of the switch knives and performs a voltage test, verifying the load side of the switch is either fully energized or fully deenergized.

- Terminations, fasteners, and mounting bolts should be checked for proper torque, and then marked in some manner as having been checked.
- Cable, wire, and bus terminations should be closely examined for discoloration and evidence of arcing. Repairs should be made on identified issues.
- Incoming and outgoing cables should be carefully examined for displaced insulation around conduit bushings and any racking elements located in the gear. Cable should never rest on the equipment bus. Displaced insulation observations should be documented both in writing, and by photography to provide a baseline for further observation. Extra insulation elements, such as sheet mastic, can be installed to provide additional insulation.
- Grills, vents, and fans should be thoroughly cleaned. If filter media is present, it should be replaced with new stock.
- The equipment grounding elements, both incoming and outgoing, should be thoroughly checked for continuity and torque. This includes grounding bushings.
- A good quality vacuum with a new filter and the proper accessories is a must-have tool. Plant compressed air may seem like a good alternative, but compressed air merely blows material around while a good vacuum will contain the dirt and grime. Additionally, it is possible to blow conductive material into the gear using compressed air.
- Clean, lint-free rags with an appropriate solvent are another good way to clean dirt and grime from electrical equipment. Be sure to use and dispose of the solvent as per the container recommendations.
- It is extremely important that all circuit breakers and fusible switches be exercised on a timetable at least consistent with the manufacturers' recommendations. Exercising assures the device lubrication has not degraded to a paste and the device remains operable. Issues should be documented and immediately brought to a supervisor's attention.
- Inventory everything that goes into an electrical enclosure, because everything that goes in must come back out. This can be done by photography or by a simple checklist.

Figure 5-5   ATS Undergoing Maintenance

Figure 5-5. ATS equipment must undergo maintenance procedures that include cleaning and torque tests. Courtesy of Lawson Electric Co., Chattanooga, TN

Nothing is as bad to a worker, an employer, or a facility as a blow-up caused by carelessness.

- If safety grounds are used, make certain and double-check that they have been removed using the established procedure, including any required PPE, before reenergizing equipment. Upstream overcurrent protection devices will certainly open, but the unnecessary stress on upstream equipment and feeders is not good.
- Should the replacement of fuses or circuit breakers be on the task list, be certain the new overcurrent protection device has appropriate ratings for both overcurrent as well as interrupting ratings consistent with the equipment and the system. Careful calculation and evaluation should happen with this step. Installing overcurrent protective devices with interrupting ratings lower than system requirements runs the risk of serious equipment damage, or fire, in the event of a bolted fault.

Proper maintenance of switchgear, switchboards, and panelboards in health care facilities is an important part of keeping the electrical system functioning. Documented and well-established maintenance programs provide confidence in the operation of the electrical system and are a CMS requirement. Safety programs provided to employees by the employee or owner of the facility will reduce chances of worker injury and costly unscheduled shut-downs of essential electrical systems. **See Figure 5-5.**

Wet Stacking

When diesel engines do not come up to operating temperature in an appropriate time period, a condition known as wet stacking can occur. Wet stacking is a particularly nasty condition that can damage exhaust valves, fuel injectors, and damage turbochargers. Wet stacking can also reduce the effectiveness of engine lubricating oil, causing issues with crankcase bearings and seals. Diesel engines typically do not come up to proper operating temperature when they are operated under loads less than a certain percentage of their full load range. It is counter-intuitive, but running a diesel engine at less than full load can seriously damage the engine.

Wet stacking causes problems for health care maintenance workers who are charged with testing diesel generator operation but may not, for obvious operational reasons, have a connected electrical load that will properly load the generator's diesel engine. Recently, health care facilities have used both portable and permanently installed load banks, which are essentially large resistors, to provide the necessary electrical load to bring the diesel up to temperature. One of the real advantages load banks bring to the testing process is that they can be staged in and out of the testing period. For example, a diesel generator test can begin with the load provided by the automatic transfer switch(es) that are part of the test. After about 15 minutes, load banks can be periodically brought in to increase the electrical load, and upon the conclusion of the test can be dropped out periodically to provide a cool-down period for the generator.

SUMMARY

Maintenance of electrical distribution equipment in health care facilities is a significant part of the electrical industry. Many electrical contractors are discovering that maintenance work is a vital and profitable part of doing business. Following equipment manufacturer recommendations, *NFPA 99*, and *NFPA 70B* guidance for well-timed, frequent maintenance procedures reduces downtime and accidents. Providing a reliable and safe supply of electrical power for critical life support and life safety is a vital element of any health care facility providing a high quality of care to a community. Several codes and standards, most recently *NFPA 99*, regulating electrical systems have adopted requirements for maintenance. Equipment maintenance programs must be in writing, detail rationale for the program, and document all crucial data. The most valuable NFPA document covering electrical systems maintenance is *NFPA 70B: Recommended Practice for Electrical Equipment Maintenance.* Because this document is not a standard or a code, but rather a recommended practice, until the next edition is release as a standard, it is not enforceable by the AHJ. However, it does play a vital role in guiding the work of the Electrical Worker. Due to the sensitive and critical role that these facilities play in communities, special care must be taken when performing such maintenance activities. Understanding the codes, standards, and documents that regulate these protocols and procedures is what sets a skilled Electrical Worker apart.

REVIEW QUESTIONS

1. **For health care facilities to be eligible to receive Medicare and Medicaid payments from the United States Department of Health and Human Services, facilities must conform to the __?__ .**
   a. Center for Disease Control
   b. Centers for Medicare and Medicaid Services (CMS) Conditions of Participation
   c. Hospital Association of America
   d. *NFPA 99: Health Care Facilities Code*

2. **CMS requires that maintenance shall be performed on hospital electrical equipment in accordance with the __?__ .**
   a. American Hospital Association Guidelines
   b. equipment manufacturer's recommendation
   c. hospital governing body maintenance guidelines
   d. industry standards

3. **Essential electrical system generation specifically requires that equipment to be maintained to come online in __?__ upon a power outage. It also requires that generator sets be tested __?__ times a year in intervals of not less than 20, but no more than 40 days, as well as specific main and feeder circuit breaker inspection and exercise requirements.**
   a. 10 seconds / 12
   b. 30 seconds / 6
   c. 60 seconds / 12
   d. 120 seconds / 6

4. ***NFPA 70B: Recommended Practice for Electrical Equipment Maintenance* is not a standard or code, and therefore, not enforceable by an AHJ; however, when considering maintenance and testing, *NFPA 70B* is just as important to an Electrical Worker as *NFPA 70* is when installing electrical systems.**
   a. True   b. False

5. **When health care facilities engage outside electrical contractors to perform maintenance on the facility's electrical system, it is generally to perform specific preventive maintenance procedures on specific electrical equipment, or at the far end of the maintenance spectrum, on the entire branch of an essential electrical system.**
   a. True   b. False

REVIEW QUESTIONS

6. Which of the following are questions used as a consideration of maintenance protocol?

    I. Are the facility's standard electrical system placards up to date?

    II. Are the placards easily understood by the average worker?

    III. Has a contingency plan been formulated in the event the out of service equipment cannot be brought online in the required timeframe?

    IV. Have one-line diagrams been studied to obtain an understanding of how the proposed work affects the entire electrical system?

    a. I., II., III., and IV.
    b. I., II., and IV.
    c. II., III., and IV.
    d. IV. only

7. Phase rotation tests are required before any power distribution work or disconnection of service conductors.

    a. True   b. False

8. When performing maintenance work on hospital equipment that is not locked out and tagged out or placed in an electrically safe work condition, what is the risk exposure to an Electrical Worker performing the work?

    a. High
    b. Low
    c. Medium
    d. Very low

9. "Qualified Electrical Worker" is defined as those who have demonstrated the skills and knowledge related to the construction and operation of electrical equipment and installations and can perform work on or near energized equipment.

    a. True   b. False

10. Before starting each job that involves exposure to electrical hazards, the employee in charge shall complete a job safety plan and conduct a job briefing with the employees involved.

    a. True   b. False

11. In addition to meeting all requirements of Article 120 per 110.2, establishing and verifying an electrically safe condition consists of which of the following steps?

    I. After interrupting any loads, open all applicable disconnecting means.

    II. Apply proper lockout/tagout devices in accordance with the employer's written policy.

    III. Determine all possible sources of the electrical supply.

    IV. If possible, visually verify all blades or cutout devices are open or fully drawn out.

    V. Push any start buttons or activation switches to make sure the equipment does not start.

    VI. Using an adequately rated test instrument, verify that the conductors or circuit parts are deenergized.

    VII. Where induced voltages or stored energy exists, ground the phase conductors or circuit parts.

    a. I., II., III., IV., and VII.
    b. I., II., and VII.
    c. III., IV., V., VI., and VII.
    d. III., V., and VI.

12. Proper maintenance of switchgear, switchboards, and panelboards in health care facilities is an important part of keeping the electrical system functioning and documented. In addition, well-established maintenance programs provide confidence in the operation of the electrical system, and are a CMS requirement.

    a. True   b. False

13. A(n) __?__ is required when hot work is performed within the restricted approach boundary and when energized equipment, conductors, or circuit parts are not exposed but an increased likelihood of injury from arc flash exposure exists.

    a. energized electrical work permit
    b. first aid / AED / CPR training
    c. host employer safety review
    d. insulated tool evaluation

14. A critical part of a safe work procedure is completing a job briefing or "pre-task" report before beginning the work.

    a. True   b. False

Work in Existing Health Care Facilities

A growing trend in health care facility construction is the almost constant changes to existing facilities as health care organizations adopt new technology and medical processes to assure patients receive the best care science can provide. Recent studies have shown that the demolition and construction processes negatively impact patients and others with compromised immune systems. These facts have driven wide-ranging changes in the construction work environment, changes that affect every Electrical Worker engaged in their trade at an existing health care facility. Furthermore, patient information privacy laws and regulations, as well as appearance expectations, all affect existing health care facility workplaces.

Objectives

» Explain why an Electrical Worker's appearance and conduct is especially important when working in a health care facility.

» Describe who should be involved in the development of a risk assessment and what items should be addressed.

» Understand why an Infection Control Risk Mitigation Plan (ICRMP) is important and how it is enforced.

» Distinguish and describe the differences between barriers used in health care facilities during construction projects.

Chapter 6

Table of Contents

CASE STUDY

Case Study: "Joe" Requires Surgery

"Joe" has been telling everyone on the job that he will be taking the kids on vacation soon. Joe's general foreman is the only person on the job that knows the truth: Joe's parents are taking the kids for a few days, because Joe has been having some issues that require surgery and a few nights' stay at the local hospital. Joe is a private person and would rather get through this surgery and hospital stay with the privacy that he and his family are entitled.

Joe and his wife arrive at the hospital early on the morning of his surgery. As they settle into the surgical preparation area, Joe thinks to himself, "I am just glad that no one knows that I am here and I cannot wait to get the whole thing over with and be home."

Several of the hospital staff members move Joe to the surgery suite ready room on the ninth floor. As they wheel Joe into the elevator lobby, he notices several pairs of concrete dust prints from work boots on the floor. As the elevator doors open, a worker in a hard hat and safety vest comes out of the cab. Joe hears the worker exclaim - "Holy smokes, it's Joe. What are you doing here?" Joe raises his head and sees "Sam," a fellow Electrical Worker who is apparently working on a project at the hospital. Joe notices that Sam is covered in concrete dust and that his work clothes are in bad shape. As Sam leaves the elevator and the doors close, Joe hears the hospital staffers talking to one another about how disruptive the remodel project has been.

Joe's surgery goes very well. Joe wakes up the morning after surgery and, as he surveys his hospital room, is puzzled to see one of his co-workers from his workplace in the room as well. The co-worker asks Joe how he is doing, and proceeds to say that Joe gave his fellow workers quite a scare after Sam alerted them that he was in the hospital rather than on vacation. Joe's co-worker said she was sorry to intrude, but she was certainly glad to see that he seemed to be doing fine.

This fictional story helps define several issues Electrical Workers face when working at health care facilities.

- Concerning his medical condition and subsequent procedure, Joe has every right to absolute privacy, and there are a multitude of state and federal regulations in place to ensure this medical privacy is upheld. While Sam may have been well-intentioned, he should not have reported Joe's condition to others without Joe's permission. The fact that Sam disclosed Joe's condition, which he "discovered" while employed at the hospital, expressly violates several elements of federal law designed to protect patients' confidentiality. Sam's actions expose him, his employer/contractor, and the health care organization itself to potential legal action on behalf of the patient. An Electrical Worker employed in any health care facility must keep any knowledge of any patient, medical condition, procedure, or diagnosis entirely confidential.

- While it may be something construction workers have grown accustomed to, construction dust in any form is dangerous in a health care environment. Seasoned workers will comment that they have been exposed to this dust their entire working life with no problem (the recent OSHA silica standard notwithstanding), but health care facilities are full of people with compromised immune systems, and exposure to airborne dust is a big problem for patients recovering from disease. From a strictly housekeeping perspective, health care facilities are spotless for a reason—to prevent the spread of disease and infection. The dusty boot prints, while common on a normal construction site, are an anathema in a health care facility.

- Consider Sam's appearance from the viewpoint of a patient who is not an Electrical Worker. Just like Joe, patients come to a health care facility to take care of conditions that are negatively impacting their life in some manner. Patients expect health care organizations to employ skilled, professional staff who have the patients' best interest foremost. With that expectation, any worker in a health care facility, including outside contractors and their employees, should, in dress and behavior, meet the patients' expectations. While no one expects an Electrical Worker to wear a sports jacket and tie to work, clean work boots, clean trousers that do not have holes, a proper belt, and a clean and appropriate shirt are expected of an electrical professional. In addition, foul language should never be used.

REMODEL AND RETROFIT

For most medium- to large-sized hospitals, ambulatory surgery centers, nursing homes, and clinics, as well as other regional health care facilities, the demolition and construction of existing spaces is a fact of life. Rapid advances in medical science coupled with staggering advances in technology and engineering produce new diagnostic and treatment techniques and equipment that health care organizations must adopt in order to provide the best, most up-to-date care for their patients. The reconfiguring of existing spaces to accommodate new procedures or equipment is an ongoing enterprise. This type of work creates opportunities for a savvy electrical contractor, although work in an existing health care facility can be frustrating and try the patience of an Electrical Worker used to the fast pace of a new construction job. **See Figure 6-1.**

FROM A PATIENT'S POINT OF VIEW

Patients in a hospital are stressed, confused, anxious, and scared. Regardless of the circumstances that brought them into the health care facility, all patients expect up-to-date care and respectful and competent treatment in a safe, secure, and clean environment. While the work being performed to remodel the health care facility is important to the workers who are doing the work, the project is at best an unfortunate disruption to staff and patients. **See Figure 6-2.**

Construction work executed in a working health care facility brings certain risks to patient care that must be taken into consideration before and during construction. Very broadly, these concerns include:

- Utility electrical service interruptions, particularly those that are unplanned

Figure 6-1   Existing Health Care Facility Addition

Figure 6-1. *Even though a new addition is considered new work, infection control risk mitigation plans may be in place to protect patients in adjoining facilities.*

- The release of dust and other pathogens that may cause patient infection
- The relocation of services and the proper communication and signage to keep confusion for the staff, patients, and general public to a minimum
- The compromising of fire protection systems that would diminish the health care facility's defend-in-place strategies
- Dust that can damage costly, sensitive medical equipment
- Emergency helicopter service having to use an alternative landing site if construction cranes are required for the project
- Vibrations that may result in surgical blunders
- The health care facility's entrance and egress, which must be kept open and unobstructed at all times
- Tripping hazards that must be eliminated

Toward the goal of keeping staff and patients safe and secure during construction projects in existing facilities, the American Society for Healthcare Engineering (ASHE) has created a list of 13 expectations that health care organizations should oblige contractors (and their employees) who are engaged in construction in an existing health care facility:

Knowledgeable workers. Hospitals and health care organizations expect contractors to bring workers on site who are knowledgeable about both their particular trade or craft and some of the requirements specific to working in health care facilities. Organizations expect contractors to understand the codes and standards applicable to the facility, and to train their staff and any subcontractors to comply with them. Many health care organizations require some level of training or certification for contractors working in their facilities, as well as completion of an orientation process before work begins.

Worker identification. Most health care organizations require that all workers on the jobsite wear visible identification. This might be an ID badge provided by the facility, or one the contractor is

Figure 6-2   Dusty Conditions

Figure 6-2. *A block layer can create a hazardous condition by using a dry saw to cut a concrete block to size. This type of activity would certainly be prohibited by an infection control risk mitigation plan.*

required to provide for all subcontractors and staff. Usually, workers must undergo training prior to receiving an ID badge, and some organizations require background checks. The process may vary from one health care facility to the next, so it is important to understand and comply with the requirements specific to a particular facility. In many cases, workers who do not have identification will be escorted off the property.

Jobsite security. The jobsite must be secured, especially after hours. While some facilities have security staff that will make routine rounds, in most cases, it is part of the contractor's job to devise a plan for securing the site, instituting a plan, and making sure it is followed. Although this may be primarily the responsibility of the general contractor, subcontractors also need to realize the importance of keeping the site secure and the key role that everyone plays in all related precautions.

Parking. The health care organization will have specific requirements regarding parking. Patient and visitor access to the facility is a top priority, so contractors may be asked to park farther away from the facility (or the jobsite) to maintain sufficient accessible, available, and adequate parking for patients and visitors. Hospitals usually have strict policies about their parking, and repeat violations could result in workers or contractors being removed from the project.

Dining facilities. Some hospitals may not want construction workers to use the hospital dining facilities, while others may allow this as long as the workers are clean and do not track in dirt or dust. Because of this variation from one facility to the next, dining access should be clarified during the pre-construction meeting or in the specifications.

Restroom facilities. On new construction projects or additions, hospitals usually ask that their restroom facilities be reserved for the facility population only and that temporary facilities are provided for construction workers. However, in a renovation, where contractors are working in an existing facility, the health care organization may designate which restrooms can be used. As with dining facilities, this should be clarified at the pre-construction meeting.

Access and travel paths. Access to the facility and to the jobsite, including travel paths for Electrical Workers, material, and debris must all be identified and agreed to by the health care facility before the contractor begins work. This is part of the infection control risk assessment.

Smoking and tobacco use. The use of tobacco products is prohibited in health care facilities and because of associated safety and health risks, tobacco is not generally allowed on the campus or grounds. Contractors are expected to comply with the facility's tobacco policy, and failure to do so may result in dismissal.

Hot work permits. Many hospitals require the issuance of a hot work permit when torch work, welding, or similar work will be performed. The permit is usually issued by the hospital facility management department, project management department, or the safety officer.

Other hospital permits. Some facilities may have other permit requirements for certain types of work, such as penetrating smoke or fire barriers or removing ceiling tiles.

Appearance and personal hygiene of workers. Most hospitals have specific dress code requirements. Often, T-shirts are not allowed, or if workers can wear T-shirts, they must have the contractor's logo on them. Workers must also have reasonable personal hygiene, especially when working in areas where patients, staff, and visitors are present. Improperly dressed Electrical Workers or those with poor hygiene will be asked to leave.

Conduct of workers. Hospitals and health care organizations are very strict about the behavior of workers. Patients, visitors, and health care staff must be treated with respect. Crude, vulgar, or disrespectful language and actions will not be tolerated.

Patient confidentiality. Patient confidentiality is key when working in health care organizations. Workers may see patients they know or recognize, but hospitals expect workers to maintain the confidentially of those in the facility.

The expectations of a crafts worker are considerably greater in an existing health care facility than on any other type of construction project. While these expectations may seem extreme at first, when one considers that the mission of the health care facility is to provide quality service and safety for the well-being of patients, visitors, and staff, these expectations come into perspective.

DEMOLITION/ CONSTRUCTION RISK ASSESSMENT

Risk assessment is a big element of health care facility construction, as is drafting a daily organizational policy. Risk assessment plays a major role in developing a schedule and workflow process for construction performed in an existing working health care facility. While each facility's risk assessment process is unique to that facility, ASHE provides some general guidelines for healthcare facilities undergoing this type of work. ASHE suggests that, at a minimum, before undergoing a risk assessment the following should be carefully defined:

- The type of work to be done
- The affected locations, including entrance and egress
- The level of disruption the construction process will cause to the health care facility
- Which services will be negatively impacted by the construction process

ASHE goes on to suggest that the following personnel should be engaged in the risk assessment:

- Project architect
- Consulting engineers
- Construction manager
- Mechanical, electrical, and plumbing contractors
- Health care facility project manager
- Representatives from the following health care facility departments:
  o Facility management
  o Infection prevention
  o Risk management
  o Environmental services
  o Security
  o Patient care
  o Any services directly or indirectly affected by the project

The risk assessment team's work should begin well before the project begins and should continue until project completion. The team should evaluate and devise a remediation plan for each identified risk and then fully assess the effectiveness of each remediation plan. As the project changes scope and size over time, the team needs to be flexible as the job itself changes, bringing with it new unforeseen potential risks. Finally, at the conclusion of the project, the risk assessment team should submit a detailed report, including meeting minutes for use in future projects. ASHE suggests that, at a

minimum, the team should focus on these elements:

- Keeping entrances and egress points clear and unobstructed
- The mitigation of noise into patient care spaces, particularly critical care spaces
- Disruptions in water, medical gas, electrical, fire alarm, and sprinkler systems
- The mitigation of vibration into patient care spaces, particularly those spaces where delicate procedures are performed
- The prevention of infection pathogen infiltration, usually caused by dust and mold. This is a *Guidelines for the Design and Construction of Health Care Facilities* requirement, enforced by CMS
- Hazardous elements that may be found as a regular part of the demolition/construction process, such as:
  o Silica
  o Lead and lead paint
  o Asbestos
  o Mold
  o Mildew

Common Elements of Construction Risk Assessments

Each health care organization will have internal protocols on demolition and construction work performed on their facilities that remain open to the public. All of these protocols have common elements that are worth discussing.

Infection Control Risk Assessment/Mitigation Plans

Hospital acquired infections (HAI) are a monumental problem for health care facilities. The Centers for Disease Control (CDC) believes that close to two million infections occur in all types of health care facilities each year. Of these two million cases of HAI, almost 100,000 of them result in a patient's death. The CDC also estimates HAI cases add a staggering cost of $35 to $45 billion to the health care system. ASHE reports that published papers in medical journals link 5% of HAI deaths to issues raised by construction activities. These numbers are the reason why the *Guidelines for the Design and Construction of Health Care Facilities* mandates that before construction begins, health care organizations perform an infection control risk assessment that puts in place an infection control risk mitigation plan (ICRMP) for use during construction activities. The assessment and ensuing plan are designed solely to protect patients from infection risks that are elevated due to construction.

The *Guidelines for the Design and Construction of Health Care Facilities* require that the ICRMP contains at least a minimum of nine components covering the following topics:

- Patient placement and relocation
- Standards for barriers and other protective measures required to protect adjacent areas and susceptible patients from airborne contaminants
- Temporary provisions or phasing for construction or modifications of HVAC and water supply systems
- Protection from demolition
- Training for staff, visitors, and construction personnel

- The impact of potential utility outages or emergencies, including the need to protect patients during planned and unplanned utility outages and evacuation
- The impact of the movement of debris, traffic flow, cleanup, elevator use for construction materials and construction workers, and construction worker routes
- Provisions for the use of bathroom and food facilities by construction workers
- Installation of clean materials (particularly ductwork, drywall, and wood/paper/fabric materials) that have not been damaged by water
- The monitoring and evaluating of the Infection Control Risk Mitigation Plan (ICRMP) throughout the life of the project
- The governing body shall provide monitoring plans for the effective application of the ICRMP during the course of the project.
- Provisions for monitoring shall include:
  - o Written procedures for the suspension of work
  - o Protective measures indicating the responsibilities and limitations of each party (governing body, designer, contractors, and monitors)

These requirements are basically concerned with the isolation and containment of air and waterborne pathogens to areas under construction away from patient care spaces. A pathogen is defined as something that causes a disease. This can be fungus, bacterium, parasites, viruses, or mold spores that cause disease in their host. Pathogens are generally mitigated by a healthy human immune system. However, pathogens can cause sickness and death in young children and adults with compromised immune systems, such as transplant and chemotherapy patients. There are three pathogens that are particularly related to construction activities.

Mold spores can lie dormant for many years and then suddenly become

Figure 6-3   Common Mold Spores

Figure 6-3. Common mold spores can cause serious health problems to patients with compromised immune systems.

airborne when disturbed by maintenance, renovation, construction, and even housekeeping activities. Spores are usually inhaled by the host and can cause severe health problems. **See Figure 6-3.**

Legionella bacteria are found naturally in the environment and have an affinity for warm water. In health care facilities legionella can be found in cooling towers, hot water tanks, evaporative condensers, even ornamental fountains. Legionella causes Legionnaires' disease, a particularly nasty form of pneumonia that can prove quite deadly. Legionella is transmitted to humans by the inhalation of a water mist, or less commonly the ingestion of soil contaminated with the bacteria. Legionella can enter a hospital's domestic water supply by the unintentional mixing of domestic and hydronic water supplies. Legionella can also multiply rapidly in stagnant water, such as in a closed domestic water system that has been tested and capped off for a period of time. **See Figure 6-4.**

Aspergillus is a fungus that reproduces through tiny spores. Aspergillus is a major component of mildew and can also be found in soil, plants, and decomposing vegetation. Aspergillus spores can be found in a health care facility's ventilation system, non-HEPA vacuum systems, waste containers, decorative plants, domestic and hydronic water systems, and any damp surface where mildew can grow. Fungi spores stick to dust particles and are not damaged by extreme temperatures. These spores are the main reason infection control is so focused on dust control. These fungi spores cause an infection known as aspergillosis, most commonly known as lung disease, but it is not uncommon for it to infect other organs. In 2006, a well-respected medical journal reported that one-half of aspergillosis infections were directly related to construction activity in health care facilities. **See Figure 6-5.**

All ICRMPs include a worker training component that identifies these risks as well as any local pathogens.

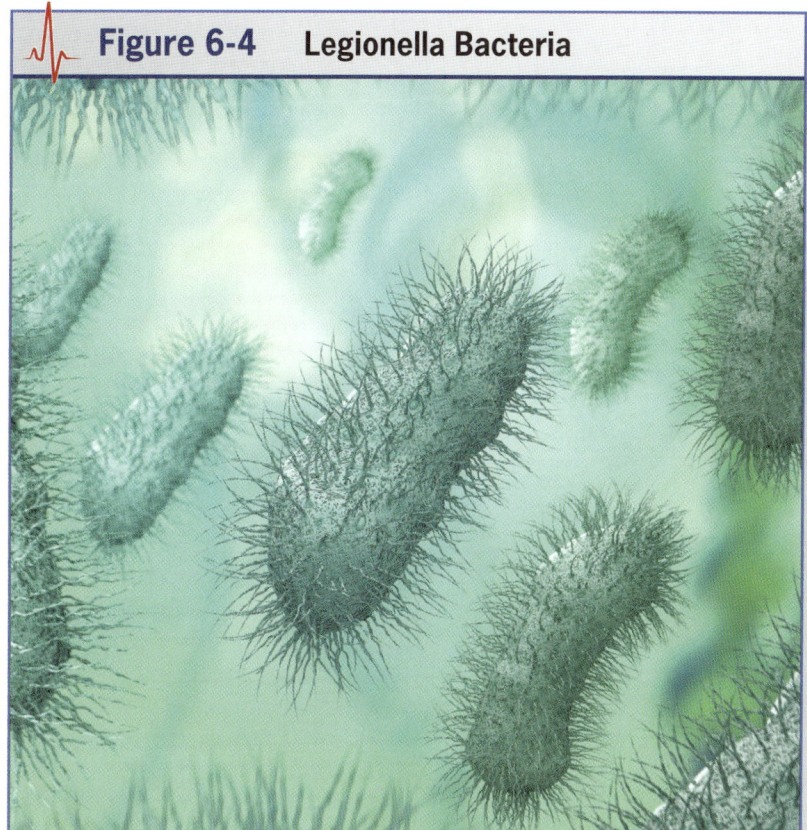

Figure 6-4   Legionella Bacteria

Figure 6-4. Legionella bacteria can cause Legionnaires' disease, a deadly form of pneumonia.

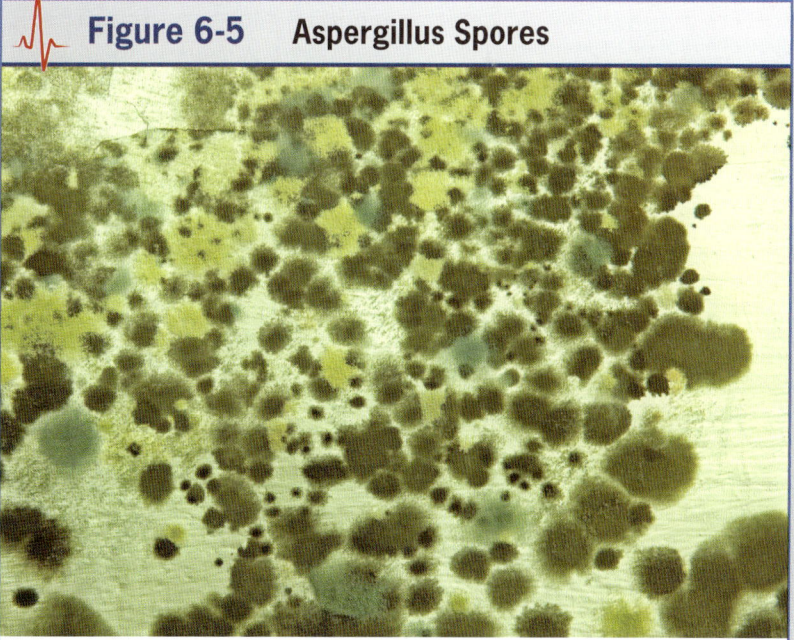

Figure 6-5   Aspergillus Spores

Figure 6-5. Microscopic aspergillus spores that cause aspergillus in patients with compromised immune systems.

This training also includes information on how pathogens infect patients, including several important terms and definitions:

- **Agent** – the pathogen and the element; for example, a dust particle that contains the pathogen.
- **Reservoir** – a space where agents may be found. These reservoirs can be behind partition walls, in and on lay-in ceilings and light fixtures, in and on ductwork, in domestic and hydronic water systems, and in cooling towers.
- **Portal of Exit** – how the agent moves from the reservoir to ambient air. This occurs when the reservoir is disturbed by construction (or housekeeping) activities. The goal of all mitigation plans is to keep pathogens isolated to the construction space.
- **Mode of Transportation** – the means by which an agent moves from a portal of exit to a compromised patient. This is the link of the chain all mitigation plans seek to break. Transportation can occur in three modes: in the air, on surfaces, and in water.
  - o Airborne pathogens are contained by surrounding the construction space with airtight soft or hard partitions that are provided with negative pressure airflows (air moving from the health care space to the construction space). The air is then filtered and exhausted to the environment. It is important that the installed health care facility's HVAC equipment not be used for this activity. ASHE strongly suggests using temporary equipment designed for this purpose.
  - o Pathogens can be transported on the surface of any material that is brought out of the construction space, including clothing, shoes, trash carts, and material carts. Many construction spaces will have a sally port where workers are required to

vacuum their clothes and clean and cover their boots with protective covers. Carts and other wheeled devices should be cleaned as directed, and their wheels driven over a tack pad to pick up any dust before entering the health care space. The very same techniques that are used in clean rooms are utilized in this area.
  - o Waterborne pathogens are a much larger problem for plumbers and pipefitters than for Electrical Workers, but it is helpful to recognize that this is a transportation mode that can cause widespread issues if domestic water becomes contaminated.
- **Portal of Entry** – how the pathogen enters the patient. Typically, the pathogen enters the patient through the respiratory mucus membranes, through an orifice, or through a break in the patient's skin.
- **Susceptible Host** – the patient that contracts an infection due to a pathogen. These patients generally have a weakened immune system, which may be the reason they are seeking care, or may be a side effect of treatment.

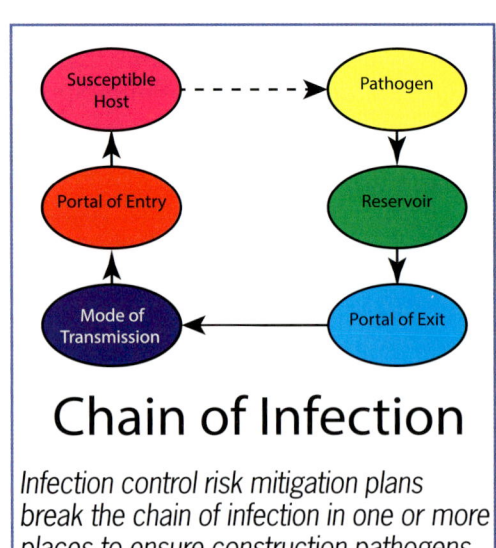

Chain of Infection

Infection control risk mitigation plans break the chain of infection in one or more places to ensure construction pathogens are not transmitted to patients.

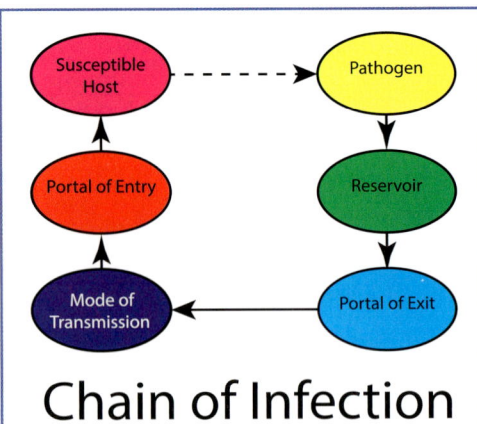

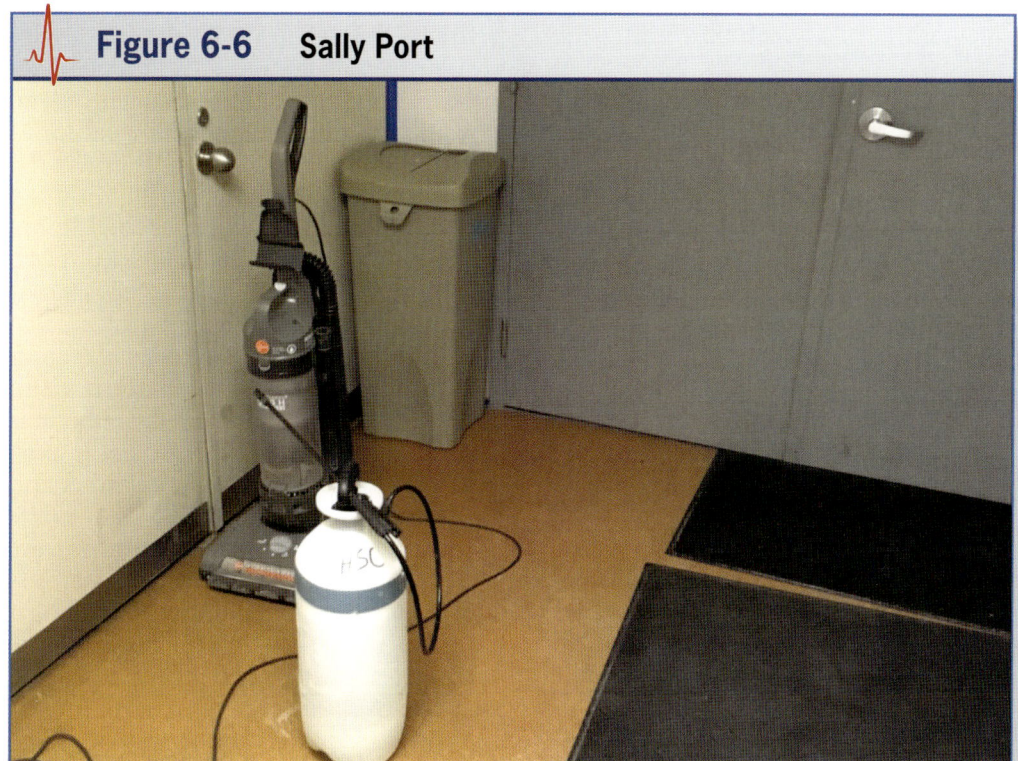

Figure 6-6   Sally Port

Figure 6-6. *A sally port, a HEPA vacuum, and a wash down pressure tank are typically used during construction at a health care facility.* Courtesy of Hatzel & Buehler, Circleville, OH

Infection control risk mitigation plans may be seen as a barrier to efficient work practices; however, it is important to realize that lives are literally depending on workers to conform to the ICRMP.

Construction Process Plans

It should come as no surprise that ICRMPs, coupled with working health care facility logistical challenges, impact the construction process plans. While all demolition and construction projects performed in health care facilities are unique, several construction management challenges seem to be more common.

Travel routes for workers, small materials and tools, exterior staging areas, delivery depots, and trash and other construction debris dumps should be well understood and completely followed, even though they may not be the most direct route. These routes have been carefully planned to minimize patient exposure to dust-borne pathogens and

the disruptions caused by the nature of the construction work. Travel may be limited to a single elevator or stairwell. In the event that certain tasks take a worker outside of the construction space and into the health care facility, it is critical that hands, clothes, shoes, tools, materials, carts, ladders, and any other objects leaving the construction zone are thoroughly cleaned and wiped down as per the ICRMP. It is also important to make certain that every item required to do the job is accounted for before leaving the construction space; extra trips back to the space to retrieve a forgotten tool may prove costly.

In certain situations, construction spaces will be segregated from the health care space by the use of sally ports, also known as anterooms. **See Figure 6-6.** These areas act as an additional safety zone between the construction space and the health care space. Sally ports have portals to both the construction and health care spaces,

Figure 6-7   Sally Port B and C

Figure 6-7. *It is critical that at least one door of a sally port be fully closed at all times. Tack mats, HEPA vacuums, and wash down pressure tanks are used to protect the hospital space from contaminants due to construction.* Courtesy of Hatzel & Buehler, Circleville, OH

Figure 6-8   Negative Pressure Machine

Figure 6-8. *A negative pressure machine with a HEPA filter covering the exhaust controls airflow in spaces under demolition/construction.* Courtesy of Hatzel & Buehler, Circleville, OH

which, under normal circumstances, are both sealed closed. When an Electrical Worker and materials need to travel from the construction space into the health care space, they enter the sally port through the portal, and seal the portal behind them. The cleaning procedures occur in the sally port. Once completed according to specification, the portal to the health care space is then opened, and the Electrical Worker along with the materials can continue into the health care space. It is critical that the portal to the sally port be sealed closed once all personnel and material are removed. When crafts workers travel from the health care space to the construction space, the sally port is utilized in reverse; again, it is very important that both portals are never opened at the same time. **See Figure 6-7.**

The barriers enclosing construction zones are generally divided into two types: soft barriers and hard barriers. Soft barriers are usually used for short-term projects, and are typically heavy-duty reinforced plastic sheeting mounted on a frame. These barriers are very susceptible to damage and should be monitored by those working on the project. Should the soft barrier become torn or compromised in some manner, the issue should be repaired as quickly as possible while bringing the matter to a supervisor's attention.

Hard barriers are typically made of drywall or a sheet wood product mounted to a metal stud assembly. While much more robust than a soft barrier, hard barriers should also be regularly monitored for damage or displacement. As with soft barriers, any compromising issues should be brought to a supervisor's immediate attention.

The erection of barriers and the placement of construction travel pathways may impact the health care facility's firefighting and other defend-in-place strategies. As part of the facility's overall life safety plan, the health care facility may initiate a series of interim life safety measures over the life of the construction project. These measures are

Figure 6-9   Airflow Monitor

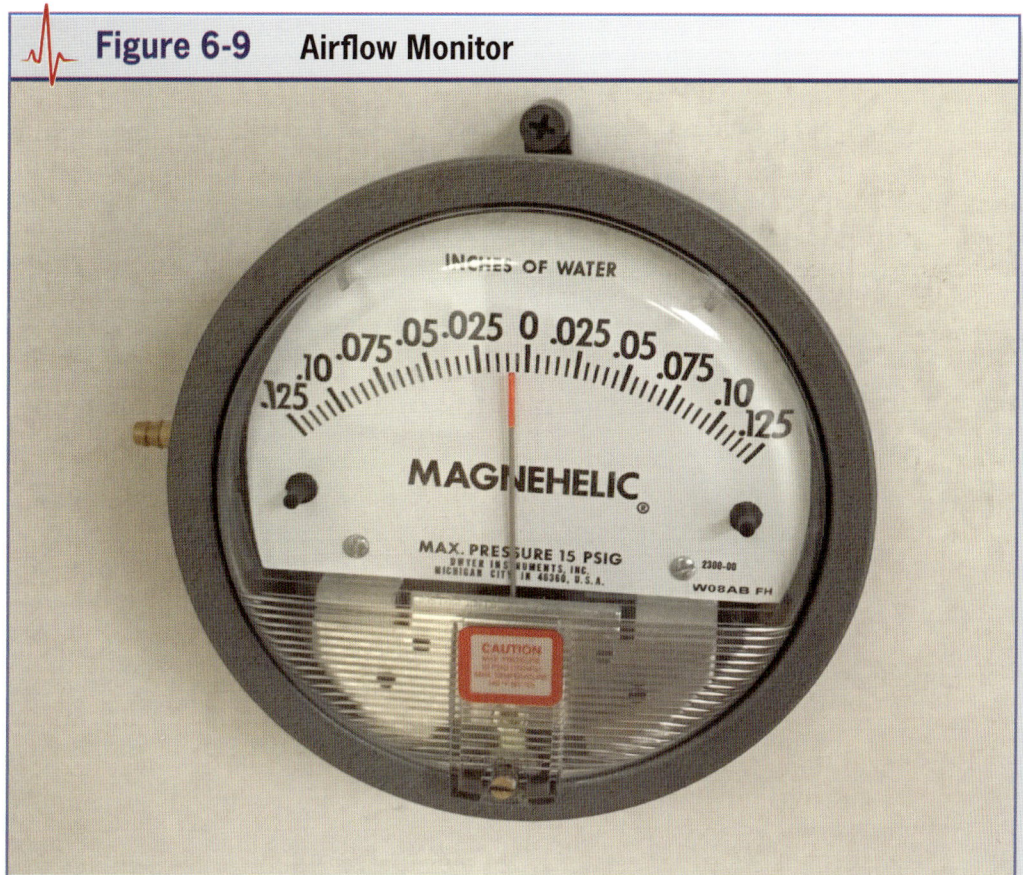

Figure 6-9. An airflow monitor ensures that a health care facility space that is under construction is held in negative pressure. *Courtesy of Hatzel & Buehler, Circleville, OH*

put in place to take care of any disruptions to the life safety plan caused by the work being done and the ICRMP. Typically, this means that the means of egress for patients and staff may be modified to accommodate barriers and construction travel pathways. For Electrical Workers, this may mean changes to corridor lighting, entrance and egress lighting, and modifications to the fire alarm system.

It is important to note that these changes are performed in a working health care facility, and the conditions of the construction risk assessment, including the ICRMP, should be followed to the letter. Furthermore, additional electrical work may be performed on the construction zone's HVAC system, which may be as simple as temporarily wiring a negative pressure machine or as complex as reprogramming the space's HVAC controls to ensure proper airflow. **See Figure 6-8.** Filtration sensors may also be added to monitor the filter's effectiveness with increased construction dust levels. It is also possible that electronic airflow monitors will be specified to ensure proper airflow patterns, particularly in high-risk spaces. These monitors will be part of an alarm system that will notify the proper personnel when and if airflow patterns are not normal. **See Figure 6-9.**

It has been said that the only facilities more regulated than health care facilities are nuclear power plants. Whether this is true or not, health care facilities are places where life and death are played out on a daily basis. Electrical professionals must do their part in this complicated process as professionally and as transparently as possible.

SUMMARY

Health care facilities are constantly changing to adapt to the needs of the communities that they serve. Because construction projects are often active alongside functioning hospitals, electrical professionals must understand that these projects pose a risk of infection to patients. The safety and privacy of these patients must be respected during the entire course of a project.

REVIEW QUESTIONS

1. Working in existing medical facilities is common because of the rapid advances in medical science coupled with the staggering advances in __?__ that produce new diagnostic and treatment techniques and equipment that health care organizations must adopt to be able to provide the best, most up-to-date, care for their patients.
   a. electrical system upgrades
   b. medical procedures
   c. technology and engineering
   d. turn-key constructor practices

2. Hospital patient privacy is required by __?__.
   a. a doctor's orders
   b. a multitude of state and federal regulations
   c. hospital security
   d. hospital staff and physicians

3. Exposure to airborne dust is a big problem for patients recovering from a disease. Therefore, __?__ in any form is a very bad thing in a health care environment.
   a. construction dust
   b. exposure to dirty work clothing
   c. leaky water systems
   d. noise and yelling

4. Patients expect health care organizations to employ skilled, professional staff who have the patients' best interest foremost. It is also expected that workers in a health care facility, including outside contractors and their employees, should, in dress and behavior, meet the patients' expectations.
   a. True   b. False

5. Which of the following items must be taken into consideration before and during construction where construction work will bring certain extra risks to a facility's patient care procedures?
   a. Dust
   b. Release of dust or other pathogens
   c. Tripping hazards
   d. Unplanned power interruptions
   e. Vibration or noise
   f. All of the above

6. All evaluations of qualified workers are dependent upon the contractor. Health care organizations do not expect workers to understand or comply with the codes and standards applicable to the facility work or completion of an orientation process before work begins.
   a. True   b. False

7. Generally, __?__ provided by the facility or the contractor are used for all subcontractors and staff and must always be present with the worker on the jobsite.
   a. company clothing with logos
   b. ID badges
   c. plans and specs
   d. tools

8. While some facilities have security staff that will make routine rounds, in most cases, it is part of the contractor's job to devise a plan for securing the site, instituting the construction plan, and making sure it is followed.
   a. True   b. False

REVIEW QUESTIONS

9. Some hospitals may not want construction workers to use the hospital dining facilities, while others may allow this if the workers are clean and do not track in dirt or dust; therefore, dining access should be clarified during the pre-construction meeting or in the specifications.

   a. True   b. False

10. The use of __?__ is prohibited in health care facilities, and because of associated safety and health risks, __?__ is not generally allowed on the campus or grounds.

    a. drugs / drug testing
    b. smoke producing tools / loud noise making tools
    c. tobacco products / tobacco
    d. none of the above

11. Workers must also have reasonable __?__, especially when working in areas where patients, staff, and visitors are present.

    a. personal hygiene
    b. PPE
    c. supervision

12. Patient confidentiality is key when working in health care organizations where workers may see patients they know or recognize; therefore, hospitals expect workers to maintain the confidentially of those they see or hear in the facility.

    a. True   b. False

The Future of Health Care

The United States health care system by design is dynamic and innovative. The adoption of new technology, new treatment processes, and new procedures are an everyday pressure on health care facilities. Additionally, the open market nature of the United States health care system provides additional pressures for health care designers and constructors to meet consumer needs and expectations. The complex nature of health care construction lends itself to innovations such as BIM and prefabrication. Facilities will be designed and built using the lessons learned during the COVID-19 pandemic, emphasizing flexibility above all else. These cutting-edge technologies and designs have far-reaching consequences for construction workers.

Objectives

» Understand how the health care industry has changed in recent years and how technology has had an impact on that change.

» Explain how advancements in drafting technology have impacted the way health care facilities are designed and built.

» Understand the effect of microgrid technology on essential electrical systems.

» Understand the benefits that prefabrication brings to the construction of health care facilities.

Chapter 7

Table of Contents

THE UNITED STATES HEALTH CARE SYSTEM IS UNIQUE

The United States health care system is very different from the health care systems in other western industrialized nations because it is really not a "system" at all. In virtually every industrialized nation, health care services are a function of the government, with all citizens receiving health care benefits as a basic privilege. These national systems may be more efficient than the United States health care system, but they often sacrifice patient services for the sake of that efficiency.

Health care in the United States is comprised of physicians, clinics, practices, and small, regional, rural, and teaching hospitals—both non-profit and for-profit. In the United States system, payers, whether they are insurance companies, the federal or state government (via Medicare or Medicaid), or self-paying individuals, can pick and choose from health care providers across the care spectrum. Their choices range from pediatricians to hospice centers and everything in-between. The United States "system" is competitive, innovative, focused on patient care, and expensive. Perhaps the most important trend in health care, the health care user movement from patient to consumer has been driven by the nature of the United States patient/payer/provider network.

Health Affairs, a well-respected journal of health care policy and research, reports that in the United States consumers spent over $3.2 trillion in 2017 for health care. This figure represents a 5.8% increase from 2014, which also averaged an astounding $9,990 outlay per person in the United States. Health care spending equaled 17.8% of the gross domestic product (GDP), up 0.4% from 2014. Health care is a huge and important sector of the United States economy. It is also a critical component of the construction sector. *Electrical Contractor* magazine projected that health care projects would bring in $25 billion worth of construction activity in 2017, up from $23 billion in 2016. During the 2007–2009 Great Recession, health care construction was the one sector of the economy that remained steady for both workers and their employers. Furthermore, the health care facilities built during the Hilton-Burton Act (1946 to 1975) are reaching the end of life and in need of replacement. This fact, coupled with the aging of the general population, means health care, as a market for construction services, will be a critical sector for the foreseeable future.

The COVID-19 pandemic brought unforeseen stresses to bear on the United States health care system. While these stresses were across the spectrum, the lesson learned from the pandemic from a design and build prospective, point to facility flexibility as a key takeaway. This is especially true in HVAC systems, where the ability to switch from positive to negative pressure in a particular space became a critical need in spaces treating COVID-19 patients.

HEALTH CARE TRENDS

Health care as an economic sector is undergoing vast changes. These changes impact the health care construction market in significant ways. Understanding the general trends in the health care sector will provide insight into the future of health care construction activities and projects.

Trend From Patient to Consumer

The amount and diversity of choice that the United States health care system provides users is unique in the developed world and is a recent occurrence. As little as 60 years ago, most family health care was provided by a practicing physician located in the neighborhood or community. In addition to the physician, the practice would employ people to administrate and provide secondary care to the patients. The practice's scope of work encompassed everyone in the community; it was not unusual for the community physician to be the sole medical provider for the young and the old of the entire town. The only exception to this would be when a patient's condition required care at a hospital where the local physician would engage specialists to provide care for the patient. Although some families had employer-provided medical insurance, the great majority of patients paid for services out of their own pocket. It was not unusual for the physician to become one of the most beloved members of the community.

As transportation, health insurance, medical science, and technology continued to march forward, the role between the patient and the community physician began to change, slowly at first, then drastically over the last 20 years. As the cost of health care began to skyrocket, insurance companies began to see the community-based practice as an inefficient delivery mechanism. They provided reduced premiums if customers would agree to seek care at larger, regional practices where as many as 50 physicians may be partners, saving building and support costs. Hospitals supported this transition as the larger practices were easier to engage and provided a steady patient bed count. While this transition may have provided benefits for both insurance companies and hospitals, the transition away from community health care irrevocably damaged the personal doctor-patient relationship.

Currently, both the health care providers and the health care users understand that the basis of the relationship has moved from a physician–patient personal relationship to a purchaser/consumer relationship. While many employer-provided plans still provide an incentive to seek services at a particular health care organization, those buying private insurance, and most importantly, those on Medicare or Medicaid, can go virtually anywhere for care. This competition between health care organizations for the patient's "business" is what sets the United States system apart. Studies show that just like any other consumer, health care consumers are looking for value.

Trend to Flexibility

As of this writing, the primary lesson learned from the COVID-19 pandemic has been the importance of flexibility in health care facility patient care spaces. Patient care spaces that were designed and built to serve a particular sector of medicine have proven problematic when the spaces must be used for care in which they were not designed. COVID-19 patients with respiratory issues receiving care in spaces designed for orthopedics presented issues for facility managers and caregivers, particularly when air-flow patterns had to be reconfigured to provide negative pressures in these spaces to provide assurance that the airborne virus was not carried though out the entire facility. Future facility design will almost certainly include flexible air flow schemes, increased decontamination spaces, and provisions to provide the greatest possible care in a particular patient care area.

Trend to Value

People tend to think of *value* as "something that can be bought for a low or fair price." While technically correct, it is difficult to determine a *low or fair price* for something as diverse and intensely personal as a health care

Acuity-Adaptable Patient Care Rooms

The concept of acuity-adaptable patient care rooms was born to combat health care acquired infections; the idea being to provide as much care as possible to an individual patient in one patient care room. Avoiding transporting the patient from floor to floor, ward to ward, room to room would minimize patients' exposure to infection. Acuity-adaptable patient care rooms have gained additional traction as a result of the COVID-19 pandemic's stress on health care facilities. These rooms are designed to provide an extraordinary range of service in one location; everything from basic care to intensive care at a level slightly below an ICU. The cost of acuity-adaptable patient care rooms is greater than a normal patient care space, however their flexibility—particularly in pandemic situations—provide value to the facility.

provider. Health care advertising is an excellent portal into what health care organizations feel are "value-added" elements for the health care consumer in their area. Generally, these campaigns seem to fall into three categories from the perspective of the health care organization:

- The health care organization has the newest facilities/procedures/equipment and the best physicians/specialists/innovation, and is closer to the community—both from a physical location aspect, as well as being a good social member of the community.
- The health care organization has been selected as one of the top 5/10/50/100 health care organizations in the nation for general/cardiac/neonatal/orthopedic/etc. care.
- The health care organization has the greatest expertise in joint replacement/transplants/neurosurgery/etc. and will get the patient home in an average of "x number of days."

A focus group study was recently commissioned by a physician's association to determine how consumers define value when shopping for health care services. When asked what the group valued more between a low health care organization mortality rate (essentially the number of people who die in the facility) or ease of parking, ease of parking won out every time. This may impact future construction, as the trend toward value may lead to more small, local facilities.

Trend to Smaller Facilities

Because health care consumers value community care, health care organizations are moving back to the neighborhoods, suburbs, and rural small towns. This is quite ironic when one considers that the great majority of health care was delivered locally during the middle part of the twentieth century. This movement takes health care to the consumer's locale. The community facilities can range in size from a group physician's practice, to a clinic, to an OB/GYN center, to an urgent care facility. This benefits the health care organization, which once again becomes part of the local community and ensures a steady flow of patients to the regional hospital. This is known as a *spoke and hub* strategy, or, more unkindly, the *pods and mothership* strategy. These outlying facilities represent a substantial benefit for the community from both a building inventory and job perspective and have generally been viewed very positively. **See Figure 7-1.**

Recently, the trend to smaller facilities has shown an interesting twist beyond the spoke and hub model. Microhospitals are essentially small (16,000 to 50,000 square feet) facilities that offer full service to patients, on site. Built primarily in rural areas, these facilities are designed to provide all but the most extreme care—a significant change from the spoke and hub model. Microhospitals have all the systems and treatment options found in a full-size hospital, just in a smaller footprint. As the square foot build costs of these facilities are much greater than a standard hospital, it will be interesting to see if this particular trend has stability.

Surgical procedures, such as some plastic and bariatric surgeries, are usually not covered by insurance and tend

Figure 7-1   Rural Health Care Facility

Figure 7-1. *The trend toward smaller regional health care facilities is generally seen as a benefit to the community.*

to be performed more for aesthetic improvement rather than addressing a health care issue. These surgeries are often performed at a site-specific special-purpose surgical center located in a discrete area. In the trade, these facilities are known as boutique clinics and are often not owned by a health care organization, but by a group of surgeons. These types of facilities have been growing as a market sector for some time, and projections show continued growth. It is important to note that even though these centers are not normal "hospitals," all the code and standards required of any other health care organization apply to these centers equally. **See Figure 7-2.**

The changes in care environments for an aging population are also significant and impactful. Recent changes in the *International Building Code* now permit nursing home residents to live in a more home-like environment. Perhaps the most significant of these changes allows residents to cook meals for themselves and other residents in communal kitchens. Another trend, pioneered by the Veterans Administration, focuses on the value of home-based care. These programs place emphasis on keeping the patients in their own home environment for as long as possible by providing visiting health care case workers as long as feasible. As a patient's health declines and staying at home alone is no longer an option, the next placement is in a residence where two to four additional patients are accommodated. The homeowner has full-time responsibility for the well-being of the patients. Initial studies show that this scheme may have promise, although there are grave concerns from some communities regarding the ability of a homeowner to safely manage patients in the event of a fire or other emergency situation.

Trend to Increasing Regulation

Federal Medicare and Medicaid are growing segments in the health care payers sector. This is driven by a couple of elements: the aging of America's population, meaning more people are

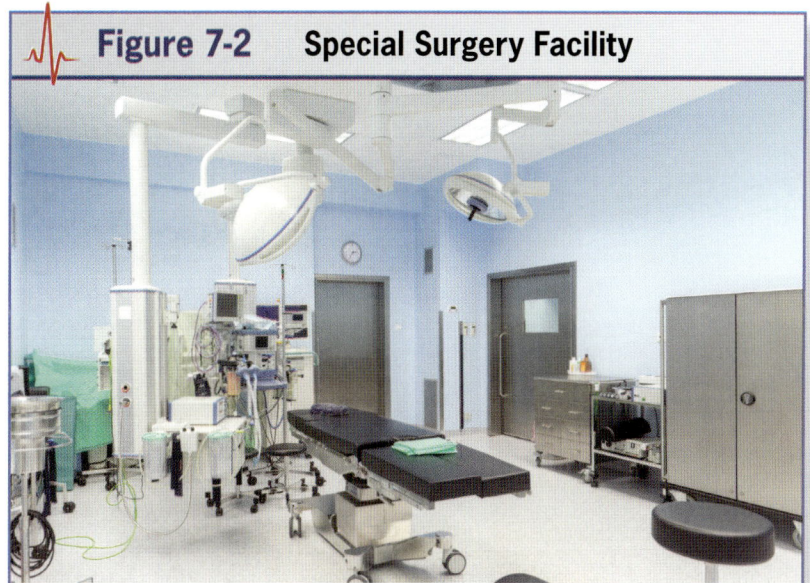

Figure 7-2   Special Surgery Facility

Figure 7-2. Specialty surgery centers—for example, those located in strip malls—are a growing trend in health care construction. All of the requirements of NFPA 70 and NFPA 99 apply to these types of facilities.

becoming eligible for Medicare benefits as they qualify for Social Security benefits; and the increasing use of Medicare as part of a national health care policy. The growth of the federal payer sector means health care organizations must remain qualified to receive these payments. Payments for federal health insurance programs are processed through the Centers for Medicare and Medicaid Service (CMS). This agency has strict standards of care that health care facilities must conform to in order to be eligible to receive payments from CMS. In this fashion, CMS, through several accreditation organizations, acts as a nationwide enforcer of standards of care.

One of the trends driven by CMS has been the adoption of a risk assessment strategy for individual health care organizations. These regulations require health care facilities to perform risk assessments whenever a change occurs in standard operating procedure, facility use, or maintenance. Risk assessments often uncover previously unrecognized potential issues, which, in turn, require the development of a contingency plan to mitigate these newly-discovered issues. Sometimes the contingency plans are reasonably simple, sometimes complex, and sometimes the plan requires the modification of the physical plant itself and the utilities serving the area. For example, in the wake of Hurricane Katrina and Superstorm Sandy, reports indicated that the loss of environmentally conditioned air was a large factor in the inability of health care facilities to provide services to patients. CMS issued a directive that conditioned environmental air shall be able to be delivered to patients and patient storage areas in the event of an emergency. Prior to this new requirement, health care facilities were not required to provide conditioned environmental air to patients. Because of this new directive, the risk assessments performed by many older health care facilities indicate that existing essential electrical systems do not have the design capacity to provide essential electrical service to patient HVAC systems.

Pandemic Temporary Health Care Facilities

In April of 2020, the NFPA published an extraordinary white paper entitled *Temporary Compliance Options for Code Modifications, Alternate Care Sites, and Facilities Related to Health Care*. The purpose of this document is to provide guidance to authorities having jurisdiction (AHJ) who found themselves in the highly unusual situation of converting convention centers, sports arenas, and the like to temporary health care facilities to contend with the explosion of patients who contracted COVID-19. Recognizing the hand that had been dealt, the document suggested that AHJs provide relief for these temporary facilities from such regulations involving sprinkler systems, egress requirements, smoke compartments, fire alarm systems, and the handling of medical gases. Electrical systems must remain redundant, relying on utility and portable generation, however the essential electrical system's three branches were often permitted to be served by a single transfer switch. Fortunately, as of this writing, these facilities have remained unused, however should future events require temporary facilities, there is guidance regarding the development of temporary health care facilities.

Although not affecting Electrical Workers as dramatically as CMS directives, the increasing awareness of infection control is also finding its way into health care design and construction, both in new builds and remodels. While these modifications are primarily based on ensuring proper airflows and filtering, new control schemes and monitoring systems will provide new horizons for Electrical Workers.

Trend to Revolutionary Health Care Technology

Advancement in practical medical science is introduced to the general public via health care facilities. In recent years, these advancements have become exponential, growing in three basic categories:

- **Procedures and Techniques.** Every year new procedures and medical techniques are developed that enable health care professionals to treat medical conditions faster and more effectively. These new processes enable patients to recover with less trauma and resume their normal lives sooner. Often these new procedures and techniques also have a cost-saving component.

- **Technological Advancement.** The technological advancement in medical equipment has increased very rapidly. Medical imaging equipment alone has seen enormous advancement in the last 20 years, and the future of this technology may be even more impressive. Radiology, nuclear medicine, fluoroscopy, angiography, mammography, computerized tomography (CT scan), and magnetic resonance imaging (MRI) have provided windows into the human body with unparalleled resolution.

- **Digital Information.** Data transmission, communication, and storage have become a critical feature for health care facilities of every size. All health care information, whether the patient's chart, the image of a recent CT scan, or the real-time collection of biometric data on a patient in the emergency department, is digitized, and the protection of this vital information has become extremely important for proper patient care. Furthermore, the staff communication systems of many health care facilities have become very sophisticated. Individual staffers may carry wireless communicators that allow real-time, instantaneous communication with other staff, facility-wide. The reliance on these IT systems places additional importance on the electrical systems serving this equipment. Permitted to be placed on the equipment branch, these systems are often additionally served by uninterruptable power systems (UPS) that provide clean uninterrupted power to this critical equipment. Recent advances in technology have lowered both the cost and footprint of these units, making them and attractive option.

HEALTH CARE CONSTRUCTION TRENDS

There are a number of health care construction trends that Electrical Workers need to be aware of. These include health care microgrids and the introduction of building information modelling (BIM) systems. While neither microgrids nor BIM are new to the electrical industry, their role in health care design and construction is evolving and taking on a greater role and importance.

Health Care Microgrids

The 2021 edition of *NFPA 99: Health Care Facilities Code* has new provisions that permit the use of health care microgrids as an approved means of providing power (emergency power supply, or EPS) to the essential electrical system in a health care facility. While the language adopted in *NFPA 99–2021* has not yet made it into *NFPA 70: The National Electrical Code (NEC)*, many public inputs have been submitted to revise *NFPA 70* to allow the use of

health care microgrids as an acceptable EPS. The chances are very good that the 2023 *NEC* will permit the use of health care microgrids as EPS.

Conceptually, microgrids are not new. Microgrids are a system of different equipment and apparatus that can produce or store electrical power. Microgrids put these disparate elements on a common bus and use a high technology controller to switch between these different elements to provide power to a particular load. A simple microgrid could consist of a utility supply, a solar array, and a battery storage system. When the sun is shining, the controller calls on the solar array to power the load and charge the batteries. When the day becomes overcast and the efficiency of the solar array diminishes the controller may call upon the batteries to supplement the solar array to power the load. In the evening, the controller calls upon the utility to power the load and deep charge the batteries.

These systems allow a facility to choose a wide variety of power sources to provide energy for their electrical needs. This allows the facility to optimize rates and keep energy costs to a minimum. More importantly from an essential electrical system standpoint, microgrid systems have the ability to diversify loads between various generation or storage elements, assuring a redundant source(s) of reliable power are available for critical loads.

Because the word *microgrid* can mean different things to different industries, *NFPA 99* carves out its own definition of both *health care microgrid* and *health care microgrid controller*:

3.3.75 Health Care Microgrid

A group of interconnected loads and distributed energy resources within clearly defined boundaries that acts as a single controllable entity with respect to the utility.

3.3.76 Health Care Microgrid Controller

A system including health care microgrid control functions that can manage itself, operate autonomously, and connect to and disconnect from the utility for the exchange of power and the supply of ancillary services.

Health care microgrids are designed to be very robust with high-performing controllers that are capable of making decisions on power supplies independently without human intervention. The optimum health care facility microgrid would have a number of elements on the common bus, some of which may include the utility, solar arrays, battery storage, diesel generators, wind turbines, gas turbine generators, and even hydroelectric power. The specialized health care microgrid controller decides what source feeds the load based on programmed data. In the event of a normal system power outage, the health care microgrid feeds the essential side of the transfer switches, providing power to the essential electrical system. **See Figure 7-3.**

Section 6.7.1.6 of the 2021 *NFPA 99* document provides the enabling language that permits health care microgrids to act as an EPS. New Section 6.10 details the requirements of health care microgrid systems.

Building Information Modelling (BIM)

The unparalleled complexity of health care construction projects lends itself to the implementation of new construction technology. These advances have occurred at every phase of a health care construction project. The initiation, permitting, design, engineering, installation, and commissioning processes have all been affected by improvements in construction technology. Perhaps the most profound of these technologies has been the introduction of building information modelling (BIM) systems. **See Figure 7-4.**

In the early 1990s, construction documents were "blueprints" that were hand-drawn by draftsmen, architects, and engineers. These hand-crafted construction drawings were in many ways

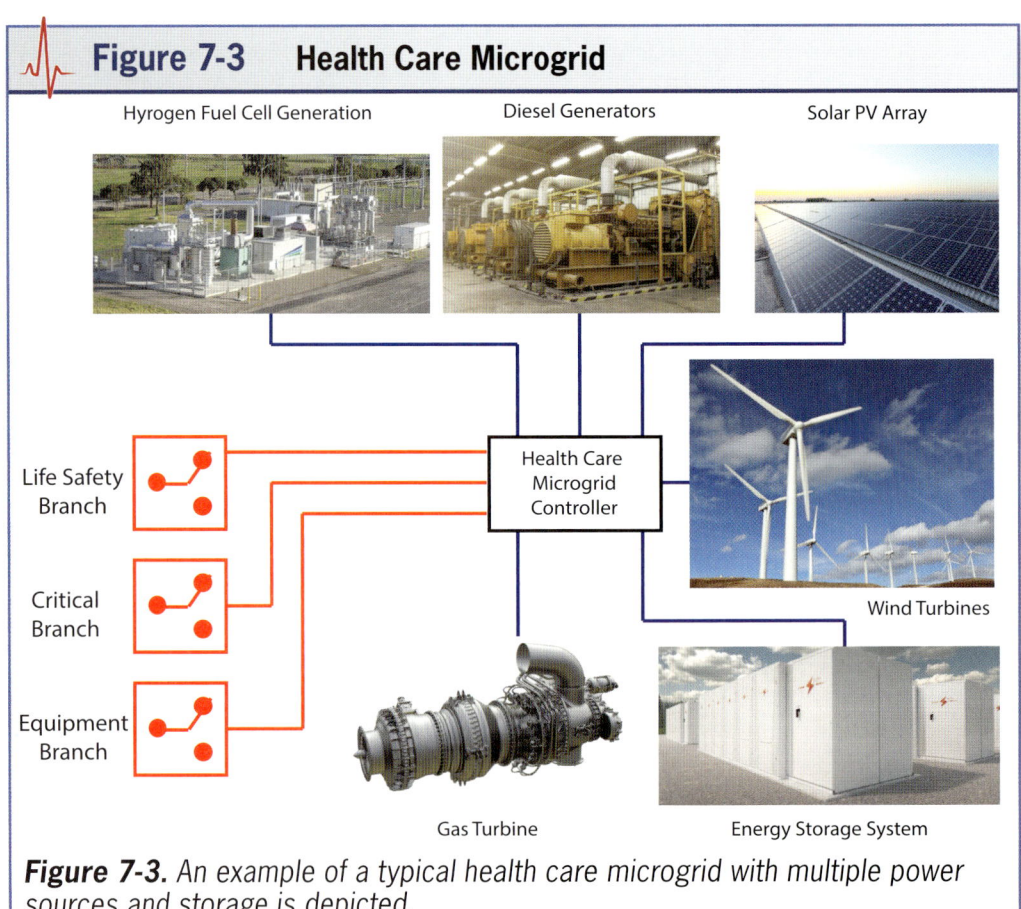

Figure 7-3   Health Care Microgrid

Hyrogen Fuel Cell Generation   Diesel Generators   Solar PV Array

Life Safety Branch

Critical Branch

Equipment Branch

Health Care Microgrid Controller

Wind Turbines

Gas Turbine   Energy Storage System

Figure 7-3. An example of a typical health care microgrid with multiple power sources and storage is depicted.

works of art, but they had serious drawbacks when trade coordination and change orders were required. By the middle of the decade, computer systems had advanced to the point where computer-aided drafting (CAD) was a viable option for architects, engineers, and contractors. CAD brought many improvements to the construction process. Changes to construction plans could be completed in minutes, rather than days. The change could also be communicated to all parties via email, and new drawings could be issued to the workforce almost immediately. Whereas the printed drawings would need to be scaled down to accommodate common paper sizes, drawings could now be rendered in full scale, eliminating the human scaling errors that were occasionally present in hand-made documents.

Prior to the introduction of CAD systems, *as-built drawings* were the final paper construction drawings marked up in colored pencils. It did not take long for owners to realize that a final as-built drawing CAD file precisely indicated the true position of the utilities. End-users began to insist that their projects be designed using CAD systems.

Through the first decade of the twenty-first century, CAD systems became indispensable elements of the construction process. They grew in capability and efficiency as CAD programs became more powerful and file sizes became smaller and easier to distribute via email. Field drawings were still printed for the construction crews, but by using the built-in power of CAD, these paper field drawings could include very detailed elements that would not have been possible with hand-rendered "blueprints." As both computers, computer operating systems, and CAD programs grew in power, it became possible to begin to design buildings on three axes (X, Y, and Z), which allowed users to design in three dimensions. This innovation allowed the different trades to address collision avoidance during the design stage, rather than the installation stage.

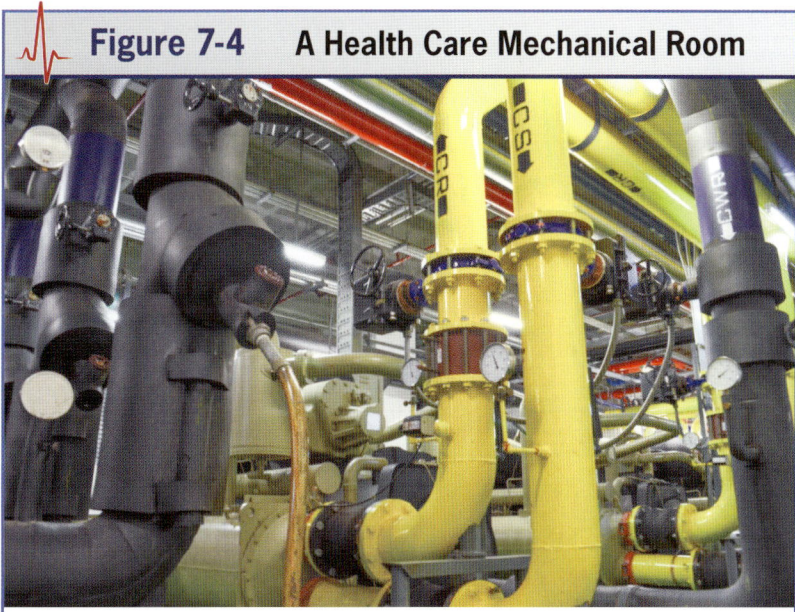

Figure 7-4   A Health Care Mechanical Room

Figure 7-4. Mechanical systems in health care facilities are quite complex, and space for various systems is always at a premium. These conditions lend themselves well to the use of BIM.

Previously, it was not unusual for multiple trades to have to fight for overhead space, especially in mechanical rooms.

In the early 2010s, CAD programs had progressed to the point that they were no longer CAD programs at all, but BIM systems. Using wireframe technology developed for the computer gaming industry, these systems were now able to essentially build the entire structure digitally (including items as detailed as branch circuit receptacle placements) before ground was ever broken on the physical structure. Not only does this level of resolution make things like utility conflicts/collisions a thing of the past, contractors can now get accurate estimates for material, including exact footage on feeder and branch circuit cables and wires, making the guesswork (and errors) of a hand take-off estimate a thing of the past. The degree of accuracy BIM systems provide is changing the construction process in huge ways. It is not unusual in today's health care construction space to have elements of the structure prefabricated off-site and properly placed during construction. It is no exaggeration to say that the prefabrication process, driven by BIM, is a game-changing disruptor for the construction industry.

As CAD morphed into BIM, improvements in hand-held devices (particularly tablets), wireless networks, GPS systems, and cloud technology brought an end to printed construction documents. Using these technologies, BIM systems allow real-time data collection and dissemination across the many layers of the project. Everyone from the crew foreman, to the construction manager, to the architect, to the owner can be notified in real time when an issue is uncovered and when a solution has been identified.

BIM AND HEALTH CARE CONSTRUCTION

Among leaders in the industry, *BIM* is defined as "An intelligent 3D model-based process that gives architecture, engineering, and construction (AEC) professionals the insight and tools to more efficiently plan, design, construct, and manage buildings and infrastructure." The three dimensional (3D), paperless aspect of BIM—coupled with modern wireless, cloud, and digital technology—has moved BIM from a novelty to the accepted method to design medium to large construction projects in a few short years. Although BIM has moved into virtually every other construction sector, due to the very complex nature of health care construction projects, the BIM process was first used extensively for health care construction.

BIM brings eight primary benefits to health care construction:

- BIM provides a platform to bring visualization to reality. The end-user has access to an extremely well-defined 3D model of the proposed facility, and has input during the design stage on every aspect of the structure. Everything from exterior finishes to the clearance requirements for a new piece of medical equipment can be easily visualized, revised,

and modified during the early phases of the project. Furthermore, the use of 3D forms allows staff and maintenance the opportunity to opine on building conditions, whereas they may not be able to interpret two-dimensional paper drawings.

- The opportunities for meaningful collaboration are exponentially greater with BIM. The ability to gain valuable feedback from the people who will work in the proposed spaces is a benefit unique to BIM systems. Not only does the design team gather insight into real-world conditions, but the health care workers can now be treated as stakeholders in the construction process, and as such may be more tolerant of any construction-caused disruptions.

- The construction schedule can be closely monitored using BIM. Potential construction delays can be discovered sooner and solutions identified faster, keeping the project on time. In many cases, the extreme detail that BIM brings to the project allows for "just in time" deliveries of materials and equipment, keeping material flowing while minimizing the issues of on-site storage and lay-down.

- BIM offers unparalleled levels of coordination between the health care project's electrical, mechanical, plumbing, structural, and architectural teams. Further benefits are realized on remodel projects where the health care staff can be brought in for consultation. The benefits of BIM from an infection control risk assessment team perspective are also significant. Being able to view spaces in 3D and view potential airflow patterns even before the initiation of the project is invaluable from this perspective.

- Studies show that health care construction projects using BIM systems are completed in a more timely manner. The main factor in this acceleration is the ability of

BIM to cut layout time to a fraction of what it used to be. Using GPS technology and laser locating units, BIM technology can perform everything from rack hanger location to structural alignment instantaneously, removing all guesswork and scaling and measurement errors from this critical construction process.

- Although hard data to back up this claim is still pending, the general feeling is that BIM seems to move the regulatory approval process along at a faster rate, perhaps because 3D modeling is easier for the processors to visualize and interpret.

- The ability to layout new medical equipment in 3D and then design the facility around the equipment, including all manufacturers' recommended structural elements, safety clearances, and utility requirements, is a huge advantage to BIM systems for health care construction.

- Perhaps the most important benefit from an end-user standpoint is the accuracy of the "as-built" model that is passed along to the health care organization after commissioning. Health care facilities are under constant re-purposing, and a full-scale, extremely detailed building model may prove helpful as the building ages.

PREFABRICATION

From an installer's perspective, the most revolutionary process BIM brings to the table is prefabrication: the process of fabricating structures or elements of structures off-site, under controlled conditions, and transporting these structures to the build site for placement. Until recently, prefabrication remained, for all intents and purposes, a dream. BIM allows this dream to become reality, with huge consequences for workers who make their livelihoods on construction sites. **See Figure 7-5.**

Previously, construction was performed by skilled craftworkers on site using local materials. Skilled construction workers often followed the work from city to city. Using BIM and modern manufacturing techniques, it is no longer necessary to build the structure on site. The only limiting factor to the elements that can be manufactured off-site are the physical limits inherent in transportation. BIM creates an international market for precisely-manufactured architectural units, made to order and perfectly fit, unit to unit, in a construction space. Obviously, this radically changes the roles of construction installers of most trades, especially the highly skilled crafts.

Figure 7-5   Patient Care Bathroom Pods

Figure 7-5. Patient care area bathrooms can be fabricated off the construction site at a local warehouse. The finished units will be transported to the job site and lifted to the proper floor for final placement.

Beginning in the late 1990s, patient bed vicinity headwalls were the first thing on health care construction sites to arrive on the job prefabricated. These units contained the correct number of receptacles (and circuitry), the complete medical gas outlets, the medical air and suction outlets, and the controls required for the patient bed positioning and television remote control. Electrical Workers and plumbers would then connect them to the appropriate installed building utility system and test the units for integrity. Prefabricated headwalls were much more cost effective than building the same set of systems in place, and prefabricated headwalls soon became the industry norm.

In early 2010, BIM had progressed to the point that it was possible to build large multi-craft racks of electrical conduit, domestic water, hydronics, waste, storm, supply air, return air, and exhaust air utilities off-site and ship them to the construction site where they would be elevated into position and secured to large all-thread rods that had been laid out and installed before the deck had been poured. These racks joined together on hangers that had been installed months before. These racks also had provisions for the utility service of the facility. For instance, the racks would have branch circuit conduit and the correct plumbing pipes to service the prefabricated headwalls found in patient care areas across the facility. The Electrical Worker merely runs a raceway from the rack stub out to the headwall connection to complete the branch circuit conduit work. **See Figure 7-6.**

The use of prefabrication has progressed to the point that complete architectural elements, such as patient care bathrooms, can be manufactured off-site on special palettes, transported to the jobsite, craned to the proper floor, dollied into position, and set in place. The appropriate connections are then made to the plumbing, electrical, and HVAC systems. This innovation is considered by some as the most historically disruptive innovation in a tried-and-true construction process.

Figure 7-6   A Multi-Craft Rack

Figure 7-6. BIM technology allows large multi-craft racks to be built off-site and transported to the job for final placement.

Legionnaires Case Study

BIM and prefabrication is a game-changing fact of life for new health care construction. A few important lessons can be gleaned from early modularized prefabrication health care construction. The prefabrication techniques used in 2008 to 2010 on the Miami Valley Hospital's new 12-story Heart Tower is a useful case study. The use of prefabrication was hailed as a triumph of flexibility of design and construction by *Healthcare Design* magazine. It is reported that work on the prefabricated units was so far ahead of schedule that additional storage space had to be rented to warehouse the units as the construction site was not yet ready for their installation.

Shortly after the opening of the Tower in 2011, Miami Valley Hospital suffered an outbreak of Legionnaires disease that killed at least one patient and made many more sick. The ensuing court records regarding the outbreak show that much of the litigation focused on the hospital, project architect, construction manager, general contractors, and the mechanical contractor. Eventually, in 2015, in the only litigation that was not settled out of court, the Second Court of Appeals found the architect did not carry the proper insurance to cover this type of event as alleged in the construction contract.

Interestingly enough, there are no public records as to how the legionella bacteria was introduced to the domestic water system of the hospital. Miami Valley Hospital produced a white paper as part of the internal investigation, but declined to release the report to the public. On March 5, 2015, *Engineering News-Record* published a long article on the controversy, quoting a settled lawsuit alleging the legionella bacteria was introduced to the hospital's domestic water system via a prefabricated plumbing system that was tested under pressure and capped with water in the system. The theory is that the bacteria developed in the prefabricated piping systems as they were stored waiting for transportation and installation.

While the public record is officially silent on how the outbreak occurred, the *Engineering News-Record* article raises a potentially serious issue for prefabricated units in health care construction.

SUMMARY

No other industry has been impacted by the rapid changes of modern technology as much as the health care industry. Keeping up with the ways these advancements constantly mold the industry can be a full-time job. When examining how health care facilities have evolved over the last several decades, the important role technology plays in the health care system can be seen not only in patient treatment, but also in the development of the facilities in which they are treated.

REVIEW QUESTIONS

1. Health care policy and research reports indicate that in the United States, consumers spent over __?__ in 2017 for health care.
   a. $1.2 billion
   b. $1.7 billion
   c. $2.9 trillion
   d. $3.2 trillion

2. Because health care consumers value __?__, health care organizations are moving facilities back to the neighborhoods, suburbs, and rural small towns to provide easy access, better care, and more personal access.
   a. community care
   b. easy access
   c. low cost providers
   d. quality of care

3. Surgical procedures, such as some plastic and bariatric surgeries, are usually not covered by insurance and tend to be more for one's aesthetic improvement rather than addressing a health care issue. Therefore, these surgeries are often performed at a site-specific special-purpose built surgical center located in a discrete area.
   a. True   b. False

4. Federal Medicare and Medicaid are growing segments in the health care payers sector and is driven by a couple of elements. As Americans reach retirement age, more people are becoming eligible for Medicare benefits as they qualify for __?__ benefits, making the increasing use of Medicare part of a national health care policy.
   a. company insurance provider
   b. company pension
   c. local or State funded
   d. Social Security

5. Payments for federal health insurance programs are processed through the Centers for Medicare and Medicaid Service (CMS). This agency has strict standards of care that health care facilities must conform to be eligible to receive payments from CMS.
   a. True   b. False

6. CMS issued a directive that __?__ air shall be able to be delivered to patients, and patient storage areas, in the event of an emergency.
   a. clean
   b. conditioned environmental
   c. both a. and b.
   d. neither a. nor b.

7. Beginning in the late 1990s, patient bed vicinity __?__ were the first thing on health care construction sites to arrive on the job prefabricated. These units contained the correct number of receptacles (and circuitry), the complete medical gas outlets, the medical air and suction outlets, as well as the controls required for the patient bed positioning and television remote control.
   a. headwalls
   b. luminaires
   c. outlets
   d. task lighting

8. The use of prefabrication has progressed to the point where complete architectural elements, such as patient care bathrooms, can be manufactured off-site on special palettes, transported to the job site, craned to the proper floor, dollied into position, and set in place.
   a. True   b. False

Working in Existing Health Care Facilities During the COVID-19 Pandemic

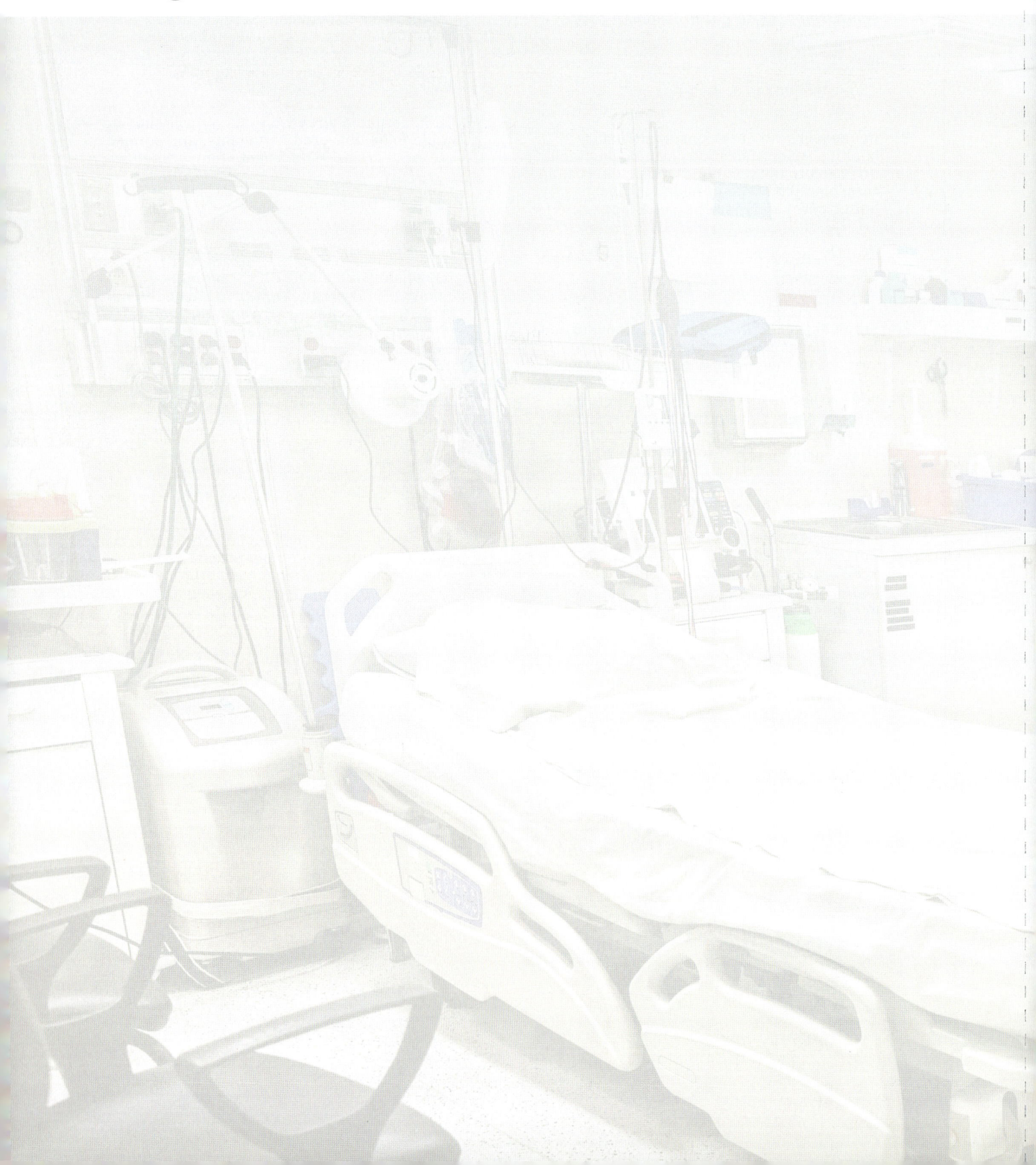

Appendix

INTRODUCTION

At the time of this writing, many valuable lessons of the COVID-19 pandemic are still being learned. It is not an exaggeration to say that the pandemic has reinforced the wisdom of Infection Control Risk Assessment/Mitigation Plans (ICRAMP). At the same time, it is challenging to perform an effective ICRAMP when the threat is not entirely understood. Health care organizations have taken a four-pronged approach when reviewing construction activities during the crisis:

- Issue a stop-work order on projects that are not considered vital to the health care organization's newly focused mission. Some projects have been delayed and will resume when the pandemic has passed. Others, particularly those in the planning stages, have been canceled and funds reallocated to other more critical activities.

- Build temporary facilities in buildings not designed for health care activities, such as convention centers and athletic facilities, or build stand-alone temporary facilities on undeveloped property. Because these facilities are temporary, the local authority having jurisdiction (AHJ), working in concert with an accreditation organization, may allow the temporary facility some respite from code and standard requirements. From an Electrical Worker's perspective, these are "new builds" and may not require an ICRAMP. Under any conditions, the procedures and protocols an employer has in place to protect one another from the transmission of COVID-19 must be carefully followed.

- Continue existing projects deemed essential, with enhanced ICRAMP protocols and procedures to combat the spread of the novel coronavirus.

- Begin emergency fast-track remodel and retrofit activities to address specific physical plant alterations needed to treat patients with COVID-19 more effectively.

WORKING DURING THE PANDEMIC

Addressing the final two bullet points above will be the focus, as those scenarios impact the Electrical Worker employed in a functioning health care facility. While each project in a working health care facility is unique, with a unique set of ICRAMP protocols and procedures, specific COVID-19 additions to these procedures generally apply to several fronts.

Increased use of PPE, especially face masks and gloves, is mandated to help contain the spread of the virus. At the time of this writing, COVID-19 is thought to be primarily transferred from person-to-person via airborne contact; secondarily, the virus is believed to be transferred via surface contact from surface-to-person. The face mask requirement is designed to protect both the wearer and those that may come inside the six-foot social distancing boundary. The use of face masks has been shown to minimize transmission by trapping respiration droplets containing the virus. The use of rubber or vinyl gloves is employed as a means to stop the spread of the virus from surfaces to human respiratory systems. It is critical when wearing gloves not to touch the face or eyes, and it is crucial to change gloves as often as instructed. This will allow maximum benefit from the PPE to be achieved.

Increased cleaning protocols are also in place to combat the surface transmission of the virus. The daily cleaning and mop-down of workspaces is a requirement as well as the regular cleaning of shared hand tools and power tools. Hand tools should be cleaned with an approved disinfectant. Power tools are another matter altogether as the cleaning solution may damage the plastic handles and surfaces of the tools, essentially ruining the tool. Batteries are particularly vulnerable to cleaner damage, with some manufacturers suggesting a 72-hour rest period before batteries are once again placed in service. It would be wise to use the tool manufacturer's web site and learn specific instructions for properly cleaning power tools without damaging them.

For additional information, visit qr.njatcdb.org Item #6256

Milwaukee Tool COVID-19 Resources

Workspaces will almost certainly be under negative pressure as work is underway. This pressurization is thought to be very useful in keeping the airborne transmission of the virus from infecting patients with compromised respiratory and or immune systems. As detailed earlier, this critical protection must be continuously monitored, and workers must do their part for it to be effective.

Daily wellness checks can also be implemented. Workers will be asked to complete a health checklist before entering the site that will be reviewed by a medical professional. Body temperature may be taken as part of the wellness check. Those with symptoms of COVID-19 will be sent home and possibly quarantined.

Access and egress pathways will be sharply defined and closely monitored. This is done to combat the spread of the virus as well as to provide additional security for the health care facility.

Planning Successful and Safe Health Care Construction Projects During the Global Pandemic

For additional information, visit qr.njatcdb.org Item #6489

Construction COVID-19 Checklists for Employers and Employees

For additional information, visit qr.njatcdb.org Item #6490

SUMMARY

For an Electrical Worker and their employer, one of the most important lessons learned from the COVID-19 pandemic is the value to the health care facilities customer of a contractor and workforce that is agile and able to adapt to changing environments seamlessly without significant disruption. This especially applies to jobs preformed on an "emergency" basis, when one patient care area requires transformation into an entirely different occupancy. On every job, it is essential to follow the health and safety protocols and procedures put in place by the employer, local public health agency, and the Center for Disease Control. These requirements may seem burdensome, but they are in place for everyone's safety. Whatever political aspect of the pandemic individuals embrace, the protocols are in place to keep each and every worker and the people they come in contact with safe as possible.

What Construction Workers Need to Know About COVID-19

For additional information, visit qr.njatcdb.org Item #6257

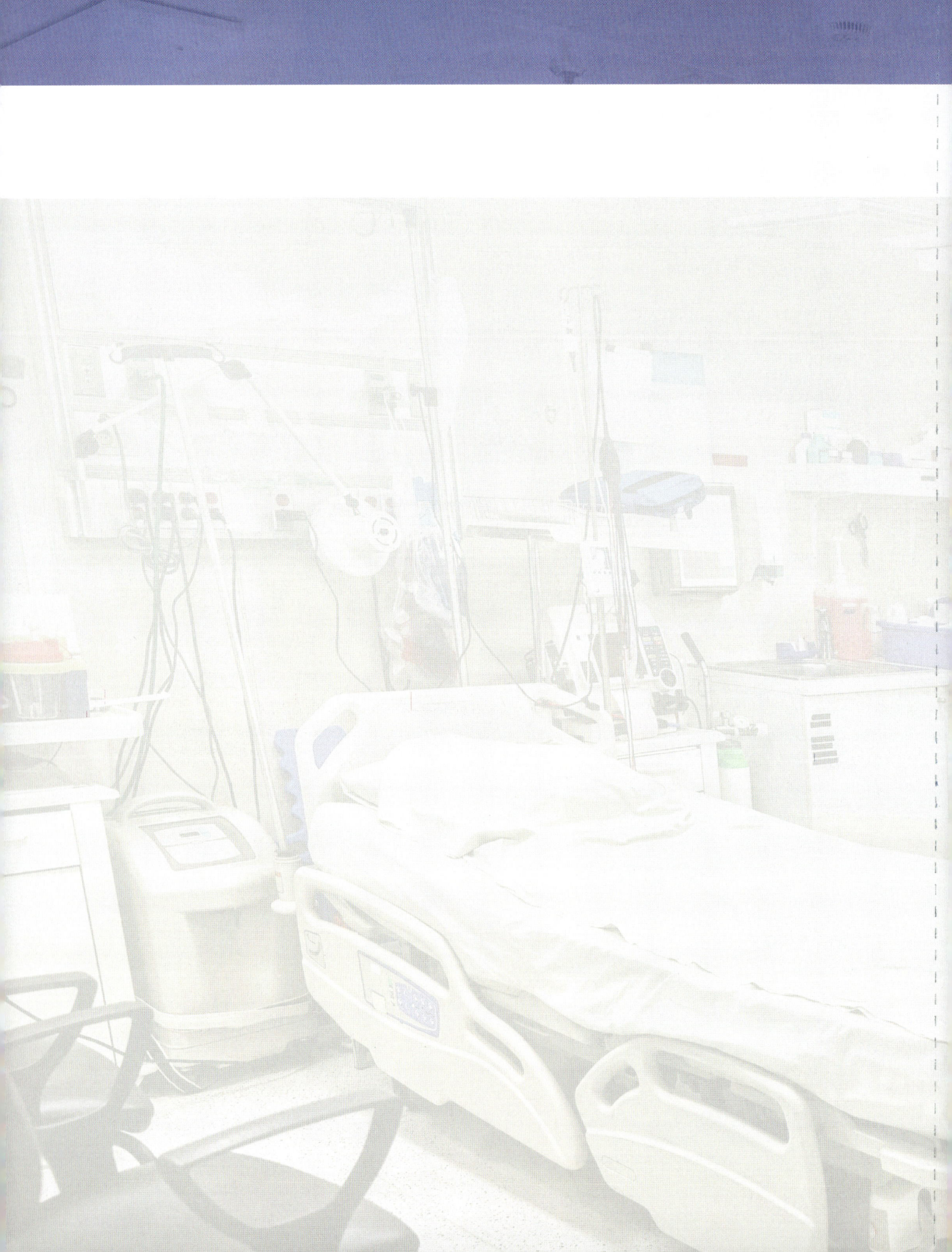

Glossary

To aid the student's ability to comprehend the vast diversity of codes and standards within health care facilities, each definition within the Glossary has been supplemented with the addition of the citation of the origination document and section number within the document that the definition can be found.

A

Accreditation Organization. A third party organization that performs an evaluative process in which a health care organization undergoes an examination of its policies, procedures, and performance by a third party external organization to ensure that it is meeting the predetermined criteria. It usually involves both on- and off-site surveys. Approval by a CMS approved accreditation organization is required for the health care organization to receive Medicare payments. [**CMS**]

Alternate Power Source. One or more generator sets, or battery systems where permitted, intended to provide power during the interruption of the normal electrical services; or the public utility electrical service intended to provide power during interruption of service normally provided by the generating facilities on the premises. [**99**:3.3.4]

Ambulatory Health Care Occupancy. An occupancy used to provide services or treatment simultaneously to four or more patients that provides, on an outpatient basis, one or more of the following:

(1) Treatment for patients that renders the patients incapable of taking action for self-preservation under emergency conditions without the assistance of others.

(2) Anesthesia that renders the patients incapable of taking action for self-preservation under emergency conditions without the assistance of others.

(3) Treatment for patients who, due to the nature of their injury or illness, incapable of taking action for self-preservation under emergency without assistance of others. [**99**:3.3.5]

Anesthetizing Location. Any area of a facility that has been designated to be used for the administration of any flammable or nonflammable inhalation anesthetic agent in the course of examination or treatment, including the use of such agents for relative analgesia. [**70**:517.2]

Authority Having Jurisdiction. An organization, office, or individual responsible for enforcing the requirements of a code or standard, or for approving equipment, materials, an installation, or a procedure. [**70**:100]

B

Battery-Powered Lighting Units. Individual unit equipment for backup illumination consisting of the following:

(1) Rechargeable battery

(2) Battery-charging means

(3) Provisions for one or more lamps mounted on the equipment, or with terminals for remote lamps, or both

(4) Relaying device arranged to energize the lamps automatically upon failure of the supply to the unit equipment [**70**:517.2]

CITATION KEY:

70 - *NFPA 70: 2020 National Electrical Code*

99 - *NFPA 99: 2021 Health Care Facilities Code*

110 - *NFPA 110: 2019 Standard for Emergency and Standy Power Systems*

CMS - Centers for Medicare and Medicaid Services

For instance, the definition of *Anesthetizing Location* can be found within *NFPA 70: National Electrical Code*, in Section 517.2.

A

Accreditation Organization. A third party organization that performs an evaluative process in which a health care organization undergoes an examination of its policies, procedures, and performance by a third party external organization to ensure that it is meeting the predetermined criteria. It usually involves both on- and off-site surveys. Approval by a CMS approved accreditation organization is required for the health care organization to receive Medicare payments. [**CMS**]

Alternate Power Source. One or more generator sets, or battery systems where permitted, intended to provide power during the interruption of the normal electrical services; or the public utility electrical service intended to provide power during interruption of service normally provided by the generating facilities on the premises. [**99**:3.3.4]

Ambulatory Health Care Occupancy. An occupancy used to provide services or treatment simultaneously to four or more patients that provides, on an outpatient basis, one or more of the following:

(1) Treatment for patients that renders the patients incapable of taking action for self-preservation under emergency conditions without the assistance of others.

(2) Anesthesia that renders the patients incapable of taking action for self-preservation under emergency conditions without the assistance of others.

(3) Treatment for patients who, due to the nature of their injury or illness, are incapable of taking action for self-preservation under emergency conditions without assistance of others. [**99**:3.3.5]

Anesthetizing Location. Any area of a facility that has been designated to be used for the administration of any flammable or nonflammable inhalation anesthetic agent in the course of examination or treatment, including the use of such agents for relative analgesia. [**70**:517.2]

Authority Having Jurisdiction. An organization, office, or individual responsible for enforcing the requirements of a code or standard, or for approving equipment, materials, an installation, or a procedure. [**70**:100]

B

Battery-Powered Lighting Units. Individual unit equipment for backup illumination consisting of the following:

(1) Rechargeable battery

(2) Battery-charging means

(3) Provisions for one or more lamps mounted on the equipment, or with terminals for remote lamps, or both

(4) Relaying device arranged to energize the lamps automatically upon failure of the supply to the unit equipment [**70**:517.2]

Bonded (Bonding). Connected to establish electrical continuity and conductivity. [**70**:100]

Branch Circuit. The circuit conductors between the final overcurrent device protecting the circuit and the outlet(s). [**70**:100]

Branch Circuit, Appliance. A branch circuit that supplies energy to one or more outlets to which appliances are to be connected and that has no permanently connected luminaires that are not a part of an appliance. [**70**:100]

Branch Circuit, General Purpose. A branch circuit that supplies two or more receptacles or outlets for lighting and appliances. [**70**:100]

Branch Circuit, Individual. A branch circuit that supplies only one utilization equipment. [**70**:100]

Branch Circuit, Multiwire. A branch circuit that consists of two or more ungrounded conductors that have a voltage between them, and a grounded conductor that has equal voltage between it and each ungrounded conductor of the circuit and that is connected to the neutral or grounded conductor of the system. [**70**:100]

> Revised for the 2011 *NEC*, 517.18(A) and 19(A) both prohibit the use of multiwire branch circuits from serving patient bed locations in both general care and critical care areas (spaces) of all health care facilities. This prohibition includes multiwire branch circuits supplied from the critical branch and the normal branch. Multiwire branch circuits are permitted to be used for other circuits and locations.
>
> Section 210.4(B) requires that ungrounded conductors of multiwire branch circuits be provided with a means to be simultaneously disconnected at the point where the branch circuit originates. This is generally accomplished using multi-pole circuit breakers or identified handle ties. Section 210.4(D) also addresses multiwire branch circuits from the standpoint that they must be grouped with their associated grounded (neutral) conductor at least once as the circuit conductors enter the enclosure where the branch circuit originates.
>
> The reason the *Code* prohibits multiwire branch circuits in patient bed locations is that a short circuit or overload on one circuit could effectively cause two other circuits of the multiwire branch circuit to automatically disconnect leaving all three circuits of the multiwire branch circuit without power. Since patient care receptacles may be used for life support equipment, this interruption could endanger the life of a patient.

C

Centers for Medicare and Medicaid Services, The (CMS). Is part of the United States Department of Health and Human Services. The agency administers Medicare, Medicaid, the Children's Health Insurance Program (CHIP), and the Health Insurance Marketplace. [**CMS**]

Critical Branch. A system of feeders and branch circuits supplying power for task illumination, fixed equipment, select receptacles, and select power circuits serving areas and functions related to patient care and that are automatically connected to alternate power sources by one or more transfer switches during interruption of the normal power source. [**99**:3.3.30]

E

Electrical Life-Support Equipment. Electrically powered equipment whose continuous operation is necessary to maintain a patient's life. [**99**:3.3.45]

Emergency Power Supply (EPS). The source of electric power of the required capacity and quality for an emergency power supply system (EPSS). [**110**:3.3.3]

Emergency Power Supply System (EPSS). A complete functioning (EPS) system coupled to a system of conductors, disconnecting means and overcurrent protective devices, transfer switches, and all control, supervisory, and support devices up to and including the load terminals of the transfer equipment needed for the system to operate as a safe and reliable source of electric power. [**110**:3.3.4]

Equipment Branch. A system of feeders and branch circuits arranged for delayed, automatic, or manual connection to the alternate power source and that serves primarily 3-phase power equipment. [**99**:3.3.50]

Essential Electrical System. A system comprised of alternate sources of power and all connected distribution systems and ancillary equipment, designed to ensure continuity of electrical power to designated areas and functions of a health care facility during disruption of normal power sources, and also to minimize disruption within the internal wiring system. [**99**:3.3.52]

Exposed Conductive Surfaces. Those surfaces that are capable of carrying electric current and that are unprotected, uninsulated, unenclosed, or unguarded, permitting personal contact. [**99**:3.3.54]

F

Fault Hazard Current. See *Hazard Current.*

Feeder. All circuit conductors between the service equipment, the source of a separately derived system, or other power supply source and the final branch-circuit overcurrent device. [**70**:100]

Flammable Anesthetics. Gases or vapors, such as fluroxene, cyclopropane, divinyl ether, ethyl chloride, ethyl ether, and ethylene, which may form flammable or explosive mixtures with air, oxygen, or reducing gases such as nitrous oxide. [**70**:517.2]

Flammable Anesthetizing Location. Any area of the facility that has been designated to be used for the administration of any flammable inhalation anesthetic agents in the normal course of examination or treatment. [**70**:517.2]

G

Governing Body. See *Health Care Facility's Governing Body*

Ground Fault. An unintentional, electrically conductive connection between an ungrounded conductor of an electrical circuit and the normally non–current-carrying conductors, metallic enclosures, metallic raceways, metallic equipment, or earth. [**70**:100]

Grounded (Grounding). Connected (connecting) to ground or to a conductive body that extends the ground connection. [**70**:100]

Ground-Fault Circuit Interrupter (GFCI). A device intended for the protection of personnel that functions to de-energize a circuit or portion thereof within an established period of time when a current to ground exceeds the values established for a Class A device.

> Informational Note: Class A ground-fault circuit interrupters trip when the current to ground is 6 mA or higher and do not trip when the current to ground is less than 4 mA. For further information, see UL 943, Standard for Ground-Fault Circuit Interrupters. [**70**:100]

Ground-Fault Current Path. An electrically conductive path from the point of a ground-fault on a wiring system through normally non–current-carrying conductors, equipment, or the earth to the electrical supply source.

> Informational Note: Examples of ground-fault current paths are any combination of equipment grounding conductors, metallic raceways, metallic cable sheaths, electrical equipment, and any other electrically conductive material such as metal, water, and gas piping; steel framing members; stucco mesh; metal ducting; reinforcing steel; shields of communications cables; and the earth itself. [**70**:100]

Ground-Fault Protection of Equipment. A system intended to provide protection of equipment from damaging line-to-ground fault currents by operating to cause a disconnecting means to open all ungrounded conductors of the faulted circuit. This protection is provided at current levels less than those required to protect conductors from damage through the operation of a supply circuit overcurrent device. [**70**:100]

Grounding Conductor, Equipment (EGC). The conductive path(s) that provides a ground-fault current path and connects normally non–current-carrying metal parts of equipment together and to the system grounded conductor or to the grounding electrode conductor, or both.

> Informational Note No. 1 it is recognized that the equipment grounding conductor also performs bonding.

> Informational Note No. 2 See *NEC* 250.118 for a list of acceptable equipment grounding conductors. [**70**:100]

H

Health Care Facility's Governing Body. The person or persons who have the overall legal responsibility for the operation of a health care facility. [**99**:3.3.74]

Hazard Current. For a given set of connections in an isolated power system, the total current that would flow through a low impedance if it were connected between either isolated conductor and ground. [**99**:3.3.72]

> **Fault Hazard Current.** The hazard current of a given isolated system with all devices connected except the line isolation monitor. [**99**:3.3.72.1]

> **Monitor Hazard Current.** The hazard current of the line isolation monitor alone. [**99**:3.3.72.2]

> **Total Hazard Current.** The hazard current of a given isolated system with all devices, including the line isolation monitor, connected. [**99**:3.3.72.3]

Health Care Facilities. Buildings or portions of buildings or mobile enclosures in which medical, dental, psychiatric, nursing, obstetrical, or surgical care is provided. [**99**:3.3.73]

Hospital. A building or portion thereof used on a 24-hour basis for the medical, psychiatric, obstetrical, or surgical care of four or more inpatients. [**101**:3.3.152]

I

Isolated Power System. A system comprising an isolating transformer or its equivalent, a line isolation monitor, and its ungrounded circuit conductors. [**99**:3.3.93]

Isolation Transformer. A transformer of the multiple-winding type, with the primary and secondary windings physically separated, which inductively couples its secondary winding(s) to circuit conductors connected to its primary winding(s). [**99**:3.3.94]

L

Life Safety Branch. A system of feeders and branch circuits supplying power for lighting, receptacles, and equipment essential for life safety that is automatically connected to alternate power sources by one or more transfer switches during interruption of the normal power source. [**99**:3.3.97]

Limited Care Facility. A building or portion thereof used on a 24-hour basis for the housing of four or more persons who are incapable of self-preservation because of age; physical limitation due to accident or illness; or limitations such as mental retardation/ developmental disability, mental illness, or chemical dependency. [**70**:517.2]

Line Isolation Monitor. A test instrument designed to continually check the balanced and unbalanced impedance from each line of an isolated circuit to ground and equipped with a built-in test circuit to exercise the alarm without adding to the leakage current hazard. [**99**:3.3.99]

M

Microgrid, Health Care. A group of interconnected loads and distributed energy resources within clearly defined boundaries that acts as a single controllable entity with respect to the utility. [**99**:3.3.75]

Microgrid Controller, Health Care. A system including health care microgrid control functions that can manage itself, operate autonomously, and connect to and disconnect from the utility for the exchange of power and the supply of ancillary services. [**99**:3.3.76]

Monitor Hazard Current. See *Hazard Current*.

N

Nursing Home. A building or portion of a building used on a 24-hour basis for the housing and nursing care of four or more persons who, because of mental or physical incapacity, might be unable to provide for their own needs and safety without the assistance of another person. [**99**:3.3.127]

P

Patient Bed Location. The location of a patient sleeping bed, or the bed or procedure table of a Category 1 Space. [**99**:3.3.138]

Patient Care Space. Space within a health care facility wherein patients are intended to be examined or treated.

> **Category 1 (Critical Care) Space.** Space in which failure of equipment or a system is likely to cause major injury or death to patients or caregivers.
>
> **Category 2 (General Care) Space.** Space in which failure of equipment or a system is likely to cause minor injury to patients or caregivers.
>
> **Category 3 (Basic Care) Space.** Space in which failure of equipment or a system is not likely to cause injury to the patients or caregivers but may cause patient discomfort.
>
> **Category 4 (Support) Space.** Space in which failure of equipment or a system is not likely to have a physical impact on patients or caregivers.

Informational Note No. 1: The governing body of the facility designates patient care space in accordance with the type of patient care anticipated and with the definitions of the area classification. Business offices, corridors, lounges, day rooms, dining rooms, or similar areas typically are not classified as patient care space.

Informational Note No. 2: Basic care space is typically a location where basic medical or dental care, treatment, or examinations are performed. Examples include, but are not limited to, examination or treatment rooms in clinics, medical and dental offices, nursing homes, and limited care facilities.

Informational Note No. 3: General care space includes areas such as patient bedrooms, examining rooms, treatment rooms, clinics, and similar areas where the patient may come into contact with electromedical devices or ordinary appliances such as a nurse call system, electric beds, examining lamps, telephones, and entertainment devices.

Informational Note No. 4: Critical care space includes special care units, intensive care units, coronary care units, angiography laboratories, cardiac catheterization laboratories, delivery rooms, operating rooms, and similar areas in which are patients are intended to be subjected to invasive procedures and are connected to line-operated, electromedical devices.

Informational Note No. 5: Spaces where a procedure is performed that subjects patients or staff to wet conditions are considered as wet procedure areas. Wet conditions include standing fluids on the floor or drenching of the work area. Routine housekeeping procedures and incidental spillage of liquids do not define wet procedure areas. It is the responsibility of the governing body of the health care facility to designate the wet procedure areas. [**70**:517.2]

Patient Care Vicinity. A space, within a location intended for the examination and treatment of patients, extending 1.8 m (6 ft) beyond the normal location of the patient bed, chair, table, treadmill, or other device that supports the patient during examination and treatment and extending vertically to 2.3 m (7 ft 6 in.) above the floor. [**99**:3.3.141]

Patient Equipment Grounding Point. A jack or terminal that serves as the collection point for redundant grounding of electric appliances serving a patient care vicinity or for grounding other items in order to eliminate electromagnetic interference problems. [**99**:3.3.142]

Q

Qualified Person. One who has skills and knowledge related to the construction and operation of the electrical equipment and installations and has received safety training to recognize and avoid the hazards involved. [**70**:100]

Qualified Person. One who has skills and knowledge related to the operation, maintenance, repair, and testing of the EPSS equipment and installations and has received safety training to recognize and avoid the hazards involved. [**110**:3.3.11]

R

Reference Grounding Point. The ground bus of the panelboard or isolated power system panel supplying the patient care area. [**99**:3.3.158]

Relative Analgesia. A state of sedation and partial block of pain perception produced in a patient by the inhalation of concentrations of nitrous oxide insufficient to produce loss of consciousness (conscious sedation). [**70**:517.2]

Risk Categories. [**99**:3.3.162]

> **Category 1.** Activities, systems, or equipment whose failure is likely to cause major injury or death to patients, staff, or visitors. [**99**:3.3.162.1]

> **Category 2.** Activities, systems, or equipment whose failure is likely to cause minor injury to patients, staff, or visitors. [**99**:3.3.162.2]

> **Category 3.** Activities, systems, or equipment whose failure is not likely to cause injury to patients, staff, or visitors but can cause discomfort. [**99**:3.3.162.3]

> **Category 4.** Activities, systems, or equipment whose failure would have no impact on patient care. [**99**:3.3.162.4]

S

Selected Receptacles. A minimum number of electrical receptacles selected by the health care facility's governing body as necessary to provide essential patient care and facility services during loss of normal power. [**99**:3.3.160]

Switch. [**110**:3.3.12]

Automatic Transfer Switch. Self-acting equipment for transferring one or more load conductor connections from one power source to another. [**110**:3.3.12.1]

Bypass-Isolation Switch. A manually operated device used in conjunction with an automatic transfer switch to provide a means of directly connecting load conductors to a power source and disconnecting the automatic transfer switch. [**110**:3.3.12.2]

Nonautomatic Transfer Switch. A device, operated manually by a physical action or electrically by either a local or remote control, for transferring a common load between a normal and alternate supply. [**110**:3.3.12.3]

T

Task Illumination. Provision for the minimum lighting required to carry out necessary tasks in the described areas, including safe access to supplies and equipment, and access to exits. [**99**:3.3.177]

Total Hazard Current. See *Hazard Current*.

U

Ungrounded. Not connected to ground or a conductive body that extends the ground connection. [**70**:100]

W

Wet Procedure Location. The area in a patient care space where a procedure is performed that is normally subject to wet conditions while patients are present, including standing fluids on the floor or drenching of the work area, where either such condition is intimate to the patient or staff. [**99**:3.3.187]

Routine housekeeping procedures and incidental spillage of liquids do not define a wet procedure location. [**99**:A.3.3.187]

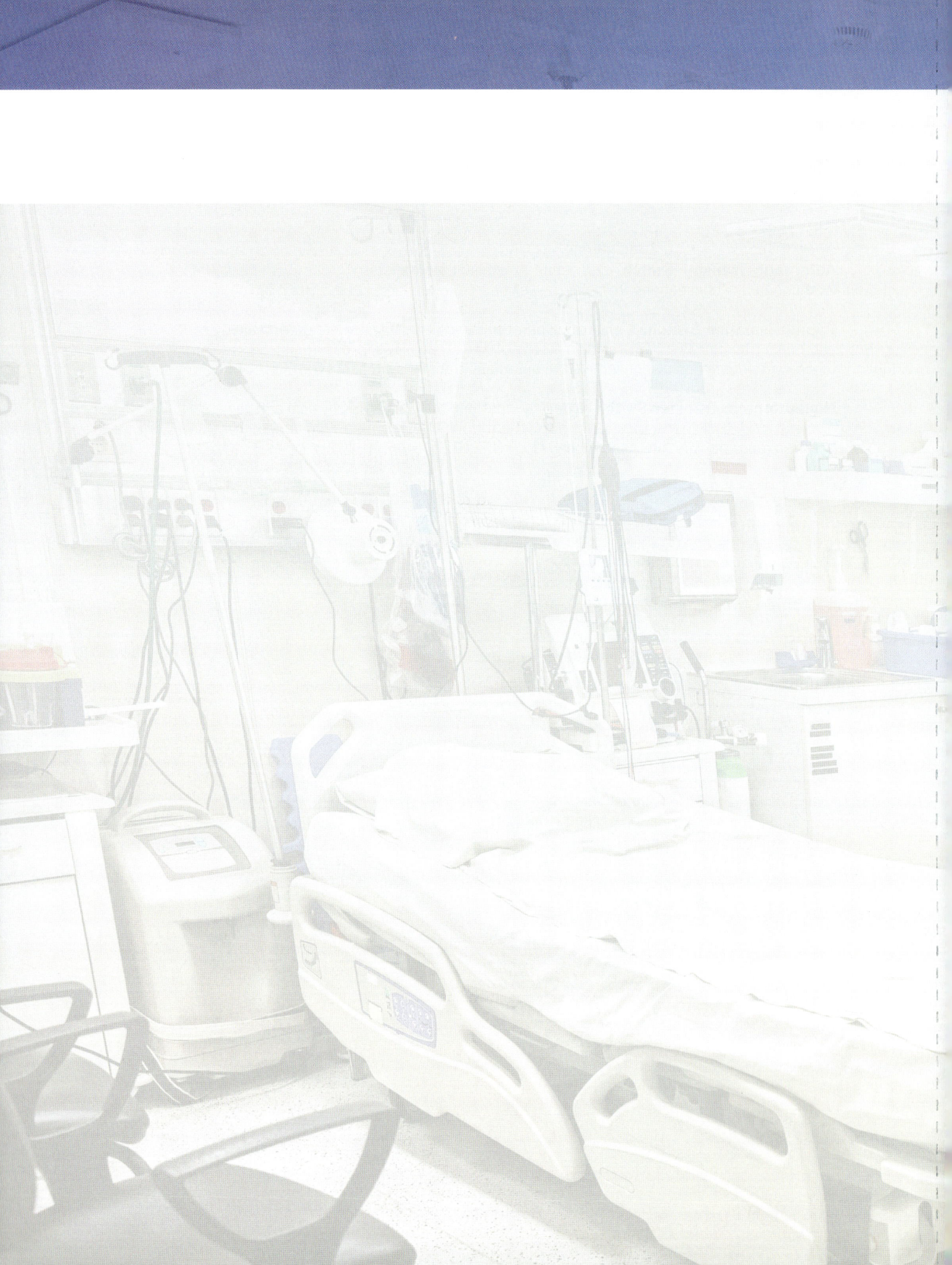

Index